FDR AND HIS CONTEMPORARIES

The Franklin and Eleanor Roosevelt Institute Series on Diplomatic and Economic History

General Editors: **Arthur M. Schlesinger, Jr., Willliam J. vanden Heuvel and Douglas Brinkley**

1. **FDR AND HIS CONTEMPORARIES: Foreign Perceptions of an American President**
   Edited by Cornelis A. van Minnen and John F. Sears

2. **NATO: THE CREATION OF THE ATLANTIC ALLIANCE AND THE INTEGRATION OF EUROPE**
   Edited by Francis H. Heller and John R. Gillingham

FDR AND HIS CONTEMPORARIES

Foreign Perceptions of an American President

Edited by
Cornelis A. van Minnen and John F. Sears

St. Martin's Press
New York
In Association with the Roosevelt Study Center

 For information, write:
Scholarly and Reference Division,
St. Martin's Press, Inc., 175 Fifth Avenue, New York, NY 10010

First Published in the United States of America in 1992

Printed in the United States of America

ISBN 0-312-06712-7

Library of Congress Cataloging-in-Publication Data

FDR and his contemporaries : foreign perceptions of an American president / edited by Cornelis A. van Minnen and John F. Sears.
p. cm.
Includes index.
ISBN 0-312-06712-7
1. Roosevelt, Franklin D. (Franklin Delano), 1882-1945—Public opinion. 2. United States—Foreign relations—1933-1945.
I. Minnen, Cornelis A. van. II. Sears, John F., 1941- .
E807.F33 1991
973.917'092—dc20 91-21814
CIP

CONTENTS

FOREWORD

On 16-18 May 1990, a group of prominent historians and political scientists from some fifteen different countries around the world met at the Roosevelt Study Center in Middelburg, the Netherlands, to discuss the topic, "Franklin D. Roosevelt As Seen By His European, Latin American, and Asian Contemporaries." Although innumerable books and articles have been published over the years about FDR and U.S. foreign policy in the 1930s and 1940s, President Roosevelt's personal relationship with his allies and foes and their perceptions of him have never been as directly addressed from so many perspectives as during this conference.

We were particularly pleased that colleagues from the Soviet Union, Poland, and Yugoslavia participated in the meeting. Their presence ensured a more balanced view of the multifaceted Roosevelt and his impact on the entire world. It also helped fulfill the Roosevelt Study Center's goal of serving as a pan-European venue for scholars at which a candid exchange of opinions can take place. The conference participants were especially engaged by the eyewitness report of Dr. Valentin Berezhkov, who had served as the personal interpreter for Stalin and Molotov and in that capacity had met Hitler, von Ribbentrop, Roosevelt, and Churchill.

As organizers of this conference, we want to express our thanks to the speakers who so graciously accepted our invitation to share their knowledge and advance our understanding of the relationship between FDR and the foreign leaders with whom he dealt. The atmosphere at the conference was so stimulating and congenial that we could have continued our discussions for several days more. We also gratefully acknowledge the support of the conference sponsors: the AT&T Foundation, the Netherland-America Foundation, Inc., the Franklin and Eleanor Roosevelt Institute, the Roosevelt Study Center, USIS The Hague, and the vanden Heuvel Family Fund.

We have divided the essays written for the conference into four parts: part 1 deals with Franklin D. Roosevelt's internationalism; parts 2 and 3 focus on the relationships between Roosevelt and his allies and foes; and part

4 is devoted to the legacy of FDR's internationalism in the period after the Second World War.

We hope that this volume will stimulate further research and discussion about one of the most important political leaders of the twentieth century, a man who, almost half a century after his death, continues to fascinate people and whose shadow looms large over today's world.

Cornelis A. van Minnen
John F. Sears

Part I

INTRODUCTION

1

FRANKLIN D. ROOSEVELT'S INTERNATIONALISM

Arthur M. Schlesinger, Jr.

Thanks to the initiative of the Roosevelt Study Center and the Franklin and Eleanor Roosevelt Institute, to the hospitality of the province of Zeeland and the government of the Netherlands, and to the generosity of the several sponsors listed in the program, we are happily assembled in this serene and cheerful place—historians from across the world joining together to recollect in tranquility a past that when it happened was indeed far from tranquil.

The great freemasonry of scholarship unites us today. But exactly half a century ago countries from which we come were bitterly opposed in what was to be the greatest war in history: on one side in May 1940, Germany, allied with Italy, Japan, and the Soviet Union, supported by fascists and communists everywhere; on the other, Great Britain, France, the smaller West European democracies, and China, supported by the United States and by liberal democrats everywhere.

The world has changed much since then—never more so than in the last couple of years. And though I doubt that even today we will achieve total agreement on all matters, I know we will witness that free and candid exchange of views which is of the essence in the writing of history. Especially here in the Netherlands, we can hardly forget the great Dutch historian Pieter Geyl's splendid definition of history as "an argument without end."[1]

History is also a means by which the present seeks to repossess the past. Today is the sixteenth of May 1990. Cast your minds back exactly fifty years—to the sixteenth of May 1940. The more venerable among us can still remember the shock and anguish that spoiled an exceptionally lovely spring. As we meet in this quiet town, it is hard to believe that half a century ago the land shook under the rumble of tanks, the crash of bombs, and the cries of the wounded and dying.

It was fifty years ago last Thursday when Nazi divisions roared into the Netherlands and Belgium. It was fifty years ago yesterday when the Dutch army surrendered to Adolf Hitler. French forces remained in Zeeland, and fifty years ago tomorrow Middelburg itself was subjected to one of the severest bombings of the war.

And fifty years ago today German forces had driven Belgian, French, and British units out of eastern Belgium to positions behind the Scheldt river. German Panzer divisions had crossed the Meuse on a broad front and were thrusting into northern France. Rommel's 7th Division had nearly reached Cambrai. Guderian was sixty miles east of Sedan. The French army under General Gamelin was falling back in confusion and disarray.

And it was also on this very day half a century ago that Winston Churchill, British prime minister for less than a week, flew to Paris to find out what had happened to the great French army—the army that he himself had called "an incomparable machine."[2] The military situation, Churchill discovered, was "incomparably worse than we had imagined." He met, fifty years ago today, with Paul Reynaud, Edouard Daladier, and Maurice Gamelin at the Quai d'Orsay. "Utter dejection," Churchill later recalled, "was written on every face." The Germans, he was told, were expected in Paris in a few days. Churchill asked Gamelin where he had placed the strategic reserve. Gamelin shrugged and replied, "*Aucune*."[3] Churchill looked out the window and saw clouds of smoke rising from bonfires of official documents in the garden of the Quai d'Orsay—a memory that must chill historians. The next morning he flew back to London and directed his cabinet to consider the consequences of the fall of France. One inescapable consequence was that Britain would stand alone in military resistance to Hitler's conquest of Europe.

And fifty years ago today across the Atlantic in Washington Franklin D. Roosevelt told the American Congress: "These are ominous days—days whose swift and shocking developments force every neutral nation to look to its defenses . . . . The brutal force of modern offensive war has been loosed in all its horror." He cited motorized divisions, parachute troops, infantry landed from planes, the fifth column, and laid particular stress on the vulnerability of the United States itself to air attack. "The American people," he said, "must recast their thinking about national protection"; and he asked Congress for a defense appropriation of $1,184 billion—an equivalent of about $15 billion in 1990 dollars. "I should like," he said, "to see this nation geared up to the ability to turn out at least 50,000 planes a year"—a goal that seemed a little fanciful for a nation that the year before had produced but six thousand.[4]

What brought the American president to the point where he would deliver such a speech to a nation far from persuaded that American interests were vitally at stake in a European war? Our collective effort will be to analyze and assess Roosevelt and his policies. My contribution will be to offer one historian's account of the origins and evolution of Roosevelt's outlook on the world.

I must emphasize the word "one," for the subject is far from uncontroversial even in the United States. Indeed, American scholars have portrayed Roosevelt across the spectrum—as an isolationist, as an appeaser, as an incorrigible vacillator, as the cunning defender of capitalism, as a closet socialist dedicated to the subversion of the market economy, as a Machiavellian schemer plotting to embroil his country in foreign wars, as a dreamy idealist gullibly dedicated to naive visions of world peace and harmony as an arrogant imperialist serving the interests of American economic hegemony. No one can be finally sure what was going on in that welcoming, enigmatic, elusive, teasing, devious, calculating, spontaneous, manipulative, superficially frivolous, ultimately decent, finally impenetrable mind—in what his friend the playwright Robert E. Sherwood called "Roosevelt's heavily forested interior."[5]

Roosevelt was one of those mixtures of complexity and simplicity that fascinate and baffle biographers. Recall his answer when a reporter asked him his philosophy. "Philosophy?" he replied. "Philosophy? I am a Christian and a Democrat—that's all."[6] It was far from all, but it suggests the naïveté in ends that licensed infinite sophistication in means. With all the camouflage, it is possible, I think, to see a pattern in Roosevelt's approach to foreign policy, to discern a figure in the carpet.

What he wrote in 1938 about his domestic policy in the introduction to his public papers applies equally to his foreign policy:

> Those who seek inconsistencies will find them. There were inconsistencies of method, inconsistencies caused by ceaseless efforts to find ways to solve problems for the future as well as for the present. There were inconsistencies born of insufficient knowledge. There were inconsistencies springing from the need of experimentation. But through them all, I trust that there also will be found a consistency and continuity of broad purpose.[7]

Wherein did this consistency and continuity lie? As a statesman on the world stage, Roosevelt was formed by family traditions, by personal experience, by influential models, and by objective national and international necessities. He was born into what was by American standards a cosmopolitan family. His father knew Europe well and as a young man had marched with Garibaldi. His mother's family, the Delanos, had been in the China trade; his mother herself had lived for two years in Hong Kong as a small child. FDR made his first trip to Europe at the age of three and spent every summer there from ninth to his fourteenth years. By the time he was elected president, he had crossed the Atlantic and back thirteen times and had lived almost three years of his life in Europe.

He came of age in those exciting years after the turn of the century when the United States was bursting into the international arena—doing so, moreover, under the exhilarating leadership of his kinsman Theodore Roosevelt. TR became one of the two polar figures shaping FDR's internationalism, with a strong assist from the great naval geopolitician Admiral Alfred Thayer Mahan, who was a friend of both Roosevelts and whose treatises on seapower young Franklin began to read before he was sixteen.

Theodore Roosevelt and Mahan had a lucid and realistic view of international relations. They saw the world in terms of national interest and the balance of power. Maintaining the balance of power seemed the key to the preservation both of international order and of American security. This was not a novel doctrine. The fathers of the American republic had seen the world the same way. As Thomas Jefferson put it in 1814, "It cannot be to our interest that all Europe should be reduced to a single monarchy." Though the United States was then fighting Britain, Jefferson said that, if Napoleon again advanced to Moscow, he would prefer the survival of Britain than to see "the whole force of Europe wielded by a single hand."[8]

This geopolitical realism waned when the United States withdrew from European conflicts after 1815. Most Americans thereafter developed a righteous conviction of moral superiority to what came to be known dismissively as "power politics." Theodore Roosevelt sought to revive the realistic analysis. Like Jefferson, he had no doubt that, if the whole force of Europe were wielded by a single hand, it would be a grave threat to vital American interests. "As long as England succeeds in keeping 'the balance of power' in Europe, not only in principle, but in reality, well and good," he told a German diplomat four years before the First World War. "Should she however for some reason or other fail in doing so, the United States would be obliged to step in . . . in order to restore the balance of power in Europe, never mind against which country or group of countries our efforts may have to be directed."[9]

FDR admired TR greatly, deserted the Democratic party to cast his first presidential vote for him, married his niece, and proudly succeeded in 1913 to the office TR had occupied fifteen years earlier, assistant secretary of the navy. The next year, despite TR's warning, the Kaiser's Germany threatened to gather the whole force of Europe in a single hand. As the First World War began, young FDR from his office in the Navy Department was sure that the American interest lay in Allied victory, even though the president who had appointed him, Woodrow Wilson, was determined that America stay out of the war. "I just *know*," FDR wrote his wife in the spring of 1915, "that I shall do some awful unneutral thing before I get through!"[10]

The United States, it can be convincingly argued, entered the First World War in 1917 for the balance-of-power reasons expounded by Jefferson and Theodore Roosevelt. But Wilson disdained such ignoble motives and demanded higher justification before he would offer up the lives of young Americans. He set forth a radiant vision of a world beyond national interest and alliances, beyond spheres of influence and balances of power, a world not of organized rivalries but an organized common peace, founded on democracy, self-determination, and collective punishment of aggression. This vision quickly captured the imagination of ardent young men and women—Franklin Roosevelt among them. Theodore Roosevelt had taught FDR geopolitics. Woodrow Wilson now gave him a context of international idealism in which the principles of power had a strong but secondary role.

Theodore Roosevelt in certain moods saw war as a positive good, as a means of fostering stern and virile virtues and of strengthening a nation's honor and soul. The First World War, however, was very different from that romantic charge up San Juan Hill. For the younger Roosevelt, the awful carnage on the Western front certified the necessity of the Wilsonian dream. "I have seen war," FDR said in a speech in 1936. ". . . I have seen blood running from the wounded. I have seen men coughing out their gassed lungs. I have seen the dead in the mud. I have seen cities destroyed. I have seen two hundred limping, exhausted men come out of the line — the survivors of a regiment of one thousand that went forward forty-eight hours before. I have seen children starving. I have seen agony of mothers and wives. I hate war."[11]

Wilson now held out the hope of a world in which nations might join together to abolish such horrors. The Wilsonian vision enlarged young Roosevelt's horizons: He now saw not only war but peace; not only the United States but the world; not only a balance of power but a community of power. Those two polar figures, Theodore Roosevelt and Woodrow

Wilson, detested each other. But they joined to construct the framework within which Franklin Roosevelt, who admired them both, approached foreign affairs for the rest of his life.

FDR deeply believed, as he said in 1919, that America had "taken on for all time a new relationship" to the world; it would commit a grievous wrong "if it were ever to attempt to go backwards towards an old Chinese wall policy of isolationism."[12] As the Democratic party's vice presidential candidate in 1920, he campaigned vigorously for Wilson's League of Nations. "If the World War showed anything more than another," he said, "it showed the American people the futility of imagining that they could live in smug content while the rest of the world burned in the conflagration of war."[13]

In 1928, as foreign policy spokesman for the Democratic party, he contended in an article for the Council on Foreign Relations quarterly *Foreign Affairs* that "the outside world almost unanimously views us with less good will today than at any previous period" and that only through a policy of international collaboration could the United States "regain the world's trust and friendship." He called for cooperation with the League, "the first great agency for the maintenance of peace and for the solution of common problems ever known to civilization."[14]

But in the aftermath of war a disillusioned America had turned back with heartfelt relief to traditional isolationism. The nature of this isolationism requires specification. American isolationism never meant economic or intellectual withdrawal from the world. It meant, quite narrowly, the rejection of political commitments and "entangling alliances," the insistence on national freedom of decision in the conduct of foreign affairs. Such political unilateralism had coexisted from the start with the promotion of commercial, financial, and cultural ties between the United States and other nations.

The onset of the Great Depression after 1929 accentuated the American determination to look homeward. The Hoover administration resorted to the time-honored Republican remedy for economic distress: raising the tariff. The highly protective Smoot-Hawley tariff of 1930 had, as Roosevelt observed, "the inevitable result of bringing about retaliations by the other nations of the world. Forty of them set up, just as you and I would have done, their own tariff defenses against us."[15] The multiplying trade barriers, he said, were "symptoms of economic insanity . . . . If the present tariff war continues, the world will go back a thousand years."[16] The spread of economic warfare helped sabotage the Wilsonian dream of collective action to keep the peace.

In the meantime the Japanese invasion of Manchuria in 1931 struck a decisive blow against the peace system. Then Hitler's conquest of power in

1933 meant a resurgent Germany and new threats to the stability of Europe. By the time Roosevelt became president five weeks later, the peace system was in deep trouble.

The new American president brought to the White House an international outlook based on four basic principles. One was TR's belief in the preservation of the balance of world power. A second was Wilson's dream of concerted international action to keep the peace. The third was the conviction that peace and political collaboration rested on commercial harmony among nations and therefore required a freely trading world. The fourth principle was the imperative necessity in a democracy of basing foreign policy on domestic consent. The first three principles were inevitably qualified and compromised by the fourth.

The deepening depression made the domestic economy the first priority for the American people, and for the new president too. But, for all the necessary domestic distraction, Roosevelt followed the rise of aggression in the world with acute foreboding. He devoted a great part of his second cabinet meeting to the possibility of war with Japan. The hope of deterring Japanese aggression was primary in the decision to establish diplomatic relations with the Soviet Union.

At the London Economic Conference later in 1933 Roosevelt refused to sacrifice his national recovery program to ill-judged European demands for an international gold standard; but, as he subsequently wrote the aggrieved British prime minister, "I am concerned by events in Germany, for I feel that an insane rush to further armaments in Continental Europe is infinitely more dangerous than any number of squabbles over gold or stabilization or tariffs."[17] When Stafford Cripps of Britain, at that time a Labour M.P., came to luncheon at the White House in 1935 and assured Roosevelt that in the end Germany would wriggle out of actual fighting, the president wrote ironically to his ambassador to Moscow, "He told me, with a straight face, that Hitler does not feel he can count on the German people to back him up in a war."[18]

German aggression, Roosevelt believed, was bound to undermine the fragile international order and threaten the safety of the republic. His annual message to Congress in January 1936, with its condemnation of "autocratic institutions that beget slavery at home and aggression abroad,"[19] began his long labor of public education to prepare the American people to meet the danger. In August 1936 he went on to denounce the "new-born fanaticisms, convictions on the part of certain peoples that they have become the unique depositories of ultimate truth and right."[20]

But American foreign policy can range only as far as domestic consent will allow. The Constitution divides the control of foreign policy between the president and the Congress. In particular, Congress has the exclusive power to make appropriations, to determine the size of the armed forces, to set neutrality standards, and to authorize war. And Congress in the 1930s reflected the postwar isolationist cynicism about world affairs, even more compelling and irritable as the international order began to break up.

Thus in the first months of his presidency Roosevelt authorized the American representative in Geneva to say that, in case of a threat to the peace, the United States under certain conditions would cooperate with collective efforts made by other states to restore peace. Congress quickly disallowed this initiative by requiring that the administration's proposed embargo on arms shipments to aggressor nations apply equally to victims of aggression. Soon Roosevelt was forced to accept rigid neutrality legislation that, by forbidding the president to discriminate between aggressor and victim, nullified American power to act forcefully against aggression. Congress also rejected FDR's proposal that the United States join the World Court. "Today, quite frankly," Roosevelt wrote after his last defeat, "the wind everywhere blows against us."[21]

What could be done to arrest the world's drift to war? FDR could do something to moderate economic conflict through his program of reciprocal trade agreements. But he was not under any illusion that free trade would check the dictators. "We do not maintain," he said in 1936, "that a more liberal international trade will stop war; but we fear that without a more liberal international trade, war is a natural sequence."[22] The next year he described "an economic approach to peace" as "a pretty weak reed for Europe to lean on . . . . How can it ever avert war in the long run if the armament process continues at its present pace?"[23]

What then? Disarmament conferences? By the mid-thirties, an exhausted art form. The League of Nations? Hitler, Mussolini, the Japanese had rendered collective security impotent. Given the eclipse of the Wilsonian vision, the remaining hope, as FDR evidently saw it, was to return to the realism of Theodore Roosevelt and strengthen the European balance of power against Hitler's Germany, saving Wilson for the world after Hitler.

The restoration of the European balance became his objective in foreign affairs. There were vivid political limits on how far he could go. The American people were strongly opposed to Hitler but were just as strongly opposed to the idea of going to war to stop Hitler. Congress felt the same way. So indeed did Roosevelt himself. His hope almost to the end was that Hitler could be beaten by all aid short of war. Some isolationists feared that any aid to the Allies would make American participation inevitable, and Roosevelt faced constant hostility in his efforts to modify the neutrality statutes and to encourage international resistance to aggression.

So he pressed his campaign of public education, striving in speeches and press conferences to awaken American public opinion to the troubles he discerned ahead. Hitler provided indispensible confirmation by annexing Austria, overrunning Czechoslovakia, and invading Poland — developments urgently conveyed to America in press reports and radio broadcasts by an uncommonly talented corps of foreign correspondents.

Behind the scenes FDR used the discretionary powers of the executive to build a front against Hitler. This did not violate the neutrality statutes, which were drafted to prevent economic involvements in foreign wars, not to prohibit personal preferences about the outcome. As FDR put it after the outbreak of war in 1939, "I cannot ask that every American remain neutral in thought."[24] Certainly he did not. But, given the paranoia of the isolationists, he had to proceed cautiously, deviously, very often in secrecy, in exploring possibilities with European governments.

Britain, France, and the Soviet Union were obviously the vital components of the anti-Hitler coalition. For Roosevelt, Britain, still in those remote days a great power, was the key to the restoration of the balance, and he spent much time and concern trying to promote Anglo-American cooperation and to stiffen British opposition to Hitler. The British, however, found his diplomatic methods unduly personal and informal. "Half the battle in talking with people," he once said, "is to look them in the eye and let them look you in the eye."[25] Ignoring formal diplomatic channels, he entertained a succession of British visitors with hints, suggestions, lectures, and overtures looking to the exchange of military information and to forms of joint diplomatic action.

His signals were received with skepticism. FDR's approaches struck Whitehall as hopelessly unprofessional. His ideas seemed off the cuff, visionary, and irresponsible. And his State Department appeared to be transmitting American policy on a different wavelength. In any case, the British, for understandable reasons, discounted Roosevelt on the ground that Americans were far more given to words than to deeds.

Sir Ronald Lindsay, the astute British ambassador to Washington, tried to get London to take the American president seriously. FDR's "purpose," Sir Ronald cabled the Foreign Office early in 1937 after a White House visit by Walter Runciman, the president of the Board of Trade, "was in my mind unquestionably to try to get closer to His Majesty's Government with a view to preventing a war or shortening it if it should come."[26] In time Lindsay convinced Anthony Eden, the foreign secretary, and Robert Vansittart, the Foreign Office's top professional, but Neville Chamberlain, the prime minister, neither liked nor trusted Americans, FDR especially, and could never be persuaded that a positive response to FDR was worth the effort. Quite the contrary: Fearing that Roosevelt's "meddling" would run athwart his own cherished program of peace through appeasement, he hoped to exclude the American president from Europe altogether.

In 1938 the French government, less persuaded of the virtues of appeasement and alarmed by the growth of Hitler's *Luftwaffe*, sent Baron Amaury de La Grange across the Atlantic to buy American aircraft. As La Grange reported to Paris, he found Roosevelt, "who is Francophile and fears German expansion, . . . well informed about what is going on in Germany" and "completely in favor" of strengthening the French air force.[27] When it developed that the American aircraft industry was not up to producing modern combat aircraft in quantity, the French sent Jean Monnet on a second air mission to the United States. Monnet and Henry Morgenthau, Jr., the secretary of the treasury, used French purchases to expand American aircraft production, laying the industrial basis for the annual 50,000 planes Roosevelt demanded fifty years ago today.

As for the Soviet Union, diplomatic recognition had been intended as a warning to Germany as well as to Japan. After William Bullitt, Roosevelt's first ambassador to Moscow, soured on Soviet communism, Roosevelt replaced him with Joseph E. Davies, who did his sometimes effusive best to improve relations between the two countries. The hope of incorporating the Soviet Union in the anti-Hitler front collapsed, however, in August 1939 when Stalin decided to cast his lot with Hitler.

In the current moment of democratic triumph, we forget how precarious the position of democracy was half a century ago, how pervasive the contempt was, among intellectuals and masses alike, for parliamentary methods, for government by discussion, for liberties of expression and opposition, for bourgeois individualism. Discipline, order, massed strength, submergence of the individual were the talismans of the day.

The First World War had shattered old structures of security and order and unleashed angry energies of revolution — revolution not for democracy, as in the eighteenth and nineteenth centuries, but precisely *against* democracy. Bolshevism and fascism had acute doctrinal differences, but their structural similarities—a single leader, a single party, a single body of infallible dogma—meant that each had more in common with the other than with democracy. Both despised, denounced, and, wherever they could, destroyed regimes based on free elections, parliaments, human rights, and individual liberties.

The Great War was followed in a short dozen years by the Great Depression. History, it appeared, was pronouncing its final verdict on the experiment in self-government. Democracy could secure neither peace nor prosperity. Economic collapse now seemed to verify the Marxian prophecy that capitalism would perish of its internal contradictions. The impotence of democratic regimes before mass unemployment seemed to verify the fascist claim that parliamentary methods were bankrupt.

The millennial creeds of fascism, nazism, communism, promised a new heaven and a new earth. The totalitarian gospel appealed to the fears of the rich, to the frustrations of the lower middle class, to the yearnings of the workers, to the illusions of the intellectuals. As Hitler's divisions stormed across Scandinavia, the Low Countries, and France, many in the West saw totalitarianism, in the title of a poisonous little book Anne Morrow Lindbergh was writing that spring in the United States, as "the wave of the future."

While her husband, the famous aviator, predicted Nazi victory and opposed American aid to the democracies, the gentle Mrs. Lindbergh lamented "the beautiful things . . . lost in the dying of an age," saw totalitarianism as free society's predestined successor, a "new, and perhaps even ultimately good, conception of humanity trying to come to birth," discounted the evils of Hitlerism and Stalinism as merely "scum on the wave of the future," and concluded that "the wave of the future is coming and there is no fighting it."[28] In America *The Wave of the Future* went through seven printings by December 1940. In Western Europe many—far too many—arrived independently at the same defeatist conclusion.

Roosevelt did not. His New Deal had demonstrated the vitality of liberal democracy in face of the cruelties of uncontrolled capitalism and the agonies of mass unemployment, and now he proposed to rally democracy against totalitarian aggression. "There are some," Roosevelt told Congress fifty years ago today, "who say that democracy cannot cope with the new techniques of Government developed in recent years by . . . a few countries which deny the freedoms that we maintain are essential to our democratic way of life. That I reject." And he concluded: "Our security is not a matter of weapons alone. The arm that wields them must be strong, the eye that guides them clear, the will that directs them indomitable. These are the characteristics of a free people."[29]

This ringing faith in the power of free society undergirded Roosevelt's internationalism. It found memorable expression eight months later when in another address to Congress he looked forward "to a world founded upon four essential human freedoms," a world which would see "the supremacy of human rights everywhere" and would therefore be "the very antithesis of the so-called new order of tyranny which the dictators seek to create with the crash of a bomb."[30] And the Four Freedoms acquired its program when Roosevelt and Churchill met at sea off Newfoundland in August 1941 and promulgated the Atlantic Charter.

The Atlantic Charter embodied the Wilsonian vision of self- determination, no territorial aggrandizement, and "a wider and permanent system of general security." And it emphasized the economic dimension Roosevelt added to Wilsonianism—"access, on equal terms, to the trade and to the raw materials of the world" and "fullest collaboration between all Nations in the economic field with the object of securing, for all, improved labor standards, economic advancement, and social security."[31]

After America's entry into the war, the need for postwar planning crystallized Roosevelt's international outlook. I should perhaps mention a theory that had brief currency awhile back — the theory that Roosevelt's fatal error was to subordinate political to military objectives; that he neglected everything else in the interests of victory. Roosevelt was in fact the most political of politicians, political in every reflex and to his fingertips—and just as political in war as he had been in peace. As a virtuoso politician, he understood perfectly that there could be no better cloak for the pursuit of political objectives in wartime than the claim of total absorption in winning the war.

And he was more than a virtuoso politician. He was also a statesman with an instinct for the broad emergent movements of history. As he had been ahead of most European leaders in his conviction that Hitler meant war, he was also ahead in his conviction that war against Hitler meant dramatic changes in the world.

Roosevelt took care during the war to minimize damage to American lives and property; and after the war, he believed, America would be the most powerful country on the planet. He expected it to use that power to promote a New Deal for the world—democratic societies based on human rights, economic growth, social reform, the development of natural resources and a freely trading international economy; a trading system that would, incidentally, assure markets and raw materials for the United States. American prosperity, FDR believed, required in an increasingly interdependent world rising living standards in all countries. "Poverty anywhere constitutes a danger to prosperity everywhere," he declared in 1944, endorsing the Declaration of the International Labor Organization.[32]

He moved quietly and methodically to prepare the American people for an enlarged international role. By the end of 1944 a series of international conferences, held mostly at American initiative and dominated mostly by American agendas, had begun to outline the postwar world: most vitally perhaps at Bretton Woods (finance, trade, development) and also at Dumbarton Oaks (international organization), Hot Springs (food and agriculture), Washington (relief and rehabilitation), and Chicago (civil aviation). Upon his death in April 1945 Roosevelt left an encompassing and relatively enduring framework for the world after the war—an interesting achievement for a president who was supposed to subordinate political to military goals.

The Soviet Union, he believed, had proved itself a great power and had to be incorporated within this framework. Roosevelt is often criticized for naïveté in thinking that he could charm Stalin into amiable postwar collaboration. Perhaps he was not so naive after all. Stalin was not the helpless prisoner of ideology. The Soviet dictator saw himself less as the disciple of Marx and Lenin than as their fellow prophet. Roosevelt was surely right in regarding Stalin as the *only* lever capable of changing the Soviet course. Only Stalin had the power to rewrite communist doctrine, as he had already rewritten Russian history. Roosevelt's determination to work on and through Stalin was, it seems in retrospect, based on shrewd insight. It was the only chance the West had. As Walter Lippmann observed, Roosevelt was too cynical to think he could charm Stalin. "He distrusted everybody. What he thought he could do was outwit Stalin, which is quite a different thing."[33]

FDR had learned realism from TR long before he had learned idealism from Wilson. The balance of power continued to shape his basic thoughts about foreign policy. But he always cherished the Wilsonian hope, and he knew that it was the Wilsonian dream, and not the balance of power, that moved his countrymen. His task now was to reconcile international geopolitical inevitabilities, such as Soviet predominance in Eastern Europe, with domestic political myths, such as the wickedness of spheres of influence. He talked idealism but played the power game, withholding the atomic secret from Stalin and keeping the Soviets out of occupation policy in Western Europe. At Yalta he concentrated on luring the Soviet Union into the United Nations, the new world organization that would, he hoped, fix up the loose ends later.

In the short run, Stalin appeared to gain from democratic confusions. But statesmanship is tested by the long run. Yalta is often condemned for the alleged surrender of Eastern Europe to Moscow. In fact, far from decreeing the partition of Europe, the Yalta Declarations on Liberated Europe and Poland envisaged an Eastern Europe based on self-determination and free elections—the very Eastern Europe that has emerged in these last exciting months, not as the repudiation but as the fulfillment of Yalta.

In the long run too Roosevelt anticipated a narrowing of differences, a measure of convergence, between democratic and communist societies. He told Under Secretary of State Sumner Welles that, marking American democracy as 100 and Soviet communism as zero, the American system, as it moved away from *laissez-faire*, might reach the figure of 60 and the Soviet system, as it moved toward political democracy, might reach the figure of 40.[34] The illustration was typically slapdash, but the anticipation looks a good deal less foolish in 1990 than it did in, say, 1950.

Roosevelt also was sure that Western colonialism was finished in Asia and Africa. Here again his intuitions about the course of history can hardly be gainsaid. He tried to persuade the British to leave India and to prevent the French from returning to Indochina; and he pressed the idea of international trusteeships as the means of the liquidation of colonial empires.

He believed too that China would in due course become a great power and that it should be installed as one of the Four Policemen charged with supervising the postwar international system. For this thought Roosevelt suffered much ridicule from Churchill at the time and from historians since. Roosevelt, responding to Churchill's objections, observed at the Teheran Conference that he wanted China as one of the Big Four "not because he did not realize the weakness of China at present, but he was thinking farther into the future . . . . After all China was a nation of 400 million people, and it was better to have them as friends rather than as a potential source of trouble."[35] At Yalta he told Churchill that it would take "three generations of education and training . . . before China could become a serious factor."[36] Now that two of these three generations have passed and China has grown from 400 million to a billion people, FDR's assessment seems perhaps wiser than Churchill's scornful dismissal of "the pigtails" as the "Great American Illusion."[37]

FDR's internationalism was generally a success in shaping his times, not alone because of his adroit and flexible merger of the tough-minded realism of Theodore Roosevelt with the soaring idealism of Woodrow Wilson, but most of all because Franklin Roosevelt, for all his insouciance, improvisation, and persiflage, saw more deeply than his contemporaries into the great currents of modern history.

Part II

FDR'S ALLIES

2

CHURCHILL AND FRANKLIN D. ROOSEVELT: A MARRIAGE OF CONVENIENCE

David K. Adams

The story of the glory of the Churchill-Roosevelt partnership in the wars against Japan and Nazi Germany has been told many times and there is perhaps little new to say about it, either about their comradeship or their squabbles over policy,[1] but there is also a curious lacuna in the historiography. This concerns the very ambivalent set of attitudes that Churchill held about the United States until very late, and his failure to cultivate the attention of Franklin Roosevelt until the crisis in European affairs had reached breaking point and the president had made the first moves.

David Reynolds has said that whereas earlier writing on the 1930s "was prone to sentimentality, the recent work has emphasised and even exaggerated the hostility and suspicion between the two governments." British Foreign Office prejudices about the United States have been well established. As late as May 1938 Frank Ashton-Gwatkin could write that although one day Anglo-American cooperation would save the world, that day had not yet arrived. In February 1939, Jay Pierrepont Moffat, head of the European division of the Department of State, could write that the "British do regard us as a Dominion gone wrong, but if they frankly regarded us as a foreign country, albeit a friendly one, relations would be better."[2] Even Winston Churchill, born to an American mother and an English father—the perfect man, therefore, according to Mark Twain—shared to a considerable extent in such attitudes, despite his WASPish invocation of the unity of the English-speaking peoples.[3]

Language, institutions, and heritage clearly have given a special quality to the Anglo-American relationship from the Revolution onward, but as the United States expanded and developed its own ways the two societies diverged. Frequent transatlantic visitors took pleasure in pointing to cultural differences: The images of America from Britain were of a rather vulgar and materialistic democracy; for many Americans Britain was an elitist, class-ridden, and rather decadent mother country of empire. Culturally the two countries were frequently at odds. The British caste system, with an innate conviction of its own superiority, clashed with the American commitment to republican democracy, equality of opportunity, and vigorous attempts to define cultural values in ways that would facilitate absorption of immigrant masses and accommodate ethnic minorities.[4]

Rivalry between the two countries was also geopolitical. Imperial designs emanating from both countries hesitated on a number of horizons: Canada, Texas, Latin America. But after the War of 1812 there were sufficient common interests, sustained by American dependence on British capital investment and by Britain's preoccupations with a global empire that was perpetually challenged by the aspirations of rival continental European powers, for the peace to be kept between them after 1815. By the end of the nineteenth century, with Britain aware of the ambitions of a United Germany, the United States came to seem like a desirable "kissing cousin," a balancing force in the game of international power politics that might be used to serve British ends. After tensions momentarily threatened war over Venezuela in 1895, a new rapprochement came about that was characterized by British neutrality in the Spanish-American War of 1898 and American "hands off" in the Boer War, despite strongly critical opinion about British policies in southern Africa. No doubt there was also in both countries some subscription to Anglo-Saxon racism in the age of the "new imperialism." Moreover, as the United States spread its wings, and during Theodore Roosevelt's presidency began to compete with Britain in naval terms, Britain took heed.[5]

Both cultural and political ambiguities are embodied in President Theodore Roosevelt's comment to a correspondent in 1904 that "the average Englishman is not a being whom I find congenial or with whom I care to associate . . . . England has been friendly with us since we have grown so strong as to make her friendship a matter of more moment to her than to us. If we quit building our fleet, England's friendship would immediately cool."[6]

Military power, as Paul Kennedy has recently reminded us,[7] is usually dependent on economic power, and by the turn of the century the historic relationship had been transformed. The United States had become the world's leading producer of agricultural commodities, industrial goods, and extractive minerals. Although the debtor-creditor relationship was not finally reversed until the First World War, there could already be seen an American takeover of significant sectors of the British economy. As early as the Great Exhibition in London in 1851, at which American technology had been on display to a rather astonished world, *The Economist* had noted that "the superiority of the United States to England is ultimately as certain as the next eclipse."[8] George Peabody of Massachusetts, who founded what later became the banking house of Morgan, was but one of the midcentury giants who paved the way for what was to follow in the American takeover of parts of the British economy.[9]

In the career of William Waldorf Astor, who established himself successively in ansdowne House, Carlton House Terrace, Cliveden, and Hever Castle, can be traced the migration of those who "longed for the respect and protection built into the English class system."[10] Still more symbolic of the tilting of the economic scales, which in the twentieth century was to see the old patterns turned inside out, was the cultural phenomenon of dynastic marriages: marriages of convenience and mutual gratification. Economic substance was exchanged for social status, new fortunes for old titles, New World vitality for Old World class. American wealth provided "capital regeneration" for British houses: "How perfect a meeting of circumstances. For the British aristocracy, whose titles were thought to carry far more distinction than any of their European brethren, possessed just what the newly rich Americans wanted, a social preeminence based not simply on the speculative waves of finance but on the rock of primogeniture. If one's daughter were a duchess, one's grandson would without question be a duke. It was the most pleasant of certainties."[11]

Jenny, daughter of Leonard Jerome, "the King of Wall Street" and devotee of the turf, was a pioneer in the transatlantic marriage market when she married Lord Randolph Churchill, younger son of the seventh Duke of Marlborough, in 1874. At this time the equations were not so clear and the Marlboroughs were not thrilled. But some twenty years later Consuelo Vanderbilt was married at the age of eighteen to the ninth duke; Mary, daughter of Levi Leiter of the Marshall Field department store was married to George Nathaniel Curzon; Maud Alice Burke, "the yellow canary" heiress to the Comstock Lode, ruined her chances of capturing the grandson of the last King of Poland and settled for Sir Bache Cunard of the steamship line. Known as Emerald, she showed an "astonishing competence in the commerce of life." At the age of eighty, Lord Donegall advertised for a wife who could bring in £25,000 and attracted Violet Twining.[12]

For the heiresses and their parents, social status was the lure, and many fishes were caught in the net. But there remained a tendency in British society to regard the "Big Spenders" as rather vulgar, and it was perhaps envy as well as avarice that illuminated a culture that continued to produce a stream of critical accounts of the United States that were generally sanctimonious.[13] This world into which Winston Churchill was born in 1874 was a curious one and far removed from the world of the Roosevelts in Hyde Park, New York, although as it happens FDR and Churchill were distant cousins.

The widely different backgrounds and life-styles of the James Roosevelts and the Randolph Churchills influenced their offspring with results characterized by Isaiah Berlin in this way: The "differences between the President and the Prime Minister were at least in one respect something more than the obvious differences of national character, education and even temperament . . . . Mr. Roosevelt was a typical child of the twentieth century and of the New World; while Mr. Churchill . . . remains a European of the nineteenth century." Leo Amery remarked in 1929 that "the key to Winston is to realise that he is mid-Victorian . . . and unable ever to get the modern point of view."[14]

Churchill, this nineteenth-century gentleman, had a tremendous curiosity about the United States that was accompanied by fascination with its energy, but he also lacked, until quite late in the interwar period, a full appreciation of the realities of power in the twentieth century. As his relationship with FDR developed, it contained a great deal of affection, but this could hardly disguise the profound differences in world outlook and policy objectives about which they were to have substantial disagreements throughout World War II. It has indeed been written that "the war was all they had in common."[15] Perhaps, then, the Anglo-American marriages of convenience are an appropriate metaphor for the Churchill-Roosevelt relationship.

It was not that Churchill's view of the United States, which of course underlaid his relationship with FDR, was not based on direct experience. In 1895 the young subaltern of the 4th Hussars had set off across the Atlantic on the Cunarder *Etruria*, passing through New York en route for Cuba, where he would observe the action as Spanish troops gathered in Havana to suppress the Cuban revolt. Bourke Cockran, his mother's friend, awaited him on the pier and gave him a social whirl: "What an extraordinary people the Americans are! Their hospitality is a revelation to me and they make you feel at home and at ease in a way that I have never before experienced." Like so many earlier British visitors, he was scornful of the American press: "vulgarity divested of truth. Their best papers write for a class of snotty housemaids and footmen"; he thought paper dollars "most disreputable," but loved the physical comforts brought about by American technology and entrepreneurship, and found American vitality infectious:

> A great, crude, strong, young people are the Americans—like a boisterous healthy boy among enervated but well bred ladies and gentleman . . . a great lusty youth who treads on all your sensibilities perpetuates every possible horror of ill manners—whom neither age nor just tradition inspire with reverence—but who moves about his affairs with a good-natured freshness which may well be the envy of older nations of the earth.[16]

Such a portrayal was par for the course, patronizing as it was.

He returned to the United States in 1900, this time, as he remarked in a letter to Cockran, pursuing "profit not pleasure." His lectures, with daring tales of escape from the Boers and vigorous support for Britain's South Africa policies, frequently met with hostile audiences. At a dinner of the New York Press Club he made remarks, later repeated elsewhere, that caused additional discomfort in multi-ethnic America: "The chief characteristic of the English-speaking peoples, as compared with other 'white' people, is that they wash, and wash at regular periods. England and America are divided by a great ocean of salt water, but united by an eternal bath-tub of soap and water." Vice president-elect Theodore Roosevelt, whom he went to see in Albany, did not particularly take to him: "I saw an Englishman, Winston Churchill here, and . . . he is not an attractive fellow."[17]

Five years later when Churchill published his life of his father, Lord Randolph, Theodore Roosevelt wrote to his son in quite extreme language that "the older one *was* a rather cheap character, and the younger one *is* a rather cheap character."[18]

The high point of Churchill's tour came in Boston, where the Lodges spoke only to Cabots and the Cabots spoke only to God. Perhaps reflecting the tensions within the city, generated in part by reactions to the massed Irish in the North End and the Italians of Little Italy, his visit became the occasion for a great pro-British demonstration orchestrated by the Anglo-American Society. In a lecture at the Tremont Temple he spoke with pride of being "the natural product of an Anglo-American alliance; not political, but stronger and more sacred, an alliance of heart to heart." The lecture was followed, appropriately enough, by dinner at the Somerset Club. However, in the Midwest, heartland of the other America, he had generally hostile audiences. Nonetheless he ended the tour some $6,000 better off.[19]

He made the tour immediately following his first election to the House of Commons. His political career need not concern us until the coming of the world war in 1914 when Churchill was serving as First Lord of the Admiralty, a post to which he had been appointed by Prime Minister Herbert Asquith in 1911 and at which he would remain until he was dismissed after the Dardanelles tragedy in 1915. Here his career first interlocks with that of FDR, then young assistant secretary of the navy, who wanted to go to London in December 1914 to observe wartime organization firsthand. Churchill was angry at U.S. neutrality, and earlier that year Asquith had recorded in a letter that the "particular 'swine' at whom he [WSC] would now like to have a fling are his kinsmen in the United States." When Roosevelt's inquiry arrived, the permanent secretary at the Admiralty reported to the naval attaché at the U.S. Embassy that the First Lord was unable because of pressure of work to offer the necessary assistance and that "in the circumstances, he will not trouble you to call upon him." This dismissive attitude is reflected later in Churchill's singularly modest attention to American problems, policies, and contributions to the war effort in his history of *The World Crisis*. When Roosevelt finally got to Europe toward the end of the war, the two men were together at a dinner party at Gray's Inn on 29 July 1918 but made little impression on each other, if they even met.[20]

As colonial secretary and then Chancellor of the Exchequer Churchill was in office throughout much of the 1920s, except for the years 1922 to 1924. Throughout this period his view of the United States is clearly that of an alien power with radically different interests. There are in fact only a few scattered references to the United States in Martin Gilbert's magisterial life of Churchill, and they are invariably hostile. The United States is seen as obstinate over the divisive issue of war debts, Japanese-American relations could be destabilizing in the Far East, and when Churchill wanted to take Britain back to the gold standard in 1925 he was worried lest this made the American "hoard of gold more valuable . . . . Shall we not be relieving them from the consequences of their selfish and extortionate policy?" As debate on the gold standard bill developed, he moderated his view somewhat and pleaded from the point of view of British interests that it was essential to act not only with the dominions but also with the United States, "our chief shop and chief customer"; but he remained highly critical of American political policies vis-à-vis Europe.[21]

In September 1928 Churchill spoke very freely about the United States to a visitor to his country home, Chartwell, who recorded in his diary: "He thinks they are very arrogant, fundamentally hostile to us, and that they wish to dominate world politics. He thinks their 'Big Navy' talk is a bluff which we ought to call." In letters to his wife about a speech by President Coolidge that was regarded as anti-British Churchill wrote: "My blood boiled too. Why can't they let us alone? They have exacted every penny owing from Europe; they say they are going to help; surely they might leave us to manage our own affairs." That same November 1928 he was strongly opposed to American pressures for naval disarmament, although the following January he was prepared to make a positive election issue of détente in Anglo-American relations over naval building. However, his wife commented that his known hostility to the United States was a possible barrier to getting the Foreign Office should the Conservatives be reelected. She advised him to "try and understand and master America and make her like you." Indeed he might have so tried![22]

With the fall of the Baldwin government in 1929, Churchill returned to the United States for the first time since 1900 to promote his books and articles. It was also a pleasure trip with three members of his family. They journeyed across Canada, were entertained by William Randolph Hearst at San Simeon, experienced Hollywood, and visited the Grand Canyon. In New York Bernard Baruch, who had assumed Cockran's earlier role, provided hospitality and entertainment. The two men had met toward the end of the Great War when Churchill was minister of munitions and Baruch a member of the War Industries Board. It seems that Churchill had made an attempt to see Governor Roosevelt for, as he had written to Baruch, he wanted "to see the country and to meet the leaders of its fortunes," but Henry Morgenthau, FDR's close friend who was at that time chairman of the New York State Agricultural Advisory Committee, wrote that Roosevelt would not be in New York at the time of Churchill's stay. In Washington he did see President Hoover.[23]

He went to America with a contract from the *Daily Telegraph* for a series of articles on his trip, and these appeared between November 1929 and February 1930. His comments were entitled "What I saw and heard in America," and he began to develop the theme of the inherent bonds of unity of the English-speaking peoples that was to be the title of his later four-volume history. He found the two nations less divided as the issues of war debts and the Irish question began to disappear, leaving naval parity and the freedom of the seas as the only outstanding points of dispute.[24]

There is a changing emphasis here that is also to be found in a number of the articles Churchill wrote after his return to England. In the *Strand*, for example, in August 1931 he compared, in friendly although still rather patronizing terms, a New World society of excesses wrapped in platitudes with the greater subtlety of the Old World. His nationalism came out strongly. Americans were a "'Frailer race'. . . . Even if the first prizes of the future should fall to the United States, the Englishman will still remain a vast enduring force for virility, sanity and good will." But nonetheless the promise for the future lay in the "union of these complimentary virtues and resources."[25]

In 1931 he was back in the United States again, this time very deliberately to replenish his coffers, having lost much of his money in the Wall Street crash. He undertook a paid lecture tour and also had articles commissioned by the *Daily Mail*. A major theme of his fully booked lectures was "The Destiny of the English-Speaking People," around which he argued for effective joint action between Great Britain and the United States. This lecture, given in Washington, D.C., produced rather tart comment from the *Washington Post*:

> Not many years ago political and economic unity with the Yankees would have been repulsive to British statesmen . . . Now the tables are turned and Mr. Churchill is trying to flatter the United States into taking over some of Great Britain's liabilities. It is rather strange for a debtor to offer a partnership to his creditors. What contribution has Britain to make to the co-operative bond Mr. Churchill suggests for the two countries?

Churchill's other substantial speech, "The World Economic Crisis," was also a plea for cooperation and also received mixed reactions, depending on place and audience.[26]

Churchill's more positive attitude toward the United States was reflected in his first speech in the House of Commons on his return to London. Referring to his tour he remarked that, whereas in 1929 he had found Britain regarded as decadent and outworn, she was now looked up to. It was up to Britain to exploit this feeling and give a lead in Anglo-American cooperation, especially in the economic sphere. The appeal for joint monetary action was repeated in his first radio broadcast to the United States two weeks later, on 8 May. This seemed to represent a change of heart, but it was contained. There is a quite petulant speech in the House on 23 November 1932 proclaiming the impossibility of British guarantees to Europe without American participation: Most difficulties could be solved "by the faithful co-operation of the English-speaking peoples. But that is not going to happen tomorrow."[27]

This was no doubt realistic, bearing in mind the political differences between the United Kingdom and the United States, but what is very odd as we move into the Roosevelt years is the singular absence of the United States in much of the Churchill literature. Despite the themes of his lectures there seems little evidence that he looked westward to the United States as a counterbalance to the rise of Germany. He had a considerable network of friends and correspondents, but they seem to have contained few if any Americans apart from Baruch. Gilbert's life of Churchill contains almost no references to the United States between May 1932 and 1938 apart from a speech in 1934 when Churchill favorably compared Britain's naval strength with that of the United States, a reference at a luncheon discussion on Ethiopia in September 1935 to America being remote and indifferent, and one in a letter to his wife (17 January 1936) in which he found the United States and Great Britain working hand in glove on naval building policy. Finally, there is a 1937 reference to the Zionist lobby in the United States.[28]

In the Companion volume evidence is also noteworthy for its spareness. Churchill wrote to a correspondent in August 1933 of "the tremendous and noble effort your President is making to set North America to work again" and expressed his confidence in the economic recovery of the United States. The following month he commended Roosevelt's action in calling a White House conference on the debt issue, and in a broadcast to the United States in January 1934 he expressed his admiration for the spirit in which Roosevelt grappled with his difficulties.[29] That is all.

The relative lack of attention given to the United States and to President Roosevelt is the more fascinating because FDR's eldest son, James, visited Chartwell in October 1933. He recorded that in a guessing game after dinner Churchill said that his fondest wish was to be prime minister and in close daily communication by telephone with the president of the United States, for "there is nothing we could not do if we were together." He apparently then drew an insignia of a pound and dollar sign intertwined and asked James to carry it to his father.[30] Churchill sent Roosevelt a copy of the first two volumes of his *Marlborough* with a hyperbolic inscription of "earnest best wishes for the success of the greatest crusade of modern times." There is no record that FDR directly responded, although Cary Grayson reported that the president had been pleased.[31]

These lacunae are also fascinating because from the late spring of 1933 Churchill was working on an article entitled "The Bond Between Us" in which he declared himself to be "an ardent admirer of the main drift and impulse which President Roosevelt has given to the economic and financial policy of the United States."[32] The following year in a profile of FDR for *Collier's* he cautiously tried, as he explained to his editor, "to strike a note of warning while at the same time expressing my sincere sympathy with the great effort the President is making." This was published in *Collier's* on 29

December 1934 as "While the World Watches President Franklin D. Roosevelt" and under its original working title as an addition to the second printing of Churchill's volume *Great Contemporaries* in 1937. Churchill's somewhat wordy profile characterizes Roosevelt as "a statesman of world renown" but only in the removal of prohibition and in his administrative measures for relief and the expansion of credit.[33]

One wonders how much Churchill's restraint was conditioned by some of the more negative responses he was getting about Roosevelt from occasional correspondents. Ambassador Ronald Lindsay wrote in December 1933, when himself acknowledging a copy of *Marlborough,* that Roosevelt has been giving us "pure hocus pocus and a continent has watched him agape"; his publisher Charles Scribner wrote in August 1935 of his friends' elation "at the setback that Roosevelt received in the elections in Rhode Island. It may mean a turn in the tide but it will be very hard to oust him next year unless there is an open split in the Democratic Party, which we cannot count on yet."[34]

The entwined sterling and dollar signs reappear in 1937 when Churchill received a letter from the French banker Réné Léon who had been an advisor to Roosevelt on monetary policy in 1933. Léon reported from New York that he had seen the president, who had been delighted to have good news of Churchill and to know that a body of British opinion favored closer collaboration in the monetary field. Léon believed the president to be "an ardent co-operator by nature, so that his quick response will always greet any genuine gesture of rapprochement." In conclusion he asked Churchill to send him another copy of the insignia drawing that he had been given on a visit to Chartwell the previous month; he had left his with Roosevelt who had it on his desk and "was gazing at it with considerable interest."[35]

There was certainly a link to Roosevelt through Bernard Baruch, with whom Churchill continued to be friends throughout the 1930s, a friendship that indeed was attacked in the German press. Baruch visited Chartwell on a number of occasions, and Churchill himself planned another trip to the United States in 1936, but this was canceled because of the abdication crisis. An intermittent correspondence witnesses Churchill praising the "cash and carry" provision of the revised neutrality act in 1937, which he came to believe had originated with Baruch, but he significantly failed to mention it in his Commons speech on the navy estimates. He welcomed it, however, in one of his regular newspaper articles as removing possible disputes such as those that had caused so much concern in 1914 and 1915; "It may be rather chilling comfort, but it is comfort nonetheless."[36]

At the Conservatives' Annual Conference at Scarborough on 7 October 1937, Churchill spoke of the close and sympathetic understanding in the United States for British problems and policies, and to cheers from his audience he stated his belief that the "understanding so perfect and spontaneous between the two branches of the English-speaking race is bound to bring an enormous contribution to the consolidation of those forces in the world which stand for peace and freedom." This may have been an oblique reference to Roosevelt's quarantine speech of 5 October 1937. In general, however, Churchill's uncertainties about the United States prevailed throughout the year. In "What We Ask of the United States" 10 December 1937, while underlining the good relations that prevailed between the two countries, he emphasized the strength of isolationism. He saw American prosperity as a major guarantor of international influences, but deeply regretted aspects of the domestic New Deal that he believed to be a ruthless "war on private enterprise." In a Commons speech on defense on 21 December he was concerned only with Anglo-French forces, which he believed would be sufficient "for some time to come"; but in January 1938 he wrote approvingly of the American naval building program.[37]

The sequence of events leading up to the resignation of Anthony Eden as foreign secretary in February 1938 is well known. Churchill's reaction underlines the puzzle about his relationship with the United States. In *The Gathering Storm,* written of course much later and in the light of the wartime experience, he hortates: "That Mr. Chamberlain, with his limited outlook and inexperience of the European scene, should have possessed the self-sufficiency to wave away the proffered hand stretched out across the Atlantic leaves one, even at this date, breathless with amazement." His contemporary reaction was not nearly so strong, and his biographer makes no reference to Roosevelt's initiative in the discussion of Eden's departure, although in a Commons' speech on 22 February Churchill did allude to reaction in the United States, where, he claimed, it would cause havoc and had rendered downcast "those who are steadily working for the closer co-operation of the two countries on parallel lines."[38]

In Gilbert's Companion volume of documents for this period there is comparable emptiness. Not until May 1938, in an article for the *News of the World,* do we find him writing of "the majestic edifice of Anglo-American friendship." But here again there are words of caution, of the "cracks in the pillars that support the mighty dome; . . . 'beneath a crust that sometimes seems too thin are bitter waters of suspicion, a march of misunderstanding'"; but nonetheless their path was one of "joint destiny." In the previous month a journalist friend had sent to Brendan Bracken, Tory M.P. and managing director of *The Economist*, notes for "your friend's two articles. They are both rather academic and objective because I imagine that he will be able to put in any epithets and abuse of the President that may be required." By July there is a flicker of something different when Churchill, in a letter to his wife, reports conversations with Baruch which suggested that the "president is breast-high on our side and will do everything in his power to help."[39]

As the dangers of Hitlerism became increasingly apparent to Churchill, he came to believe that American opinion was hardening against Germany and that in the event of war the United States would not wait as long as it had in the Great War to come in. But in an article in the *Daily Telegraph* in August, while stating that it would be foolish of the dictators to ignore such developments, he argued that it would be equally foolish of the democracies to count on direct aid from the United States.[40]

It is a pity that Churchill's projected lecture tour in the United States in the summer of 1938 did not in fact take place. FDR's commitment to friendship with Canada when he opened the International Bridge linking New York State and Ontario on 18 August 1938 perhaps opened vistas of opportunity, but the possibility of a meeting between him and Churchill at this time did not materialize.[41] However, as the Czech crisis unfolded, Churchill seemed prepared to try to use Roosevelt as a middleman with Hitler.

Gilbert's first reference to FDR in volume 5 comes on 31 August when Churchill wrote to Lord Halifax, the British foreign minister, suggesting a joint note addressed to Germany by Britain, France, and the Soviet Union that, when drafted, should be shown to Roosevelt, "and we should use every effort to induce him to do his utmost upon it." Churchill believed that such a note would encourage internal opposition to Hitler and allow the Führer "to find a way out for himself by parleying with Roosevelt." This was, of course, a very significant suggestion on Churchill's part, but there is no follow-up of concern.[42] The second of Gilbert's references comes on 26 September. In response to a telegram from Baruch urging him "in case of war send children and expectant mothers to me," he replied that "Now is the time for your man to speak." The third and final reference to FDR comes in a letter to his wife written from the South of France on 8 January 1939 in which he discussed the European situation and judged that Neville Chamberlain "in endorsing all that Roosevelt said had made a great advance."[43]

Churchill also responded favorably to Roosevelt's Peace Appeal of 14 April 1939, but there is then another blank period in Gilbert until Roosevelt's astonishing initiative of 11 September 1939. Other sources reveal at least two other speeches in which Churchill saw American public opinion as a potent factor for averting war and referred to "the intimate comprehension of the cause of freedom now at stake in Europe which is shewn by the United States,"[44] but it does not seem that Churchill made more than the most limited of efforts to bring in the New World to redress the balance of the Old. His efforts were so limited that in one of the British biographies, Robert Rhodes James's *Churchill, A Study in Failure 1900-1939* (London, 1970), there are no index references at all to either FDR or to the United States, and only three or four marginal ones in the text to the United States. Even the visit of King George VI and Queen Elizabeth to Canada and the United States in May-June 1939, which had clear political purpose, goes apparently unremarked by Churchill.[45]

On 11 September 1939 Roosevelt wrote personally to Churchill following his recall to the Admiralty, suggesting the launching of a personal correspondence. Warren Kimball has pointed out, and it is well known, that FDR conducted an extensive correspondence with numerous persons, frequently bypassing diplomatic channels, but this direct communication with Churchill is unprecedented. Churchill replied on 5 October after discussing the development with the War Cabinet, and that same evening received a telephone call from the president at his flat in Morpeth Mansions warning of the German threat to the *Iroquois*.[46] As William Manchester writes: "In bypassing No. 10 Downing Street, the Foreign Office, and his own embassy in London, the president had established a direct tie with the only man, in his view, who could save Europe from Hitler. And since Roosevelt had made this extraordinary move entirely on his own, Churchill was the passive partner in the establishment of the most momentous relationship in his life."[47]

Thereafter the relationship burgeoned as we all know, leading to a correspondence without parallel, to the wartime summit meetings, the mutual statements of strong personal regard and affection. Differences over policies and strategies remained within the relationship—the second front, interpretation of the Atlantic Charter with regard to colonial empires, and so on, but they were subordinated to the common cause of victory against common enemies. Churchill remained a full-blooded Victorian, Roosevelt the committed Democrat. They were generally harmonious but at the same time uncomfortable bedfellows. It was indeed a marriage of convenience that brought about great good, but the terms of the marriage settlement were always subject to scrutiny and interpretation. In the antecedents of war they had failed to find each other for reasons that were no doubt compelling, distinguished as they were by temperament and by exigencies of domestic politics that limited freedom of action.[48]

It has often been remarked that the tragedy of the interwar years was the separation of the United States from Europe. When Churchill was in office in the 1920s, he shared in the disregard for the United States held by many of his British colleagues, and during the 1930s, in opposition, his rhetorical faith in an Anglo-American identity was intermittent and unsustained. During the Second World War Churchill and Roosevelt needed each other, and the prime minister had to cope with what in 1938 he had called "the riddle of a Sphinx who under the mask of loquacity, affability, sentimentality, hard business, machine-made politics, wrong-feeling, right-feeling, vigour and weakness, efficiency and muddle, still preserves the power to pronounce a solemn and formidable word."[49] They made the most of it, but perhaps indeed all that they really had in common was the war, as Lord Moran has suggested so vigorously in his *Diaries*.

In that context each used the other, each exploited the other and drove hard bargains when interests conflicted. Out of their creative tension great good came and heroic myths were created. But these myths should not blind us to the evidence in the contemporary record. Statesmanship often lies in the subjection of personal feelings to the larger cause, and Roosevelt could play the Great Game as well as any other. Joseph Kennedy reports him as saying of Churchill in December 1939: "I have always disliked him since the time I went to England in 1918. He acted like a stinker at a dinner I attended, lording it all over us . . . . I'm giving him attention now because there is a strong possibility that he will become the prime minister and I want to get my hand in now."[50] Ultimately differences in culture, style and manners were subordinated to the needs of *realpolitik*; which is not to deny that *realpolitik* was guided by ethical principles in the defense of civilization when faced by the challenge of Hitlerism.

3

DE GAULLE AND FRANKLIN D. ROOSEVELT

Claude Fohlen

The relationship between Charles de Gaulle and Franklin D. Roosevelt is one of the saddest pages of Franco-American relations, which contradicts the usual cliché of a longtime friendship and has left deep scars to this day in the vision of each other's country. Recent French anti-Americanism stems directly from the tensions raised during World War II between de Gaulle and Franklin D. Roosevelt. All historians, and some other people too, know how tense and unfriendly has been the intercourse between these two statesmen who could never come to terms one with the other and enjoyed the most unpleasant relationship among all Allies during the Second World War. To explain why it was so, it is appropriate to turn first to the mere facts, which can then lead us to interpret their misunderstanding.

De Gaulle and Franklin D. Roosevelt met only twice in their lives, the first time at Anfa, in Morocco, in January 1943, shortly after the American landing in French North Africa, the second time in Washington, in July 1944, between Overlord, the invasion of Normandy, and Operation Anvil, the invasion of southern France. A third opportunity was offered by Franklin D. Roosevelt on his way back from Yalta in February 1945, but it failed, for de Gaulle refused to be invited by a foreign head of state to a meeting on French territory (Algeria), which shows better than anything else the gap between the two men. Even if they met rarely, that did not prevent de Gaulle from being very diffident toward Franklin D. Roosevelt.

The mutual suspicion goes back to the summer of 1940, which saw the defeat of France, the armistice of 25 June, and the rise of Marshall Pétain as head of the French state. De Gaulle had decided to continue to fight Germany and therefore to reach London, where he set up an administration and an army that were supposed to represent the French legitimate authority—in other words, the Third Republic. He was challenged in his claim by all governments, except the British. The Americans had no serious reason to break with the Vichy government and, because they thought they could influence it in order to moderate further demands by Germany, decided to send as ambassador a man of great stature, Admiral William Leahy, former head of naval operations, who happened to know Pétain personally[1]. They ignored de Gaulle, they ignored the Free French, they ignored the part played by those Free French forces still fighting side by side with the British. This does not mean that the sympathies of the Americans or of Franklin D. Roosevelt himself were in favor of Vichy, but the Americans considered it the only legitimate French government. It must be recognized that the splitting of France made matters difficult for other governments. France was unique among Western European powers: The United Kingdom was the only country to continue the struggle on its own territory; the Netherlands had capitulated and its government gone into exile; and Belgium had also capitulated, but the king remained in the country, considering himself a prisoner. France alone had signed an armistice with Germany and Italy and kept a government that had all the appearances of being legal, after having been legitimated, on 10 July 1940, by a massive vote of the Parliament (569 against 80).

So, from the beginning, relations were never and could not be cordial, for the very simple reason that FDR considered de Gaulle a mere adventurer who could not claim to represent France, having no legitimacy of his own. Being proud and tough, sure of himself, de Gaulle resented very much what he considered Roosevelt's signs of suspicion. There is a very nice story about it, recorded by Roosevelt. During the Anfa conference in January 1943, FDR heard de Gaulle propose to General Henri Giraud that he, de Gaulle, would be Clemenceau, "the statesman," and Giraud, Foch, "the commander in chief." Roosevelt could not help exclaiming: "Yesterday he wanted to be Joan of Arc—and now he wants to be the somewhat more worldly Clemenceau."[2] This story, which was widely circulated, infuriated de Gaulle, who was convinced that he was the only true representative of France.

The relations between de Gaulle and FDR developed in a sequence that reminds us of a Greek tragedy in three acts, starting with a family quarrel and ending with the death of one of the characters.

The first act was played in North Africa, although it opened with the occupation by the Free French of the tiny islands of St-Pierre and Miquelon, off the coast of Newfoundland, in December 1941. The American secretary of state, Cordell Hull, issued a communiqué that mentioned the "so-called Free French." To say the least, this phrasing was ungracious for those who considered themselves the true defenders of France, and they were deeply hurt. When Hull asked the Canadians to expel the French and to reinstate the status quo ante, there was an uproar in the American press, which, on the whole, supported the Free French.

Then in November 1942, the scene shifts to North Africa. The story is well known, so that it is not necessary to go into too many details. What we are concerned with is that Franklin D. Roosevelt, ignoring deliberately de Gaulle, tried to find the right man with whom to negotiate. His first choice was Admiral Jean Darlan, former prime minister of the Vichy government who had been instrumental in pushing collaboration with the Germans and who was still the head of the powerful French navy. He just happened to be in Algeria at the time of the landing to visit his son, who was in a hospital. The so-called Darlan deal, concluded between General Mark Clark and Darlan on instructions from Franklin Roosevelt three days after the landing, made Darlan the ruler of French North Africa and therefore seemed to legitimize the Vichy administration. If some people considered it a suitable expedient to win time, it is likely that Roosevelt considered it the best way to consolidate the American presence. De Gaulle was completely ignored, and he could neither forget nor forgive this slap in the face.

It was expected that, with Darlan's assassination on 24 December 1942, Roosevelt would turn to de Gaulle. Actually, he was looking for a third man whom he had already chosen: Henri Giraud, an army general of great prestige, who had just escaped from a prisoners' camp in Germany with the help of the French secret service. Giraud had pledged fidelity to Pétain and had recently been brought to North Africa in an English submarine. Yet Giraud was a poor politician who could not match de Gaulle and would become a puppet in the hands of Roosevelt and Eisenhower. Once again de Gaulle was cast aside, but this time the imbroglio took such proportions that Roosevelt summoned the two men to Casablanca/Anfa, where he was holding a conference with Churchill.

De Gaulle accepted the invitation reluctantly, because he was afraid to make any compromise under foreign pressure. He did so only after Churchill threatened to abandon him. But it was not easy, and FDR was much amused and made two unpleasant remarks about de Gaulle, one to Churchill, the other to Hull. "Here was our great hero," he told Churchill, "the winning horse that we had bred and trained in our stable; and when the day came it refused to run at all." In the other, he compared Giraud to a bridegroom and de Gaulle to the bride: "We delivered the bridegroom, General Giraud, who was most cooperative on the impending marriage . . . . However, our friends could not produce the bride, the temperamental lady de Gaulle. She has got quite snooty about the whole idea and does not want to see either of us and is showing no intention of getting into bed with Giraud."[3] Roosevelt and de Gaulle eventually met, on 17 January 1943, but could not agree on anything. In his *Memoirs*, de Gaulle writes: "Behind his patrician mask of courtesy, Roosevelt regarded me without benevolence . . . . He meant the peace to be an American peace, convinced that he must be the one to dictate its structure . . . and that France in particular should recognize him as its savior and arbiter. . . ."[4] On his side, the president "found the General rigid and unresponsive to his urgent desire to get on with the war." This is a leitmotiv in Roosevelt's writings, that de Gaulle engaged in politics and did not care about the conduct of the war, which seems unfair insofar as de Gaulle's ultimate aim was to liberate France. It is strange that a politician as experienced as Roosevelt should dismiss the importance of politics, but it may have been an excuse for disregarding de Gaulle. Actually, de Gaulle met Giraud, shook hands in front of the photographers in the presence of the president and the prime minister, and signed a communiqué that had no effect.

In any event, Roosevelt and de Gaulle could not be reconciled, while in the middle stood Giraud, who seemed to be Roosevelt's puppet and was unable and unprepared to imagine a resolution to the French quagmire. On his way to Casablanca, Harry Hopkins, FDR's close advisor, had succeeded in finding still another man fit to this task, Jean Monnet, with whom he had been associated when he was purchasing American armaments for France. Roosevelt cabled to Hull to get his opinion. Hull objected, because "Monnet had several indirect connections with the de Gaulle organization."[5] This statement is not quite accurate, since instead of joining the Free French, Monnet was serving in the British Purchase Commission. In the United States Hull suggested two other names, Alexis Léger (better known as Saint-John Perse, the winner of the Nobel Prize in literature) former secretary of the Ministry of Foreign Affairs, then in exile in Washington, and Roger Cambon, former French ambassador, in exile in Great Britain. It is difficult to assess on which side Monnet stood at this time, as he was not a politician and did not approve entirely of either de Gaulle or FDR, who, in any case, dropped him from consideration, as well as the two men suggested by Hull.[6] But, a few days later, Monnet announced himself to Giraud upon his arrival in Algiers. Officially, he was coming as a representative of the Munitions

Assignment Board, whose president was Hopkins, to supervise the distribution of American arms and ammunition to the French army. "I have been assigned by the Munitions Assignment Board to North Africa to give all possible assistance to the armament of the French Forces," he said.[7] Actually, Monnet's mission was much broader, although never made explicit by Roosevelt: to put pressure on Giraud to drop the Vichy legislation still in operation in French North Africa and, eventually, to reconcile him with de Gaulle and restore unity among the French. This is very clearly indicated in a telegram from Hull to Robert Murphy, Roosevelt's diplomatic representative in North Africa, on 23 February 1943.[8] De Gaulle did not object or interfere, as he was in London, but we know that he had no great sympathy for Monnet.

As my topic concerns de Gaulle and Roosevelt, I do not intend to tell the whole and complicated story of Monnet's mission in Algiers. The important point is that, on 4 June 1943, a French Committee of National Liberation (hereafter CFLN) was established there with de Gaulle and Giraud as copresidents and Monnet as a member. The least that can be said is that the dual leadership did not function very well, and Roosevelt always favored Giraud, on the grounds, previously stated, that de Gaulle was more involved in politics than in strategy. As emphasized by the historian, Robert Dallek, "the de Gaulle-Giraud discussions in Algiers . . . increased Roosevelt's antagonism to de Gaulle." When de Gaulle asked for the removal of the Vichyite governor of West Africa, Pierre Boisson, "Roosevelt at once advised Eisenhower and Churchill that he would not 'remain quiescent' in the face of such developments. He might send troops and naval vessels to prevent de Gaulle's control of Dakar. . . ."[9] On his side, de Gaulle did not miss any opportunity to remind the Americans of their role during the First World War, which after all was not so different from that of the French in the second one. As he told Eisenhower:

> *. . . Vous rappelez-vous, qu'au cours de la dernière guerre, la France a eu, quant à la fourniture d'armes à plusieurs pays alliés, un rôle analogue à celui qu'aujourd'hui jouent les Etats-Unis? . . . Oui! Pendant la première guerre mondiale, vous, Américains, n'avez tiré le canon qu'avec nos canons, roulé en char que dans nos chars, volé en avion que sur nos avions. Avons-nous, en contrepartie, exigé, de la Belgique, de la Serbie, de la Russie, de la Roumanie, avons-nous exigé des Etats-Unis, la désignation de tel ou tel chef ou l'institution d'un système politique déterminé?*[10]

The CFLN was eventually recognized, at least partially, by the American administration in August 1943, and de Gaulle's influence increased to the point that Giraud was forced out in November and confined to nominal control over the armies. But the Americans always refused to consider the CFLN as a government of its own, even though in the meantime they had recalled Admiral Leahy from Vichy and had broken relations with France.

The second act opens with Overlord, June 1944, the stage being set in Normandy. Once again, the two main characters are quarreling. De Gaulle had been deliberately left out of the preparation for the landing, which he heard about from General Eisenhower just before it was being launched. Two related conflicts came up, connected with the attitude of the Americans in France. The first one was about the administration of liberated areas of the French territory. The Americans had planned an administration of their own, called AMGOT (American Military Government of Occupied Territories), which was unacceptable to de Gaulle, since he considered that France was not an enemy and should have its own administration, appointed by the CFLN, which had turned, in May 1944, into the GRPF (Provisional Government of the French Republic). Now it was a matter of sovereignty, and de Gaulle was not prepared to yield on this fundamental issue. Related to this was the second reason for conflict, that of the currency. At the beginning of January 1944, Henry Morgenthau, then U.S. secretary of the treasury, proposed to FDR the printing of bank notes bearing the phrase "Republic française." Roosevelt refused, on the ground that no one knew the kind of regime France would adopt. And de Gaulle was ready to refuse any kind of American currency, because, once again, it was a matter of national sovereignty. This issue infuriated FDR, who wrote to Churchill, "I would certainly not importune de Gaulle to make any supporting statement whatever regarding the currency. . . . Provided he is clear that he acts entirely on his own responsibility . . . he can sign any statement in whatever currency he likes, even that of the King of Siam."[11] De Gaulle was blamed for not cooperating with the Allies in sending only a few liaison officers with the invading forces.

At this point of tension, one could expect the worst. But de Gaulle and FDR realized that in this crucial moment there was no more time for playing poker. De Gaulle needed the help of the Americans, if only for military reasons, and FDR understood that the support of the Gaullists would be very helpful, if only for intelligence. So de Gaulle, pressed by Churchill, accepted Roosevelt's invitation to go to Washington from 6 to 10 July. "Roosevelt had planned the meetings to be ceremonial rather than substantive, but the visit, except for the lack of a 21-gun stroke salute, was almost undistinguishable from that of a head of state."[12] De Gaulle and Roosevelt met three times at the White House and discussed general matters rather than specific French issues, except that the president briefed the general on the French underground. During three days, the tension eased very much even if the two men did not agree on anything substantial. FDR sketched his plans, writes de Gaulle, in "light touches, . . . and so skillfully that it is difficult to contradict this artist, this seducer, in any categorical way." But it was made clear to de Gaulle that the great questions of the future would be solved by the Big Four, excluding France.

> *Une telle organisation, suivant lui, implique l'installation de la force américaine sur des bases réparties dans toutes les régions du monde et dont certaines seront choisies en territoire français . . . Les propos du Président américain achèvent de me prouver que, dans les affaires entre Etats, la logique et le sentiment ne pèsent pas lourd en comparaison des réalités de la puissance . . . que la France, pour retrouver sa place, ne doit compter que sur elle-même. Je le lui dis. Il sourit et conclut, Nous ferons ce que nous pourrons. Mais il est vrai que pour servir la France, personne ne saurait remplacer le peuple français.*[13]

This encounter had, at least, one practical consequence: On 11 July while de Gaulle was welcomed in Ottawa, Roosevelt announced that the United States recognized that "the CFLN is qualified to administer France." It was a recognition de facto, short of what de Gaulle had expected, but at least it paved the way for cooperation between the Americans and the French in the liberated territories. It was only three months later, on 23 October, that de Gaulle got what he had long expected, full diplomatic recognition by the American government, the last of the Four Powers to offer it.

The tragedy is not yet over, as there was still the third act to play. Its headline: Yalta. From France, the stage moves to the Crimea, and the setting is an old-fashioned tsarist mansion in Livadia.

In the words of the historian André Kaspi, "even if the French did not yet have a constitutional government, even if there had not yet been any elections, nothing justifies that de Gaulle was not invited . . . insofar as the conference dealt with the future of Europe."[14] Before the conference, de Gaulle complained to the American ambassador in Paris, Jefferson Caffery, that he had not been invited. To be gracious, Roosevelt sent Harry Hopkins to Paris on his way to the Crimea. Hopkins met de Gaulle on 27 January 1945, and they had a long talk, a transcript of which can be found in de Gaulle's *Memoirs*. He was very bitter about Roosevelt's attitude, believing FDR did not seem to understand the latest developments in France: "*On savait que notre peuple voulait prendre part à la victoire. On mesurait ce que valait son armée renaissante. On me voyait installé à Paris et entouré par la ferveur nationale. Mais les Etats-Unis en étaients ils plus convaincus que la France fût capable de redevenir une grande puissance? Voulaient-ils l'y aider vraiment?*"[15]

Although de Gaulle was absent from Yalta, France was not mistreated. In his address to Congress after his return, President Roosevelt made that clear:

> . . . France has been invited to accept a zone of control in Germany and to participate as a fourth member of the Allied Control Council of Germany. She has been invited to join as a sponsor of the international conference of San Francisco. She will be a permanent member of the international Security Council together with the other four major powers. And finally, we have asked that France be associated with us in our joint responsibility over the liberated areas of Europe.[16]

De Gaulle was ready to be satisfied with these results, which inspired him, in his *Memoirs*, to some high-spirited comments about the rise of France as an international power, when a last incident erupted between him and FDR. On his way back from Yalta, Roosevelt had met with a number of heads of state and asked his ambassador in Paris to invite de Gaulle to pay him a visit in Algiers. De Gaulle burst out, and his anger has to be recorded in the original language:

> *[Roosevelt] fixait le lieu de notre entrevue. Ce serait Alger. Si j'acceptais de m'y rendre, il fixerait aussi la date. L'invitation de Roosevelt me parut intempestive . . . A quel titre le Président américain invitait-il le Président français à lui faire visite en France? . . . Il est vrai que, pour Franklin D. Roosevelt, Alger, peut-être, n'était pas la France. Raison de plus pour le lui rappeler . . . La souveraineté, la dignité, d'une grande nation doivent être intangibles. J'étais en charge de celles de la France.*17

And so the last opportunity to settle their differences vanished. A few weeks later, Roosevelt's sudden death inspired de Gaulle to pen these last conciliatory reflections: "*Quand la mort vint, le 12 avril, l'arracher à sa tâche gigantesque, au moment même où il allait en voir le terme victorieux, c'est d'un coeur sincère que je portai vers sa mémoire mon regret et mon admiration.*"[18]

Although the tragedy is brought to its end with the death of Franklin D. Roosevelt, this does not mean that the survivor was the winner.

The time has come to explain the attitudes of the two characters we have followed through this tragedy. If de Gaulle's line is easy to follow, Roosevelt's is more twisted and irrational.

De Gaulle was tough and uncompromising, as General Marshall recognized, "very much as John Lewis [the American labor leader]. He leads his people the same way as Lewis leads his union. And does not concede one inch . . . . He is implacable."[19] De Gaulle was also a nationalist, imbued with two ideas: to personify his country and to liberate it from the Germans. Having been a member of the last French government of the Third Republic, and the only one to refuse the armistice and to settle in England, he thought he had legitimacy on his side. For him, the Vichy government had no legality, because the vote of the Parliament in favor of Pétain had been obtained only under strong pressure from the enemies of the Republican regime, who wanted to strangle it and replace it with something akin to fascism, without the label. De Gaulle had so far been a very loyal officer in the French army, moving slowly through the rigid military establishment, because his strategic views opposed the official conceptions of the general staff. He had never been involved in active politics, except as a regular reader of the nationalist *Action Française,* Charles Maurras and Léon Dauder's newspaper. Convinced that he had a national role to play, he could not accept any compromise with other heads of state. His relations with Churchill were not easy, but at least they understood each other and were ready to find points of agreement.

With Roosevelt, things were quite different, for many reasons. FDR had strong opinions about France, which he seems to have secured from his advisors. Two of them are well known, Admiral Leahy, the former American ambassador in Vichy, already mentioned, and Robert Murphy, the former consul general in Algiers, who was instrumental in preparing the landing in North Africa. Both of them have written their memoirs, which tell a lot about their way of being informed and of informing the president.[20] Both men were honest but biased when it came to politics, because of their deep-seated conservatism. Both were men of the establishment, who did not seem to have understood the nature of the French Resistance, which they associated with fascism or nationalism. Another advisor was General William J. Donovan, head of the Office of Strategic Services, whom Franklin Roosevelt trusted very much, but Donovan underestimated the dynamism of the Resistance and the prominent part played in it by the Gaullists, at least until the eve of Overlord. The information these men and their associates provided to the president and to the Department of State reflected the official position of some circles, but not the opinion of the people, which was hard to determine, because of censorship. Roosevelt was misled by the information he got, but he also seemed to have already made up his mind and was not prepared to adapt to the quick shifts that characterize an occupied country like France. Because he did not write his memoirs, although he left an abundant record consisting of notes, letters, and addresses, it is more difficult to gauge his opinions.

Roosevelt had been deeply impressed, as had all his countrymen, by the defeat of France in 1940, and this led him to think that France was no longer a great power, which was entirely true, and that it had to be excluded forever from the decision-making powers. So France was not among the founders of the United Nations, whereas Belgium, Norway, Yugoslavia, and Poland were. This exclusion is very symbolic, because it tells a lot about FDR. France was to be treated as a second-rank European state, without much influence in the international process of peace and war. It is only at Yalta that Roosevelt began to change his mind, probably influenced by Churchill, when he realized the unbalance resulting from the advance of Soviet Russia in Eastern and Central Europe. Of course, this view could not be accepted by de Gaulle, who insists, in his *Memoires,* on the role of the French army in fighting Germany and on the efforts he made to regenerate France. A valuable statement is given by Ted Morgan, when he writes: "France had failed, and failure had to be punished. De Gaulle, even though he had dissociated himself from France's surrender by forming the Free French in London, was contaminated in Roosevelt's view. France had fallen from grace, and de Gaulle was French, and therefore did not count for much."[21]

The second point of friction was about the legitimacy of the Vichy government. This view was shared by many officials in Washington, including Secretary of State Cordell Hull. On this specific issue, Churchill and Roosevelt differed, and Churchill did not or could not convince FDR to change his mind. There is no doubt that, at the beginning, Leahy was instrumental in spreading the idea that Pétain was the legitimate heir of the Third Republic and, therefore, that the Vichy government was the only one with which to have official relations. One can guess also that the disunion among the French exiles was another reason to remain cautious. There were a number of these exiles in the United States, from former Prime Minister Camille Chautemps to Alexis Léger, from well-known journalists Pertinax, Charles Géraud and Geneviève Tabouis to Jean Monnet, who had refused to rally the Free French and continue the fight against the fascists. But the main argument was as legalistic as the one used in favor of Vichy: As long as the French people had not voted at the polls in favor of de Gaulle, he could not be considered the legitimate head of state. This would be an excellent argument in peacetime, but how to hold elections in an occupied territory?

The issue of elections explains why the United States, the number one world power, was the last of the Big Four to recognize the French provisional government in October 1944 and de Gaulle could but resent it!

All these considerations confirmed the personal feelings of Roosevelt, that de Gaulle was a troublemaker, an antidemocrat, a would-be dictator. Actually, both men were prima donnas, and prima donnas rarely work well together. The president had always used his personal charm to sway his visitors and knew very well how to employ it. But de Gaulle was entirely impervious to this kind of communication, being rational more than sentimental. FDR lost his chance, if he thought that the method which had succeeded with other people could work with de Gaulle. The relationship between both men shows at least the limits of personal diplomacy, which was FDR's secret. Let us mention here what Robert Divine wrote about his diplomacy:

> Franklin Roosevelt's claim to greatness must rest on his achievements in domestic affairs. His conduct of foreign policy never equaled his mastery of American politics and his ability to guide the nation through the perils of depression and war . . . . Roosevelt was not well equipped, either by experience or by temperament, to deal with the successive crises posed by Hitler's Germany or Stalin's Russia . . . .[22]

One can add, without erring, "and by de Gaulle's France."

Then, the last stumbling block was the French empire, the main support of de Gaulle's power during the war. Roosevelt made no secret of his commitment to decolonization and his conviction that a new era would start in the postwar period, with all colonies becoming free and independent states, and members of the United Nations. Two parts of the French empire were especially crucial for Roosevelt: French West Africa, with the naval base of Dakar, which would be converted into an international peacekeeping base, and Indochina, where the presence of the French—FDR suggested once to one of his sons—was anachronistic. De Gaulle was adamant in maintaining all overseas possessions under French authority, opposing the transfer of Dakar to any international authority. He opposed also any suggestion to transfer Indochina under a trusteeship of the UN. At the celebration of the Indochinese New Year, in the beginning of 1945, de Gaulle told the Indochinese that France wanted to make the development of Indochina the principal aim of "reborn power and greatness."[23] The question of the future of overseas territories created a permanent misunderstanding between Roosevelt and de Gaulle. Nevertheless, it seems that the president may have been slowly changing his views in this area, perhaps because of the threat posed by Soviet expansionism, perhaps also because of a more realistic approach to colonial issues. A good example of this is the help provided, in March 1945, by the US Air Force to the French army, when French troops went back to Indochina. One can only guess what would have happened had Roosevelt survived.

The relationship between de Gaulle and FDR is a sad story of misunderstanding that can be explained by many reasons, both personal—the most influential in my view—and general. Historians should not blame one man or the other, for that is not their job, but they can point out the weight of the legacy of this wartime misunderstanding in French postwar politics. Gaullism and the gaullist regime have long been associated with a specific anti-Americanism, which has been exaggerated very often on both sides. De Gaulle was not, basically, anti-American, but he never forgot the humiliations he suffered at the hands of Franklin D. Roosevelt at a critical time for France's future. He played with this legacy to influence French opinion, which needed a scapegoat on which to vent its passions, forgetting that the Americans had been instrumental in the rebirth of democracy in 1945, as they had been in rescuing France in 1918. People's memory is always short.

4

STALIN AND FRANKLIN D. ROOSEVELT

Valentin Berezhkov

FIRST MEETING

Among the foreign state figures whom I was able to observe closely, Franklin Delano Roosevelt left the greatest impression. In our country he deservedly enjoys the reputation of a realistic thinking, farsighted politician. One of the main streets in Yalta has been named after him. President Roosevelt occupies a prominent place in the modern history of the United States and in the chronicle of World War II. I remember him as a charming man, who reacted quickly and had a sense of humor. Even at Yalta, when his worsening health was especially noticeable, everyone present remarked that the president's intellect remained clear, sharp, and capable of quick reaction.

I consider a great honor my assignment to interpret Stalin's talks with Roosevelt during their first meeting in Tehran in 1943. Everything that took place then made a deep impression on me.

The Soviet delegation, which included Stalin, Molotov, and Klementiy Voroshilov, left for the Iranian capital a day before my return to Moscow from a brief trip, and I had to catch up to it. I flew out late at night to Baku and arrived there only by evening. Early in the morning I set out by plane to Tehran and, having just arrived at the Soviet Embassy at midday, learned that I was to interpret the first meeting of the two leaders. Had my aircraft arrived even an hour later, I would have been late for this meeting, which would have evoked the dissatisfaction of Stalin, who himself selected the interpreter for each meeting.

When I entered the room adjacent to the hall for the plenary sessions, Stalin was already there, in his marshal's uniform. He looked intently at me, and I hastened to apologize for being slightly late, explaining that I came directly from the airfield. Stalin nodded his head slightly, walked about the room slowly, took from the side pocket of his tunic a box with the inscription "Gertsogovina Flor," took out a cigarette and began to smoke. Narrowing his eyes, he looked less stern, and asked: "Are you not very tired from being on the road? Are you prepared to interpret? The talk will be crucial." "I am prepared, Comrade Stalin. I rested well during the night in Baku. I feel normal."

Stalin approached the table, carelessly tossed the box of Gertsogovina Flor on it. He lighted a match and then the cigarette, which had gone out. Then, having extinguished the match in a slow gesture, he pointed with it to the sofa and said: "I sit here, in the corner. Roosevelt will come in his carriage; let him station himself to the left of the armchair, where you will be sitting." "I understand," I answered. I had already interpreted for Stalin a number of times, but I had never heard him place importance on such details. Perhaps he was nervous awaiting his meeting with Roosevelt.

Stalin, of course, had no doubt that the president's attitude was extremely negative toward the system that had prevailed, through Stalin's efforts, in the Soviet Union. For Roosevelt the bloody crimes, despotism, repression, and arrests could not be a secret. The destruction of the peasant farms and forcible collectivization, which led to a terrible famine in the country and the deaths of millions; the persecutions against highly skilled specialists, scientists, and writers, who were declared "wreckers"; the extermination of talented military leaders—all this contributed to the rise of an extremely negative image of the Soviet Union in the West.

How would relations with Roosevelt turn out? Wouldn't an insurmountable barrier arise between them? Could he, Stalin, overcome the alienation? I think that FDR also understood how important it was to find common language with Stalin. And FDR was able to approach Stalin in such a way that this suspicious Eastern despot, it seemed, believed in the readiness of democratic society to accept him in its midst. At his very first meeting with the Soviet leader, Roosevelt tried to create an atmosphere of confidence. There was no stiffness, guardedness, or any awkward long pauses.

Stalin also decided to turn on his charm. Here he was a great master. Before the war our "supreme leader" rarely received foreign politicians and therefore had little experience with them. But he quickly made up for what he had missed, demonstrating his capability already in his meeting with Joachim von Ribbentrop in August 1939. After Hitler's invasion, Stalin participated directly in negotiations. Talks with Harry Hopkins, Averell Harriman, and Cordell Hull and intensive correspondence with Roosevelt gave him the opportunity to add to his impressions about Americans and work out his manner of dealing with them. But nevertheless, it can be noted that before his first talk with the president of the United States in the fall of 1943, Stalin did not feel completely confident.

Is this not why he concerned himself about where it was best to sit? Apparently he did not want his pockmarked face to be too much in the light. His marshal's tunic and trousers, with red stripes, were carefully pressed, and his soft Caucasian boots—he usually tucked them in his trousers—gleamed. Linings placed in the insole of his heels made him appear taller than he was. Even with his outward appearance Stalin attempted to produce a favorable impression. And he began the discussion with Roosevelt with typical Georgian courtesies. Does everything in his residence suit the president? Has anything been overlooked? How could he be of help? And so forth. Roosevelt kept up this game, and offered Stalin a cigarette. Stalin answered that he was used to his own. The president also asked about the "famous Stalin pipe." "The doctors forbid it," the all-powerful leader said, throwing up his hands helplessly. "One must listen to doctors," Roosevelt lectured. They inquired about each other's health, spoke about the danger of smoking, and about the benefit of being in the fresh air. In short, everything looked as if bosom buddies had met.

Discussing the situation at the front as the president requested, Stalin did not conceal the grave situation that had taken shape in the Ukraine after the Germans seized Zhitomir, an important railroad center. As a result Kiev, the Ukrainian capital, was again threatened. In turn Roosevelt also demonstrated frankness. Having outlined the fierce battles in the Pacific Ocean, he touched upon the question of the fate of the colonial empires.

"I am speaking about this in the absence of our combat friend Churchill," the president emphasized, "since he does not like to touch this topic. The United States and the Soviet Union are not colonial powers, it is easy for us to discuss such problems. I believe that the colonial empires will not long exist following the end of the war. . . ." Roosevelt said that he intended to discuss the postwar status of the colonies in more detail in the future, but that it was better to do so without the participation of Churchill, who had no plans with respect to India.

Stalin clearly was wary of being drawn into a discussion of such a delicate topic. He limited himself merely to the remark that following the war, the problem of the colonial empires might be an urgent one, and he agreed that it was easier for the Soviet Union and the United States to discuss this question than it was for countries that possessed colonies. Here I was struck by Roosevelt's initiative, for not long before I had heard Hitler propose, in talks with Molotov in Berlin in November 1940, that the Soviet Union, along with Germany, Italy, and Japan, divide up the British colonial legacy. Obviously these territories attracted many.

On the whole, I got the impression that Stalin and Roosevelt left satisfied with their first contact. But this, of course, could not change their fundamental orientations. The Roosevelt administration was guided by the formula set forth in a statement by the U.S. Department of State on 22 June 1941; that is, the day of Hitler's attack on the Soviet Union: "We must consistently adhere to a policy in accordance with which the fact that the Soviet Union is at war against Hitler in no way means that it is defending, fighting for, or adhering to those principles in international relations to which we adhere."[1]

During the war Roosevelt spoke in a very friendly way about the Soviet Union, and about Stalin personally. But here, it seems to me, he was merely giving his due to alliance relations within the framework of the anti-Hitler coalition and to the heroism of the Red Army, which had withstood the monstrous strikes of Hitler's war machine. At the same time, the president drew appropriate conclusions from the course of the battles on the Soviet-German front. Roosevelt believed that the fact that the Soviet people were continuing to resist the aggression demonstrated the stability of the system. If it withstood and remained after the war, it did not make sense to again attempt to destroy it. It was better to work out a mechanism that would enable the capitalist countries to coexist with the Soviet Union. All of this in no way meant that Roosevelt approved of the Soviet reality.

Stalin also had reasons for mistrust. Roosevelt's establishment of diplomatic relations with the Soviet Union after sixteen years of nonrecognition, his statement that he intended to support the struggle by the Soviet people against Nazi aggression, and his readiness to organize the delivery of military materiels to the Soviet Union—were all positive signs. In the actual operations of the anti-Hitler coalition, however, there were numerous facts that reinforced Stalin's suspiciousness about the United States. And in general, his deeply rooted hostility toward the capitalist system constantly fed his wariness.

I frequently heard Stalin say to Molotov: "Roosevelt makes reference to the Congress. He thinks that I believe that he is really afraid of it, and therefore cannot yield to us. He simply does not want to, and he is shielding himself with the Congress. Nonsense! He is the military leader, the supreme commander-in-chief. Who can oppose him? It's convenient for him to hide behind parliament. But he does not fool me . . . ."

When Stalin complained to Roosevelt and Churchill about unfriendly articles about the Soviet Union in the American and British press, he did not believe their explanations that they could not control the newspapers and magazines, and that the press at times did not even spare themselves. Stalin considered all this a bourgeois trap, a double game. But he saw that the Soviet side was in an unfavorable position. When rather timid critical remarks appeared in the Soviet press about the policy of the Western Allies (delay of the second front, breaking the schedule for military deliveries, rumors about separate negotiations, etc.), Roosevelt and Churchill protested and complained to Stalin, since the articles appeared in the official Soviet press.

In order to balance the situation, in 1943 Stalin decided to create a new journal, *Voyna i rabochiy klass* [The War and the Working Class], portraying it as if it were being published by Soviet trade unions. In fact, Molotov was the editor of this biweekly, although the name of a fictitious editor—some trade union figure—was on the title page. Molotov entrusted to me the technical side of preparing the sessions of the journal's editorial group, and I could see how carefully not only he but at times even Stalin metered out critical articles. Now, to the complaints of the American and British leaders, he could reply that the Soviet government did not bear responsibility for these articles, and that all complaints should be addressed to the trade union organization. Stalin was convinced that Roosevelt and Churchill manipulated the press in exactly the same way

Back in the mid-1930s Stalin attempted to establish contact with Roosevelt. A. I. Mikoyan, people's commissar of foreign trade, a Politburo member and a man close to Stalin, told me about one episode associated with this. It took place in summer 1935 at Molotov's dacha, not long before Mikoyan departed for the United States to buy equipment. An American citizen named Cone, a relative of Molotov's wife, was at the dacha. Soon Stalin appeared. After supper he called Mikoyan into the garden and said: "This Cone is a capitalist. Meet with him when you are in America. He will help us establish a political dialogue with Roosevelt." Once he arrived in Washington, Mikoyan found out that the "capitalist" Cone owned six gasoline pumps and, of course, had no access to the White House. There could be no thought about Cone acting as an intermediary. Meanwhile, during a meeting, Henry Ford, on his own initiative offered to introduce Mikoyan to Roosevelt. The then Soviet ambassador to the United States, Alexander Troyanovskiy, immediately informed Moscow of this. No answer came, and Mikoyan did not meet with Roosevelt. I was perplexed as to why he acted that way. After all,

Stalin was seeking dialogue with Roosevelt. "You don't know Stalin well," explained Mikoyan. "You see, he charged Mikoyan to act through Cone. Had I, without his sanction, used the services of Ford, he would have said: 'Well, there's Mikoyan, who wants to be smarter than we are, and has entered into big politics.' He would never have forgiven me. At some point he would have remembered without fail and used it against me. . . ."

A proposal that Stalin made to Hopkins, and then also to Harriman, before the United States entered the war, to send American troops to the Ukraine to wage combat operations on the Soviet-German front is also associated with this unique view of the United States. Naturally, Stalin's offer was refused, but what is striking is that he was very offended.[2]

No less strange was an initiative by Roosevelt that followed. On 12 January 1942—that is following Pearl Harbor—in a talk with Maxim Litvinov, the new Soviet ambassador who had just arrived in Washington, FDR expressed the opinion that American troops could replace Soviet units located in Iran, the Transcaucasus, and the area of the polar port of Murmansk. And Soviet soldiers could be transferred for operations in active sectors of the front. The president accompanied his proposal with a unique enticement: "On the American side," he said to the Soviet ambassador, "there would be no objection to the Soviet Union acquiring a non-icebound port in the north, somewhere in Norway, such as Narvik." For communications with it, Roosevelt explained, a corridor could be cut through Norwegian and Finnish territory.[3]

From the standpoint of current morality, such a proposal—made, moreover, without informing the Norwegians and Finns—seems at least cynical. Moreover, at that time Narvik, as all of Norway, was under German occupation. The Soviet government turned down the American proposal. In a telegram from Molotov, sent on 18 April, the Soviet ambassador was charged to respond to Roosevelt that the Soviet Union "does not and has not had any territorial or other claims against Norway, and, therefore, could not accept the proposal about the occupation of Narvik by Soviet troops." As for the replacement of Soviet units by Americans in the Caucasus and Murmansk, this "is not now of any practical importance, since there are no combat operations there." Further in the dispatch it was stated: "We would accept with satisfaction Roosevelt's assistance with American troops, who would have the purpose of fighting side by side with our troops against those of Hitler and his allies."[4] But the United States did not find troops for this.

This entire history left an unpleasant aftertaste in Moscow and engendered new suspicions in Stalin. He evaluated Roosevelt's proposal as infringement on the territorial integrity of the Soviet Union. He still well remembered the intervention against the Soviet Union after the revolution, when American troops occupied a number of areas of our country. At the same time, this was seen as Washington's desire to safeguard its own forces at the cost of the blood of its Soviet ally and to weaken the true main participants in the conflict—Germany and the Soviet Union.

I wish to discuss several key problems that influenced, to one degree or another, relations between Stalin and Roosevelt.

CONCERNING THE SECOND FRONT

Although our Western allies did not respond to numerous appeals from Moscow to make a landing in France, study of the possibility of such an operation had already begun in Washington in the fall of 1941. By spring of the next year a variant of an American plan for an invasion into northern France was prepared. Reporting this to President Roosevelt, General George C. Marshall stated that a landing in this area would be of maximum support to the Russian frnt. However, implementation of such an operation was made dependent on two conditions: (1) If the situation on the Russian front became desperate; in other words, if the success of German arms was so complete that the threat of an inevitable collapse of Soviet resistance was created. In this case, an attack in the West should be viewed as a sacrifice on behalf of the common cause. (2) If the German position became critical.[5]

This document throws light on the American concept of the "second front." While the Soviet Union and Germany retained the ability to continue the struggle, Washington preferred to remain on the sidelines, not suffering heavy human casualties.

On 12 April 1942 President Roosevelt reported to the head of the Soviet government that he considered it advisable to share opinions with an authoritative representative of the Soviet Union on a number of important questions of waging the war against the common enemy. He asked whether the Sovi t government was prepared to send Molotov to Washington for such talks. The Soviet side immediately agreed. To observe secrecy, this visit took place under the code name "The Mission of Mr. Brown."[6]

After a stay in London, where the Anglo-Soviet Treaty on alliance in the war against Hitler's Germany and its allies in Europe and cooperation and mutual assistance following the war was signed, Molotov set out for Washington. There, the talk with President Roosevelt mainly concerned plans for landing the Western Allies in France and the situation on the Soviet-German front. "If," stated Molotov, "the allies pulled off even forty enemy divisions from our front in 1942, the correlation of forces would change sharply in our favor, and Hitler's fate would be sealed . . . ."[7] Having listened to this statement, which Molotov made with uncharacteristic emotion, Roosevelt asked General Marshall: "Have preparations advanced sufficiently yet, so that I can inform Marshal Stalin of our readiness to open the second front?" The general answered affirmatively. And then the president solemnly pronounced: "Report to your government that it can expect the opening of a second front this year."[8] Thus the president, later joined by Churchill, officially pledged to carry out a landing. Moreover, a specific time was determined. The joint communique stated: "complete understanding has been achieved with respect to the urgent tasks of creating a second front in Europe in 1942."[9]

At that stage did Washington and London really intend to make a landing in Western Europe? Was this decision a mistake, or merely frivolousness, which, however, is not permissible for mature politicians? No doubt at that moment Roosevelt and Churchill believed that the Soviet capability to resist was waning and that the time had come to make a "sacrifice." But if they so considered, very soon they came to the conclusion that they should not hurry with the "sacrifice." The president spoke in precisely this sense in a conversation with his son, Elliot Roosevelt.[10] When after a time Roosevelt and Churchill renounced the promise given to Stalin, the president felt very awkward. In a conversation with Molotov in Washington, he justified a sharp reduction in military deliveries desperately needed by the Soviet Union by indicating they were needed for the invasion into France then in preparation. And to Molotov's question as to whether the deliveries would be curtailed and a second front not opened, Roosevelt again assured the people's commissar that the landing in France in 1942 absolutely would take place. It must be supposed that the American president breathed a sigh of relief when Churchill volunteered such an unpleasant mission as to inform Stalin in Moscow that the invasion would not in fact take place.

The decisions on that score made at the Tehran Conference are usually evaluated in our literature as an important victory for Soviet diplomacy. And in fact, finally the Western Allies named the precise date of the invasion, and in general adhered to it. Real assistance came to the Red Army, which had been fighting for three years practically one on one against Hitler's war machine. But one would like to know whether the United States and Britain, in agreeing to open up a second front in France, really yielded to the persistent demands of Stalin, who even threatened to leave Tehran. Or were they primarily guided by their own interests? Did they not consider that the situation was approaching what had been anticipated by the second point of the American plan—the impending collapse of Germany?

By the time of the Tehran Conference the decision had already been made. Crossing the Atlantic Ocean on a cruiser en route to the Iranian capital, President Roosevelt convened his closest assistants in his wardroom and shared his views about the second front. "Soviet troops," he stated, "are only sixty miles from the Polish border and forty miles from Bessarabia. If they cross the Bug River, which may take place in the next two weeks, the Red Army will be on the doorstep of Romania." From this the president concluded it was time to act. "The Americans and British," he explained, "must occupy as much of Europe as possible. France, Belgium, Luxembourg, as well as the southern part of Germany, are allotted to the British. The United States must move its ships and deliver American troops to the ports of Bremen and Hamburg and to Norway and Denmark. We must reach Berlin. Then let the Soviets occupy the territory to its east. But the United States should occupy Berlin."[11] At approximately this same time Roosevelt instructed that special air assault formations be prepared to seize the capital of the Third Reich.

Roosevelt and Churchill were in agreement that they could not put off the invasion any longer. Otherwise Soviet troops might move too far to the West. But the matter was not settled without serious differences. How was the goal to be achieved? The president believed that the shortest route to Berlin lay through France. He insisted on the landing in Normandy. The British prime minister had different views. He was most concerned that Soviet troops not be allowed to advance a significant distance beyond the borders of the Soviet Union. In his opinion, the most effective method to achieve this was to attack through the Balkans in the direction of Bulgaria, Romania, Austria, Hungary, and Czechoslovakia. As for Stalin, he continuously stated that he believed opening the second front in Western Europe would be of the most radical assistance to the Red Army.

Based on this, it seems to me that of most importance in the decision made at the Tehran Conference about the second front was not agreement on the date of the invasion but determination of the place of the landing. The fact that, in the end, Normandy was decided on was the result of the identical positions held by Roosevelt and Stalin, and this was greatly appreciated by the Soviet leader.

THE PROBLEM OF POLAND

The Polish problem occupied an important place in the relations among the main participants in the anti-Hitler coalition. Therefore, all three bear responsibility for the postwar fate of Poland.

The position of the Soviet Union, as it was then being interpreted by Moscow, seemed acceptable on the whole. Stalin expressed the desire to see Poland reborn as a strong, independent, and democratic state, friendly to the Soviet Union. Simultaneously, he insisted on recognition of the new Soviet-Polish border of 1939, which ran approximately along the Curzon Line, proposed by Britain in 1919. This corresponded to the proposal introduced by Churchill in Tehran. He presented the following formula for examination by Stalin and Roosevelt: "In principle it was approved that the center of the Polish state and people should be located between the so-called Curzon Line, and the Oder River line, including within Poland East Prussia and Oppeln Providence."[12]

The Soviets supported Churchill's proposal. As for Roosevelt, he agreed in principle with this line, although he warned that until the 1944 presidential elections he would refrain from public statements, due to the possible reaction of voters of Polish origin. Both Western leaders also understood the Soviet government's desire to have a friendly Poland as a neighbor.

During the period that followed, no progress was made on the matter, due to the negative position of the Polish government-in-exile. However, by summer 1944 the possibility of reaching an agreement came into view. In one of his conversations with U.S. Ambassador Harriman, Molotov advanced new compromise positions, which opened the way to an acceptable solution. They concerned organizing a government from Poles living in Britain, the United States, and the Soviet Union—persons untainted by fascism (and such persons truly existed in the London émigré cabinet) and favorably inclined toward the Soviet Union. Persons named as possible members of such a reorganized government included Dr. Oscar Lange, an economist lecturing at Chicago University; trade union leader Leo Krzyski, who headed the American Slavic Congress, and others. Stanislaw Mikolajczyk could remain premier of this government. After a time the U.S. government issued Lange a passport for a trip to the Soviet Union, where he was to take part in a discussion of the Polish problem. It was timed for the arrival of Churchill and Mikolajczyk in Moscow.

However, before going to the Soviet Union, Mikolajczyk decided to pay a visit to Washington. Upon meeting with Roosevelt, he asked whether the Poles should accept the Soviet proposal. And here something strange took place. The president, who quite recently in Tehran agreed with Churchill's formula about the border along the Curzon Line, recommended that Mikolajczyk "put off any settlement about borders." Immediately thereafter U.S. Secretary of State Edward Stettinius explained to the Poles that, although at that moment the Americans could not take a firm position against the Soviet Union, "in the near future Washington's policy will change, return to its basic moral principles, and be able to support Poland strongly and successfully."[13]

This unexpected turnabout of the U.S. administration did Poland a poor service. The instructions received in Washington raised the hopes of the London émigrés. Mikolajczyk did not even want to listen to Oscar Lange's arguments in favor of an understanding. He decided not to make any agreements. Matters became still more complicated due to the unsuccessful Warsaw uprising, prepared by émigré figures without the knowledge of the Soviet government.

It is still unclear to me why the White House recommended that Mikolajczyk avoid reaching an understanding. It looks as if it were associated with election considerations, since after the elections Washington's interest in the Polish problem clearly declined. Back during the negotiations that took place in Moscow in October 1944, Mikolajczyk sent Roosevelt a telegram in which he requested FDR's support for the position of the government-in-exile. He received an answer only on 17 November—after the presidential elections—and it was not at all the answer he expected. The president answered dryly that he would support any understanding that the Polish government-in-exile would reach with the Soviet Union. The border question was not mentioned at all. But reports about the administration's "firm" position on the Polish question leaked to the press, and American Poles voted for Roosevelt.[14]

No one, of course, can say with confidence how events would have developed had there been a favorable outcome to the 1944 Moscow negotiations. Had all the interested parties succeeded in coming to an agreement at that time, a reorganized government-in-exile headed by Mikolajczyk could, following the liberation of Warsaw by Soviet troops, have returned there from London, and the Polish people might have been saved many upheavals and sacrifices, and relations among the allies may have turned out less dramatically.

THE FACTOR OF THE BOMB

Although the atomic bomb turned into an important element of American policy only under President Harry S. Truman, this weapon already influenced Roosevelt's position during the process of its manufacture even when still untested, and indirectly impacted on development of U.S. postwar policy, in particular with respect to the Soviet Union. The specific nature of the means of mass destruction began, first of all, to disquiet the scientists engaged in their creation. They warned about the dangerous consequences of the appearance of an atomic bomb. However, the highest political leaders in the United States and Britain at first apparently believed that they were simply talking about a new weapon of great destructive force. They ignored the warnings of the bomb's creators, in exactly the same way as Nikita Khrushchev and Leonid Brezhnev later ignored the warnings of Academician Andrey Sakharov. The insistent demands of the scientists to reveal to the Soviet Union the secret of manufacturing the atomic bomb especially irritated Roosevelt and Churchill.

Of course, history does not yet know a case in which any country shared information about a new weapon with any other country. To the contrary, any such discoveries were always most strictly protected. But in this instance a special situation was taking shape. First, the bomb was being created under conditions of war against a common enemy, when exchange of military information and of models of the latest types of weapons was widely practiced among the Allies. Radar, complex communications systems, missile equipment, modern models of tanks and aircraft—all this and many other things became a kind of common property. Why was an exception made for the atomic bomb? Second, not only the United States, but also Britain—that is, two of the three main members of the coalition—knew about the work on the bomb. Concealment from the third partner appeared highly sinister. Third, and the scientists understood this quite well, in this case a fundamentally new type of weapon was emerging. Its creation demanded a nonstandard approach and essentially an entirely new world outlook. But could it appear under such conditions? Hardly. Almost a half century would pass before new thinking in foreign policy began to make headway.

Although Washington and London felt awkward in concealing the secret of the bomb, they decided not to yield to the persuasion of the "naive" men of science. To what extent did considerations associated with the postwar relationship toward the Soviet Union influence the position of Roosevelt and Churchill? No less important is the question: What guided Washington in the decision to use the bomb in the war against Japan? All of this concerns not only American wartime diplomacy, but also that of the subsequent period as well as the reasons for the origin of the "Cold War."

I think the leaders of the United States and Britain believed that possessing an atomic monopoly would give them unprecedented status in the world and enable them to achieve various concessions from other countries, including the Soviet Union. This was also reflected in the way that General Leslie Groves, chief of the Manhattan Project, understood his mission: "Two weeks after I took over this project, I had no doubts that Russia was our enemy, and the Manhattan Project was carried out on this basis. I did not adhere at all to the widespread opinion in the country that Russia was a valiant ally . . . . Of course, I reported on this to the President."[15] And so? The commander-in-chief did not contradict his subordinate.

The agreement concluded in summer 1943 at the Quebec Conference noted that the atomic bomb would be "the decisive factor in the postwar world, and would give absolute control to those who possess its secret." The president and the prime minister pledged not to transfer any information to a third party "without mutual agreement."[16]

Let us recall that the meeting in Quebec was held in the period of preparations for the Moscow Conference of ministers of foreign affairs of the three powers, the Soviet Union, United States, and Great Britain, just as occurred for the first meeting of the "Big Three" in Tehran. In Moscow U.S. Secretary of State Cordell Hull spoke a great deal about the importance of postwar cooperation between the United States and the Soviet Union and about the responsibility of the great powers for maintaining peace. In Tehran, in talks with Stalin, President Roosevelt repeatedly indicated the importance of American-Soviet cooperation following the victory over fascism as the decisive factor in maintaining peace and ensuring international security. And all this took place against the background of the Manhattan Project. Roosevelt discussed the "four policemen,"—the United States, Soviet Union, Great Britain, and China—who were obliged to preserve world peace, but was silent about the fact that of these four "policemen" only two would have atomic weapons.

Meeting with Churchill in mid-September at his estate in Hyde Park, the U.S. president, jointly with the British prime minister, confirmed the immutability of the decision about observing secrecy. The approved document stated: "The proposal that the world [and in reality the Soviet Union] be informed about "fusion" [the code name for atomic energy], for the purpose of achieving an international agreement about control over it and its use, is unacceptable. This matter must remain completely secret."[17]

In Livadiya, during the Crimean Conference of the leaders of the three powers in February 1945, Roosevelt asked Churchill whether they should tell Stalin about the Manhattan Project at this meeting. Churchill objected decisively, stating that he was "shocked" by such a proposal. Roosevelt did not insist.[18] Thus the last opportunity to create a more favorable atmosphere for postwar cooperation with the Soviet Union was lost.

In the public at large in the United States and Britain there was a strong mood in favor of maintaining the relations of friendship and cooperation with the Soviet Union, and Roosevelt could have relied on these feelings, opposing the pressure from the extreme right. Stalin took the silence of the Western Allies as a threat. He charged Lavrenti Beria to lead the work of creating Soviet atomic weapons. Thus began the nuclear arms race. At the same time, Stalin's suspicions, and his doubt about possible postwar cooperation, grew still stronger.

THE YALTA EXPERIENCE

The second meeting of the "Big Three," held 4-11 February 1945 in the Crimea, was marked by a most important stage in the history of the anti-Hitler coalition. It also raised to a new level the personal relations between Stalin and Roosevelt. The president's automobile trip from the Saki Airfield, near Simferopol, to Yalta enabled him to see with his own eyes the scale of the destruction in the occupied Soviet territories. He stated—quite sincerely, I believe, to Stalin that he had become "more blood thirsty" with respect to the Nazis. The president also emphasized that after the victory the United States would render economic assistance most of all to the Soviet Union. Had Roosevelt's plan been carried out, and had American equipment come to us and American specialists helped restore what had been destroyed, relations between our countries might have taken shape quite differently. And when, in Livadiya, in face-to-face discussions with Stalin, Roosevelt spoke about the future, he seemed not to exclude the possibility of Soviet-American postwar cooperation. Stalin also welcomed this possibility.

On the whole the atmosphere at the Yalta Conference was favorable, which contributed to achieving agreement on the questions that were on the agenda. At the same time, as the end of the war neared the contradictions within the coalition became more and more evident. In his talks with Stalin, Roosevelt emphasized repeatedly that with the onset of peace, forces opposing postwar U.S. cooperation with the Soviet Union were becoming more active. Therefore, the president advanced the idea for the postwar system and pushed the development of the principles on which the new international security organization was to operate.

Then all three leaders stated that they considered it especially important to preserve the unity of the great powers and provide a mechanism that would enable them to act jointly to maintain a stable peace. Did they believe in such a possibility? Or did the goals proclaimed not respond fully to their true intentions?

Stalin viewed with suspicion the formula put forth by the British and at first supported by the Americans about the rules for voting in the Security Council of the new international organization. He insisted on retaining a "veto" right, and when soon after Yalta an understanding was achieved about an acceptable procedure, the Soviet side assessed this as a sign of Washington's readiness to structure postwar relations with Moscow on the basis of equality. A tremendous amount of literature exists on the Yalta Conference. The problems that were discussed there, as well as the decisions made, are well known. Nevertheless, the myth remained alive that the division of Europe took place in the Crimea. Nothing of the sort happened there. The discussion concerned solely the division of Germany. While at the Tehran Conference both Roosevelt and Churchill energetically favored dividing Germany into several small states, at Livadiya they defended their plan rather halfheartedly.

The Soviets expressed doubt from the outset about the realism of the idea of splitting up Germany. As a result, at Yalta it was decided to shift this question to the European Consultative Commission for examination. Subsequently it was removed from the agenda altogether. Besides the already mentioned Polish question, the other Eastern European states were not discussed at all in a plan for division of spheres.

Churchill advanced the idea of a percentage relationship of the influence of the Soviet Union and Britain in a number of Eastern European states in a discussion with Stalin in Moscow in the fall of 1944. It was not mentioned at Yalta. The only decision made about territorial problems was that of transferring the city of Konigsberg and the adjacent area of East Prussia to the Soviet Union. An understanding was also reached about the conditions (including the transfer of southern Sakhalin and the Kuril Islands) under which the Soviet Union would enter the war against Japan.

It is interesting that both Stalin and Roosevelt assessed the Yalta Conference very highly. Both characterized it as an example of equal relations.

It seems to me that the Yalta experience, and the certain degree of trust between Stalin and Roosevelt that was revealed then, could have led to a new era in international affairs, and most important in relations between the Soviet Union and the United States. Yalta seemed to have opened the way to this. At least this feeling existed in Moscow. But it did not last long.

THE BERN INCIDENT

In the last weeks of Roosevelt's life, his relations with Stalin were darkened by the clash that took place in connection with the talks taking place in Bern between British and American representatives, including the American intelligence officer Allen Dulles, with SS General Karl Wolf, leader of the Gestapo in Italy. The U.S. ambassador to Moscow, Averell Harriman, informed Molotov about these contacts only on 12 March 1945, although the negotiations had been going on since mid-February.

The Soviet side reacted very sharply to these clandestine contacts. They viewed in this something akin to a separate deal by the Western Allies behind the back of the Soviet Union. The Soviet state's demand that representatives of its military command take part in the negotiations in Bern was rejected.[19] Stalin believed that under cover of the negotiations in Bern Hitler's command had begun to transfer troops from Italy to the Soviet-German front. Roosevelt answered a sharp telegram from Stalin on 1 April. His dispatch stated that surrounding the "negotiations with the Germans about the capitulation of their armed forces in Italy an atmosphere of regrettable misgivings and distrust had been created."[20]

Of course, President Roosevelt may not have known all the details of the Bern negotiations; their essence might have been concealed from him. Considerable information exists about various secret "initiatives" by the American secret services. Thus in October 1943, masquerading as a journalist, American agent Theodore A. Morde met in Turkey with German Ambassador Franz von Papen and gave him a document that was to become the basis for a political agreement between the United States, Britain, and Germany. In particular, it expressed readiness to recognize Germany's leading position in "continental Europe," including Poland, the Baltic, and the Ukraine.[21] Those who composed this document were essentially offering to split up the Soviet Union and transfer part of its territory to Germany. For this the Germans promised to open up the front in the West to the Americans and British. Having learned about this, Roosevelt prohibited any further feelers and ordered Morde's passport confiscated. However, even after this secret contacts between American intelligence and enemy emissaries did not cease.

Roosevelt's last message to Stalin about the Bern incident arrived in Moscow on 13 April 1945, the day after the president's death. The telegram noted that this entire history had "faded and receded into the past, without being of any benefit . . . in any case, there should not be mutual distrust and insignificant misunderstandings of this nature must not arise in the future. I am confident that when our armies establish contact in Germany, and link up in a fully coordinated offensive, the Nazi armies will collapse."[22]

In this message, Roosevelt emphasized the importance of relations of trust, elements of which, despite all the complexities, could still be seen in the relations between Roosevelt and Stalin. Had Roosevelt lived longer, perhaps relations in the postwar period would have taken shape more favorably. Given the certain degree of trust between Roosevelt and Stalin, it might have been possible to avoid the extremes and dangerous confrontations of the "Cold War." But, Roosevelt's untimely death and Truman's arrival in the White House fundamentally changed the situation and caused a corresponding reaction from the Soviet side.

5

SIKORSKI, MIKOLAJCZYK, AND FRANKLIN D. ROOSEVELT, 1939-1945

Lubomir W. Zyblikiewicz

In trying to re-create the contemporary image of Franklin Delano Roosevelt, I probably face more difficulties than scholars from other countries. The most obvious one is that, unlike other countries, Poland was represented during the short wartime years by two leaders[1] who were distinct in personality as well as in the policies they adopted.

The first of these men, General Wladyslaw Sikorski, not only served as Poland's prime minister and commander-in-chief, but benefited from the substantial limitation imposed by the 1935 constitution on the prerogatives of the Polish president, Wladyslaw Raczkiewicz, who was to a large degree an heir to the political forces monopolizing power in Poland up to 1939. Born in 1881, Sikorksi played a prominent role in Polish politics from at least the outbreak of World War I onward as an almost continual opponent of Jozef Pilsudski, the military leader and later dictator of Poland until his death in 1935.

His successor, Stanislaw Mikolajczyk, managed to take over the office of prime minister only after the president had recovered his prerogatives and General Kazimierz Sosnkowski had assumed the role of commander-in-chief. Both of these men held views on the cardinal problems of Polish politics that diverged sharply from those of Mikolajczyk. Mikolajczyk himself, who was twenty years younger than Sikorski, remained up to the end of the interwar period in the shadow of much more popular leaders, even in his own Polish Peasants party. Moreover, in the final period under consideration, Mikolajczyk was only a private person, having resigned his post on 7 November 1944. Even then, however, he attracted more attention from the leaders of Great Britain and the United States than anyone in the Polish "government of protest," which was headed after November 1944 by Tomasz Arciszewski, a seventy-seven-year old leader of the Polish Socialist party.

However dramatic the political and military developments for all the participants of World War II, the vicissitudes for the Poles were especially sudden and extreme. Quite naturally, these circumstances influenced the way they looked at their foreign partners. I would like to reconstruct the Polish image of the American president without overstepping the limits of action policies. Within the realm of declaratory policies we could notice—of course—many developments, but they lie outside the scope of my chapter.

The United States began to figure in Polish political calculations after the establishment of the Polish government-in-exile, although there had been sporadic and inconsequential contacts during nearly all the interwar years. Sikorski and Mikolajczyk, after he assumed the role of prime minister, met with President Roosevelt fairly often during the war years.

The most obvious determinant of their worldviews and policies was, without doubt, the changing configuration of forces among the Great Powers and its impact on the Polish case. But their policies were also heavily influenced by "domestic" politics, especially by the attitudes of Poles then in the West, particularly the troops under General Wladyslaw Anders.

During the interwar years, and even in the initial period of World War II, Sikorski continued to seek close ties with France, seeing in an alliance with that apparently strong and unassailable Great Power a cornerstone for Poland's foreign policy. Only after France's abrupt and quite surprising defeat, which brought with it the partial loss of the Polish troops that had just been reassembled with great effort, did Sikorski decide to carry out a major revision of policy. In order to maintain the continuity of the Polish state despite the German occupation and to mobilize all possible resources against the German war machine, he placed nearly all his hopes in Britain. By the middle of 1940, with the whole continent subdued by the Germans, it appeared that the willingness to continue fighting shoulder to shoulder with solitary Britain would provide Poland at last with a solid basis. Despite traditional British neglect of East Central Europe (the formal alliance of 26 August 1939 did not really change British behavior),[2] it seemed that the interests of the two countries would converge, making Poland a vital component of the new order of a postwar Europe shaped by Britain.

Sikorski's position was complicated, however, by his attitude toward the Soviet Union. Among the Polish politicians in exile, he was surrounded by hardened Russophobes who saw their nation in a war with two foes at the same time: Germany and the Soviet Union. This view was at odds with the attitude of British political leaders. From Britain's point of view, it was imperative to impede, at nearly any cost, the alliance between the Soviet Union and Germany. Also, on the sensitive territorial question, Britain's position was more distant from the Polish position than the Soviet one. Nevertheless, hardly anybody was interested in letting these differences surface, with the result that the relations between Great Britain and Poland appeared a bit closer than they actually were for more than a year after the defeat of France.

Even so, Sikorski decided to visit the United States, mainly to recruit Poles willing to fight. Although the exact number of Americans of Polish origin and their bonds with their old and new homelands are still debatable,[3] their significance was certainly recognized by both the Polish and American governments during the war, for the "Polonia" in the United States represented by far the largest population of Poles outside Poland itself. Sikorski was the first Polish prime minister to visit the United States and also the first statesman from the occupied continent to visit the still neutral United States.

Franklin D. Roosevelt and his Polish guest found common ground, first of all, in their interest in increasing the contribution of Polish-American workers in the key industrial centers that were vitally important in the process of making the United States "the arsenal of democracy." This mutual concern was sufficient to establish a warm personal climate at their meetings in April 1941 and to ensure that their discussions went smoothly.

In addition to more substantial matters, such as the question of recruiting soldiers for the Polish army and arranging urgently needed assistance through the Lend Lease program, several broad political questions were discussed. In briefing President Roosevelt before the meeting, Sumner Welles wrote: The prime minister "will wish to discuss with you postwar problems in Europe, but only in very general terms . . . . His general thesis is that no peaceful and prosperous Europe can be built up without a political and economic federation between Poland, Czechoslovakia and Hungary—and perhaps Rumania."[4]

A great part of Sikorski's first visit to the United States consisted of numerous meetings with Americans of Polish descent in order to counteract the appeals of those who argued that Roosevelt's policies risked American involvement in the war and to urge them to work more strenuously or to join the Polish forces in the West.[5] In the first case, the U.S. government undoubtedly welcomed Sikorski's activities, but it had reservations about his recruitment efforts. The final result of those efforts was strikingly modest, especially when compared to the contribution of Polish Americans to the Polish forces organized during World War I in France.

If Sikorski was anxious to make the most of his opportunity for a strategic and political *tour d'horizon* with his host, he did not succeed. Although he was well prepared, broadminded,[6] and apparently ready to take other points of view and new developments into consideration, it seems that such a dialogue did not occur. Perhaps it was too early. The visit took place two months before the outbreak of the war between Germany and the Soviet Union and seven months before Pearl Harbor—too early for the American president to air his views and expectations in the presence of a guest from a very distant and rather strange country. The president preferred to listen, without letting his guest learn his own opinion. Possibly Roosevelt would have been more open if the Polish ambassador had been more helpful, but Jan Ciechanowski was not the right go-between.[7]

Sikorski's next visit took place in March 1942. By then the war had become a protracted conflict on many fronts, a world war in the full meaning of the term. The United States was not only an active, unrestrained participant, but more and more visibly a senior partner in the Anglo-American alliance. Washington had become, in the words of one Polish authority, the "decisive center of the Great Coalition."[8] As a result, Sikorski now turned to Washington to seek support for the Polish government's political and military program, just as some months before he had transferred his loyalties from Paris to London.

This task was urgent. Aside from the changes within the power relations between Great Britain and the United States, the differing views of the British and Polish governments were coming more and more to the surface, making Great Britain less dependable as Poland's main ally, especially against the Soviet Union. Sikorski himself had accepted the necessity of collaborating as much as possible with the Soviet Union. For him, British pressure to do so served as a means of overcoming the opposition among other Polish politicians within and around the Polish government.

Two agreements signed by Sikorski, first with Ivan Maiski, the Soviet ambassador in London, only a few weeks after the outbreak of war between Germany and the Soviet Union in June 1941, and the second, with Stalin himself, in December were intended to pave the way for the establishment of a strong Polish army capable of making a significant contribution to the struggle against the Germans on the eastern front, the one nearest to Poland. At the same time, however, he decided to pass over the territorial question, in spite of strong urgings by Stalin, during their important talks in Moscow. His reason for leaving this fateful bone of contention unresolved was his conviction that important changes were taking place in the configuration of world forces. There is no foundation for placing him among the many people who completely deprecated the capabilities of the Soviet Union. But he continued to be influenced by the lessons of the last Great War, amending them only by recognizing the absence of France and acknowledging both of the great Anglo-Saxon powers as eventual masters of the military situation.

Sikorski's assessment of the military prospects, even if the eastern front was stabilized far from Polish territory and Anglo-American troops entered Poland through its southern borders and, eventually, from the Baltic Sea, became the basis for a plan for a military uprising within Poland, which he would present to both political and military leaders of Great Britain and the United States. During his second visit to the United States, this was an important item on Sikorski's agenda.

It is worthwhile remembering that his deliberations led him also to farfetched conclusions regarding the European political and economic order after the war. He believed that the Polish state should retain its eastern frontier intact and expand, more or less, at the cost of a defeated Germany.[9] So strengthened, the Polish state would become a cornerstone of the political system of postwar continental Europe.

The American ambassador to the Polish government in London, having observed the inclination of London's Polish exiles to see British public opinion as "too much at Russia's feet," reported anxiously on 20 February 1942 that Sikorski "pictures himself on the one hand as the leader of postwar Poland, on the other hand, now that France has disappeared as a dominant influence on the continent, the leader of continental Europe," and that he was attempting, though without success, to attract other governments-in-exile.[10]

A substantial part for such a plan would have been the creation of federative entities in East Central Europe itself, but a setback in Polish-Czechoslovak negotiations, the only significant development on this front at the time, had just occurred. In the meantime, Roosevelt himself had been warned about this plan and on 7 March wrote to Sumner Welles: "I think Sikorski should be definitely discouraged on this proposition. This is no time to talk about the postwar position of small [*sic*] nations, and it would cause serious trouble with Russia."[11]

It goes without saying that the agendas of Roosevelt and Sikorski for their second meeting were very different. On the other hand, the Poles seemed to act in unison with the U.S. government in regard to the negotiated British-Soviet alliance treaty.

As usual, the main burden of negotiations was assumed by Sumner Welles. During his meeting with Sikorski on 25 March 1942, just after the latter's broad-ranging conversation with the president, the Polish prime minister first of all gave a graphic account of his meetings with Stalin in December. He said repeatedly that the reason he had been able to reach such a satisfactory understanding and agreement with Stalin, with real concessions on the Soviet side, was the fact that, unlike the British, he had spoken with complete frankness. Sikorski stated emphatically that, barring German defeat or a complete defeat of the Soviet armies, he did not believe that Stalin would again enter into a separate peace with Hitler. He also said that, because of shortages of oil and manpower, he did not expect the German offensive against the Soviet Union that spring to be as powerful as the offensive of 1941.

After that introduction, Sikorski revealed his cherished plan for a federation of the Eastern European states lying between the Baltic and Aegean seas. Welles said only that he had heard of this conception, which appeared most interesting, and did not pursue the subject.[12]

Within a few days after Sikorski left the United States on 30 March, Welles thanked the American ambassador to the Polish government for giving in advance "a clear and detailed picture of the hopes, fears, and activities of the various refugee governments in London," which had turned out to be particularly helpful during the period of General Sikorski's visit. During that visit, he reported, the Polish prime minister had a number of talks with President Roosevelt and several conversations with Welles himself. The latter was favorably impressed with Sikorski's understanding of the European situation and with the vigorous and frank manner in which he presented the policies of his government. Before expressing hope for an eventual improvement in relations between the Polish prime minister and his ambassador in Washington, Welles said that he believed that Sikorski had left satisfied with the results of his visit.

This assessment sounds rather unconvincing given Welles's own statement that the American partners had managed "the shelving of General Sikorski's plan for working out immediately a post war confederation of the anti-Axis powers on the European continent."[13] Perhaps there is some explanation for this apparent contradiction. It appears that upon hearing Americans, including Roosevelt, say that all decisions on territorial questions should be postponed, both Sikorski and Count Edward Raczynski, the acting Polish foreign minister, interpreted the American position as a promising one for them. The fact that the British-Soviet treaty that was finally signed did not include the territorial stipulations the Poles had feared was greeted in Polish governmental circles as a great success and may have eased their apprehension additionally.[14]

Sikorski's third visit at the end of 1942 and the beginning of 1943 again took place in a much-altered situation. The chances of a Germany victory in the East had by then been reduced to nearly nothing and Anglo-American troops were fighting in North Africa, the alternative chosen instead of opening a second front in Western Europe. The new spirit would be expressed in the near future in the demand for "unconditional surrender" conceived by Roosevelt and accepted by his British partner.

On the Polish side the most important developments had been the departure of the Polish army commanded by General Wladyslaw Anders from the Soviet Union and the increasing tension between the Soviet Union and Poland. Although relations between the Soviet government and the Polish one in London were not definitely severed until April 1943, they had been worsening to such a degree that Sikorski may have believed even before his last visit to the United States that he urgently needed to seek support to avoid the fateful breach with the Soviet Union.[15] In my opinion, however, he remained interested, above all, in engaging the United States in his far-reaching plans for reorganizing East Central Europe, this being the cornerstone of his comprehensive political program.

Sikorski arrived in the United States on 1 December 1942 and did not depart until 10 January 1943,[16] making this last visit the longest of the three. Once again the main interlocutor was Welles, who had at least five rather lengthy meetings with the Polish prime minister. The president met with the Polish guest on 2 December and lunched with him on 5 January.

During his first meeting with Roosevelt, Sikorski tried very carefully[17] to present his plans for a postwar European order. The only effect of the meeting was the promise by Roosevelt to address a letter to the Polish prime minister that would be made public before Sikorski's departure from the United States. On 4 December, according to Welles, Sikorski handed him a draft of this letter. Welles at once voiced his reservations. Although he called his observations purely personal and preliminary, he expressed quite clearly the essential differences between the Polish and American positions.

First of all, he doubted whether the president would endorse any document stating that "Poland was to be reconstituted in her territorial limits within exactly the same boundaries as those which existed in 1939." He reminded Sikorski that, during his brief and general discussion with the president, consideration had been given only to the possibility of the elimination of the Polish Corridor and the incorporation of East Prussia into a new

Poland, provided the inhabitants of East Prussia were given the fullest right and liberty to determine their future.

Continuing the debate on the Polish proposal for an Eastern European bloc, Welles and Sikorski probed each other's ideas rather than sought any agreement. Finally, the suggestion of a Polish-Soviet military alliance, included in the last paragraph of the draft of the letter, led Welles to contrast such an alliance with the idea of the United Nations as a form of effective international security."[18]

Behind the niceties of diplomatic exchange were hidden more striking differences. Some of them are apparent in a memorandum written on 9 December by Ray Atherton, the acting chief of the Division of European Affairs. This memorandum and its annex are full of very sharp comments, perhaps the most telling of which reads:

> It is very important to observe that in the aggregate the proposals presented by General Sikorski set forth a point of view greatly at variance with the basic principles we have adopted as the real general war aims included in such documents as the Atlantic Charter and the Declaration by the United Nations. An examination of the several documents now presented shows that they cover reparations, war guilt, frontier pretensions, occupation, military booty, land and sea bases, et cetera, all in the spirit of extreme nationalism, with only a mild suggestion of Poland's own plans for international collaboration, and nothing whatever regarding some of the aspects (minorities, Jews, and rehabilitation) which particularly affect the Polish area. The proposals in effect lay down Poland's maximum nationalistic demands.[19]

Roosevelt himself, during his meeting some weeks later with Anthony Eden, apparently lost his patience in response to the British foreign minister's statement that Poland would want its original boundaries. "[A]fter all," Roosevelt answered, "the big powers would have to decide what Poland should have and that he, the President, did not intend to go to the Peace Conference and bargain with Poland or other small states; as far as Poland is concerned, the important thing is to set it up in a way that will help maintain the peace of the world."[20]

The question is whether the Polish government had any opportunity to discern the actual position of the United States on the Polish issue. I would say that to a degree it did. The fate of the letter drafted by Sikorski and presented to Welles was a serious warning. When the Department of State prepared a draft to replace the Polish one, it lacked the assurances so important to Sikorski. Moreover, when Sikorski attempted to recover some of the substance of his version, he was told on 6 January that adding the words "capable of effective defense" would involve a question of high principle because it implied "that the Polish Government intended to undertake, as soon as it was reconstituted, a program of rearmament which was entirely counter to the objectives of this Government."[21]

There is some difficulty in assessing an incident that followed Sikorski's visit. The British Foreign Office, having been informed by the Poles that its efforts, and especially Sikorski's talks with Roosevelt, had yielded results consistent with the views of the Polish government, asked Lord Halifax to verify the Polish accounts. The result was unequivocal; Halifax reported that he was told by Welles that

> the account given by General Sikorski of his conversation with the President was completely incorrect. General Sikorski had in fact done all the talking . . . . The President had made very little comment on these observations except to say that he thought the Danzig Corridor had proved a very bad arrangement and that we should all have to consider the future position of East Prussia.[22]

I would tend to exclude the possibility of intentional duplicity on Sikorski's part, seeing the source of his interpretation of the meeting in the different personalities of the two men, one a good listener and the other an eager talker. The situation of Sikorski's government, though not yet desperate, was sufficiently difficult to induce him to hear more than was actually said.

Sikorski was losing his illusions only with considerable difficulty. There are strong, though indirect, sources that make it possible to conclude that after his last trip to the United States, Sikorski began to have more and more misgivings about the chances of getting vitally needed American support for the Polish government's position and aims. Still rather reticent about admitting as much,[23] he clearly returned to London feeling more acutely the discrepancies between Roosevelt's view of the world and his own.

Jan Ciechanowski, the Polish ambassador, reported on 10 January that the Polish prime minister was gratified by the fact that Roosevelt had been "discussing with me practically all war and peace problems" and, in his own words, had "taken me into his confidence." On the other hand, he regretted that "our powerful Allies do not appear to realize the necessity of strengthening their hand in their dealings with the Soviets . . . [T]hey appear to be afraid of Soviet unfavourable reaction. And that in itself is characteristic of appeasement by which a realist like Stalin will never be taken in."[24]

At the same time, Sikorski communicated to his very close collaborator Leon Mitkiewicz, the military representative in Washington, the necessity of visiting Moscow once again. These attempts to rethink Polish strategy were not something momentary, and even the shocking news of the massacre of Polish officers at Katyn in April 1943, the appeal by the Polish government to the International Red Cross to investigate, and the decision by the Soviet Union, as a result, to break off diplomatic relations with the Polish government-in-exile, did not change this approach. We have two reliable witnesses: Tadeusz Romer, the Polish ambassador to the Soviet Union, and Michal Sokolnicki, the Polish ambassador to Turkey, who each recorded their talks with Sikorski a few days before his death.

Romer was told by the prime minister that "actually there is only one way open to us under these circumstances, namely urgent and rigorous probing to determine to what degree we can depend on the western great powers." More relevant to his American experience is the opinion Sikorski expressed to Sokolnicki: "Nevertheless we have to remain very close to the English. The Americans treat these problems in too fantastic a way. To them they are too distant and they can afford to abandon them easily .... The Englishmen offer a more solid basis. With them, we have connecting interests."[25]

Stanislaw Mikolajczyk, who became prime minister after General Sikorski's death in an airplane accident in July 1943, visited the United States, after some months of procrastination, in June 1944. Taking into consideration the correspondence before the visit and the available information about the meetings themselves between Mikolajczyk and his American hosts, it is very difficult to understand the satisfaction expressed by the Polish politicians.

The "red carpet" treatment offered the Polish guest, emphasized in Ambassador Ciechanowski's account, dimmed the real meaning of the visit. But the American insistence on having no public appearances and their proposal not to end the talks with any joint communiqué were in themselves important signs.[26] Moreover, the talks offered sufficient opportunity to learn what the actual American attitude was. Roosevelt, although he assumed an equivocal attitude in regard to the Curzon Line, nevertheless insisted that his guest thoroughly rethink Soviet-Polish relations and search for some adjustment with the Soviet Union as soon as possible. In his opinion, "when a thing becomes unavoidable, one should adapt oneself to it."

During their next meeting, on 12 June, the president once again urged his guest "to face this emergency" and to be prepared to make some concessions, especially in regard to the composition of the Polish government. Having mentioned the example of Finland, he urged Mikolajczyk to meet with the Polish-born economist Oscar Lange, who was a critic of the Polish government-in-exile. Many times the president referred to the relation of powers, seeing it as the most important reason for a meeting without delay of

Mikolajczyk with Stalin. These exhortations hardly affected Mikolajczyk's attitude.

The Polish prime minister did not realize that Roosevelt's remark about 1944 being a "political" year that confined his behavior had only one meaning: namely, that the expectation of Polish votes in the fall election placed a constraint on Roosevelt making his position in favor of the Soviet Union more manifest.

But even then the American president avoided becoming a mediator, being ready to serve only as a moderator between Poland and the Soviet Union. In response to the strong urgings of Mikolajczyk, who was unwilling to go to Moscow without strong American support, Roosevelt promised only "moral support."[27]

It remains something of a mystery why, after so much evidence, some of it circumstantial, the Polish government in London did not recognize the limits of American support and draw the necessary conclusions. Considering the infighting going on between the top Polish civil and military officials, however, the behavior may be at least partially explained.

The record of the four visits made to the United States by the Polish leaders during the war is without doubt not an edifying one. On the other hand, we should take into consideration the difficulties of any real partnership as well as the modest but concrete results of the meetings. In particular, General Sikorski seems to have been appreciated by the U.S. government as a source of knowledge when it was formulating its policies during the first phases of the war. Of course, Roosevelt and his advisors employed the information provided by his Polish guests very selectively. The items of information were "bricks" used in the construction of a world quite different from the one dreamed of by the Polish government in London.

Finally, it should be said that the differences between the two states, and between Roosevelt and his Polish wartime partners, were too fundamental to be resolved merely through more clever and efficient diplomacy.

6

REVIEW OF AMERICAN-YUGOSLAV RELATIONS IN WORLD WAR II

Ivan Cizmic

American policy toward events in Yugoslavia during World War II was very complicated.[1] Immediately after the attack on Yugoslavia in April 1941, President Roosevelt and Secretary of State Cordell Hull condemned the aggression and decided to offer moral and material help to Yugoslavia. The American government made the following announcement:

> The barbaric invasion of Yugoslavia and the attempt to destroy this state by brute force is one more chapter in the campaign for world domination and conquest. Yet another small nation has fallen victim to the conquerors' attack, which shows once again that there are no geographic borders or barriers of any sort in their campaign for world domination. The American people expresses its sympathy for the nation that has been attacked in this base manner, and we are following the brave battle of the Yugoslav people to protect its homeland and preserve its freedom. In accordance with the policy of helping those who fight against the conquerors, this government will now send military and other aid to Yugoslavia as quickly as possible."[2]

On 11 April 1941, the State Department approved the collection of aid for Yugoslavia in the United States.[3] In the beginning of June representatives of the American government made public that they recognized neither the dismemberment of Yugoslavia nor the puppet states created by the Axis powers. For the United States, the government of the kingdom of Yugoslavia remained legitimate.

The Yugoslav government itself took immediate steps to ensure that the United States did not recognize the dismemberment of Yugoslavia or the establishment of the Independent State of Croatia. On 12 May 1941 Konstantin Fotic, the Yugoslav envoy to Washington, presented a note to the State Department demanding that the American government condemn the creation of an independent state in the territory of Yugoslavia. Under Secretary of State Sumner Welles informed Fotic on 28 May that the American government would sharply protest the violation of both Yugoslavia's interests and the principles of international law that the Axis powers had committed by illegally using military occupation to alter the legal status of a country. Welles did this in the name of his government on 4 June.[4]

At a meeting on 12 May in Jerusalem, the Yugoslav government-in-exile concluded that the fate of its nation was to a large degree dependent on American aid, so a government delegation was appointed to work in the United States in order to acquire support for Yugoslavia. Envoy Fotic and Ivan Subasic, the head of this delegation, met in September with President Roosevelt and expressed their gratitude for his support for the liberation of Yugoslavia.[5] At this critical juncture, the Americans really did support in full the need to preserve the integrity of the Yugoslav state. So Edward Stettinius, director of the lend-lease administration, notified the Yugoslav delegation in Washington that, on 11 November, President Roosevelt had sent a letter in which he said that the kingdom of Yugoslavia was of vital interest to the defense of the United States. Fotic insisted to his government, which was already in London, that King Peter visit the United States. This occurred in July 1942, and the Yugoslav king was received by President Roosevelt and Winston Churchill, who at that time was also in the United States. Roosevelt and Churchill declared on this occasion that their governments wanted the restoration of a Yugoslavia that was "stable internally and not undermined by national conflicts."[6]

In January 1942 the Yugoslav government opened the Yugoslav Information Center and press bureau in New York to acquaint the American public with actual events in the country. The work of this center was directly connected with the first disagreements among politically influential Yugoslavs in the United States, which occurred over the interpretation of wartime and political events in Yugoslavia. The employees of the center, who were mostly Croats and Slovenes, did not approve of the work of Yugoslav envoy Fotic, who held Croats responsible for all the misfortunes of Yugoslavia and convinced the Americans that the future Yugoslavia would be possible only on the foundation of a Greater Serbia. Numerous Yugoslav émigrés and their powerful émigré organizations also joined in this struggle. The conflict attained such dimensions that representatives of the American government were forced to intervene. This intervention showed that the American policy toward Yugoslavia was not consistent or unified.

In an attempt to reach unanimity for the successful waging of the war, the American government tried to mediate some of the quarrels and open questions that appeared among Yugoslavs at that time. Thus Elmer Davis, who was the director of the Office of War Information, Assistant Secretary of State Adolf Berle, and Allan Cranston, director of the Foreign Language Division of the Office of War Information, called together representatives of American Yugoslavs at the State Department on 18 September 1942. Davis emphasized that the American government was aware of the quarrels and frictions among American Yugoslavs, but these tensions harmed the execution of the American war program. He said openly:

> The American government is aware that among American Croats, and to an even greater degree among American Serbs, there are battles concerning the question of the internal organization of Yugoslavia. These arguments have reached a highly undesirable level, as can be seen in the attacks of the newspaper *Srbobran* on all Croats in the old country, as well as on those here who are American citizens. These attacks are unfounded because, according to confidential information from the American State Department, the majority of Croats in the old country do not agree with the Quisling government of Pavelic and are resisting and fighting against those intruders, Hitler and Mussolini. The vast majority of Croats in America who are citizens and inhabitants here are loyal to this government, although in the beginning there were those who sympathized with Pavelic and who spread dissension between Croats and Serbs. Therefore, every attack of American Serbs on all Croats because of Pavelic's treason, as well as attacks of American Croats on Serbs as a whole because of [the Serbian Quisling] Nedic's disloyalty to the Allied cause, is not based on fact, and such attacks serve not only to weaken the American war effort and thereby weaken our cause but also aid Hitler and the fascists.[7]

At a meeting at the Office of War Information, Assistant Secretary of State Berle explained the position of the American government toward Yugoslavia and toward other friendly and Allied states. He said

> that the United States of America recognizes Yugoslavia as a state and as an ally in this war against the Axis powers, and America will extend every possible moral and material help. All three Yugoslav peoples in Yugoslavia are participating in the resistance to Hitler and Mussolini, as well as to their vassals Pavelic

> and Nedic, and our duty is to support all of the Yugoslav peoples and to extend help to all those elements that wherever and however contribute to the defeat of our common enemy. The American government does not want to become involved in the internal differences or views on particular parties or individuals on the future organization of the government in Yugoslavia, nor do Americans want to try to influence in any respect how that government will be organized, even though clearly there are different ideas and different opinions on the matter. But the duty of us Americans is not to worry now, at this moment, about these things or to waste energy on them. Our true, only, and main obligation is to overcome Hitler and his allies, and all other matters must be subordinated to that end. Every quarrel and every disturbance of the peace among Americans in relation to questions of differences in the old country, which concerns those nations and which they themselves must organize, weakens our effort and is of use to our enemies.[8]

Representatives of the American government unsuccessfully attempted to attain unified action of Yugoslav immigrants and to find some compromise between the people who worked at the Yugoslav Information Center and the Yugoslav chargé d'affaires, Fotic. Political differences among Yugoslavs in the United States, however, began to be reflected in the actions of various American politicians. Jaroslav Chyz, the head of the Foreign Language Information Service, reproached Elmer Davis and Read Lewis, the director of the Council for American Unity, for their unjustifiable attack on the Serbian nationalist newspaper *Srbobran*, which was published in the United States. Allan Cranston sharply answered Chyz by claiming that the writing in *Srbobran* was unacceptable in American politics. The conciliatory stance of several members of the Council for American Unity and their negative relations with leftist-oriented foreign-language newspapers evoked confusion. Luj Adamic, an American writer of Slovenian descent, was a council member and editor of the newspaper *Common Ground*. When he resigned from his position, Adamic sent a memorandum in which he emphasized that the council had recently often defended disruptive and harmful foreign-language newspapers and organizations under the slogan of "American Unity." Furthermore, Adamic charged, the council had permitted itself to be used as a screen for the activity of reactionary forces in the foreign-language press. All in all, Adamic believed, the council's work had inhibited, not promoted, the interests of different foreign-language groups as a whole, and the council had followed a policy of opportunism instead of promoting true democracy in the United States.[9]

Inconsistencies and discrepancies in the policy toward Yugoslavia could be observed periodically among American politicians. In one letter written to Francis Biddle of the Justice Department on 10 December 1941, Sava Kosanovic[10] expressed gratitude that, before delivering a speech at a Slavic banquet in Detroit, Biddle had corrected the words "Serbia" and "Serbs" to "Yugoslavia" and "Yugoslavs," which Kosanovic argued was exceptionally important for Yugoslav immigrants to the United States and for the Yugoslav struggle in general. Kosanovic admonished Biddle that President Roosevelt had used the term "Serb" instead of "Yugoslav" in an important speech. Such mistakes should not made, Kosanovic said, because only one-tenth of the 1,200,000 Yugoslav immigrants in the United States were Serbs. Although the current situation in Yugoslavia—particularly the creation of the Independent Croatian State and the chetnik (Serbian guerilla) resistance—seemed to permit use of "Serb" instead of "Yugoslav," the more general term should continue to be used so that all those who fought for the restoration of Yugoslavia would not feel abandoned.[11] Such mistakes, however, continued to be made. In a speech to the International Students' Congress in Washington, President Roosevelt said that the "living spirit of the struggle" was in Norway, Czechoslovakia, Poland, Serbia, and Greece. This statement created a real commotion among American Yugoslavs. The Yugoslav Information Center was asked for an explanation, and a correspondent of the New York *Daily News* received a request to question the president about this statement at a press conference.

Kosanovic wrote a letter to Mayor Fiorello La Guardia of New York warning him of the negative consequences such assertions could have for the Yugoslav struggle. Kosanovic said that such statements ignored the Croats and Slovenes, who were an incontrovertible factor in the Yugoslav state,[12] especially since guerilla warfare was most active in Slovenia and Croatia and everyone was unified in the struggle against the common enemy. Kosanovic asked La Guardia to try to establish from what quarter the suggestion came to use the term "Serb" and to take care that in the future such mistakes were not made.[13] In the meantime, the Associated Press news agency from Washington carried the following explanation:

> President Roosevelt explained today that in his speech of September 3 he praised the resistance of Serbia, and not of Yugoslavia, because he collected Serbian stamps in his youth. In certain circles this statement is considered proof that referring to the former country of Serbia is a sign that the President no longer recognizes the country of Yugoslavia. The President, however, stated that he had made this error because he had seen the name Serbia so many times on the stamps that he collected.[14]

Secretary of State Hull confirmed yet another American policy toward Yugoslavia when he stated on 9 December 1943 to newspapermen that the United States would help both the partisans and General Draza Mihailovic's forces. The basic goal of U.S. aid to Yugoslavia was a pragmatic one: to unite all groups, whatever their political ideas, in the struggle against the Germans. The American government recognized the king and the Yugoslav government in Cairo as the legitimate representative of Yugoslavia in general questions of military strategy, but the success of the Yugoslav National Liberation Army (NOVJ) was of immense usefulness to the anti-Hitler coalition. The final organization of the state and the political system in Yugoslavia was a matter that the Yugoslavs would themselves decide in the future. In the first months of 1944, the American government and the governments of Great Britain and the USSR diverged somewhat in their attitude toward events in Yugoslavia. The American government was willing to protect the chetnik movement and the interests of King Peter and his government. On 14 April 1944 Edward Stettinius, the director of the lend-lease administration, arrived in London with instructions from President Roosevelt to work out a joint Allied policy toward Yugoslavia. Stettinius's talks in London ended in favor of international affirmation of the partisans' war of national liberation.[15]

The American press was divided on reporting on events in Yugoslavia. On the basis of facts supplied by Fotic, articles in the *New York Times* contributed to the creation of the legend about Draza Mihailovic as a "hero." The *Times* was among the last newspapers that continued to publish Mihailovic's "war reports," which Fotic wrote in Washington and distributed to American newspapers.[16] Nevertheless, at the end of 1943 even this newspaper began to publish reports about the collaboration of the chetniks with the Italians. American journalist Baldwin often wrote about events in Yugoslavia and persistently put in a good word for Mihailovic, especially at the beginning of the war when he asserted that Milan Nedic, the Yugoslavian prime minister, was not a traitor but rather the Pétain of the Serbian nation.[17] The prominent American journalist Anna McCormick maintained that there were no Serbs among the partisans. The magazine *New Week* also wrote about the partisans in a hostile manner. When, at the end of 1943, a good part of the American press changed its position in relation to events in Yugoslavia, this magazine carried a picture of the chetnik Mihailovic. The *Christian Science Monitor* was still trying to promote the myth about Draza Mihailovic at the end of the war.[18]

In a letter dated 10 January 1944, Kosanovic warned DeWitt Poole, who was in charge of Foreign Nationalities at the Office of Strategic Services, that there were clear antipartisan tendencies in the daily reports from radio stations in the previous months. Kosanovic pointed out that this had occurred at a time when the partisans' military activity was actually far more intensive than before and that the American stance had completely changed to favor the partisans officially.[19]

From the very beginning of the war, some American newspapers wrote positively about Yugoslavia, and in the second phase of the war their number increased.[20] One group of journalists, among whom were Ralph G. Martin, Stoyan Pribichevich, John Talbot, and Ed Johnson, visited the partisan lines and, after their return, wrote about their stay with the partisans, about meetings with Marshal Tito who discussed the situation on the front in great detail, about the political situation in Yugoslavia, and about the program for which the National Army of Liberation was fighting. These articles were published in American newspapers. Later they were collected into a pamphlet entitled *The Yugoslav Struggle through American Eyes*.[21]

Journalist W. Bernstein wrote very positively about events in Yugoslavia. His interview with Marshal Tito was published in almost every newspaper in the United States.[22] Radio commentator Sydney Rogers in a broadcast from San Francisco at the end of 1942, said that the partisans were fighting—and that Mihailovic was not fighting—against the occupying powers in Yugoslavia. The New York *Daily Worker*, the organ of the American Communist party, wrote frequently and objectively about events in Yugoslavia from the very beginning of the war. *PM*, which followed Roosevelt's policy, went a step further in its articles on Yugoslavia, for which Luj Adamic was responsible.[23]

American public opinion in the second part of the war increasingly came over to the side of the partisans and the national war of liberation. Winifred N. Hadsel's study "The Struggle for Yugoslavia," which was published in the journal *Foreign Policy Reports*, perhaps discussed this most eloquently. Hadsel maintained that agreement between the partisans and the chetniks was impossible for a number of reasons. Mihailovic attempted to get full military control over all units, whereas the partisans sought joint military command; in addition, the power over liberated territory belonged to the newly elected individuals rather than to the prewar state apparatus. Hadsel further stressed that Tito's movement had a broad basis because the partisans were composed of both men and women as well as of members from many religions, nationalities, and political opinions. Mihailovic wanted to preserve his military forces untouched, outside the fighting, and from the time he became the minister of war in the royal government in January 1942, he began to view his opponents as traitors. The partisans, however, undertook active tactics in the belief that, in this way, they would get the support of all Yugoslav peoples. In their resistance movement the partisans tried to engage an ever greater number of German soldiers, thereby easing the position of the Red Army on the eastern front. In this way the partisan struggle became an integral part of the European front.

Hadsel commented as well on the serious conflicts that existed regarding the future organization of Yugoslavia. Mihailovic was fiercely loyal to the Karageorgevich dynasty and wanted the restoration of prewar conditions, but he made some concessions at the congress in Ravna Gora, which was held in January 1944. At this congress chetnik representatives offered constitutional and social reforms as well as a federal structure in postwar Yugoslavia. Hadsel was skeptical that Mihailovic's program would win over the broad support of the Yugoslav masses. The partisans wanted to prevent the restoration of the prewar conditions by establishing complete democracy and national equality, but they also wanted to put off all important questions concerning the organization of the state until after free elections had been held. Hadsel warned that the partisans had already replaced the old authorities in the liberated areas with new national ones and that the meeting of the Anti-Fascist Council of the Yugoslav National War of Liberation had been held in Bihac. He also mentioned the relative military strength of the two movements: Partisan forces amounted to 200,000 or 250,000 men, whereas the chetniks amounted to only 15,000. Finally, as Hadsel commented, in London and Washington it was believed that some kind of reconciliation was possible. The partisans, however, condemned the Yugoslav government in London, which condemned them. Although King Peter called for united resistance, he stuck by Mihailovic as the sole leader of resistance in Yugoslavia.

According to Hadsel, during 1942 and at the beginning of 1943 civil war in Yugoslavia threatened to provoke serious disagreements among the Allies. Moscow condemned Mihailovic because of his inactivity and for the collaboration of his units with the enemy. Public opinion and the press in the West, however, portrayed Mihailovic as a hero, and the British sent him a military mission. Only in 1943 did the Western Allies change their policy and send military missions to Tito; the United States basically followed the policy of Great Britain. Hadsel asked how the Allies would act toward Yugoslavia after the war. The Allies hoped that the partisans and the king would resolve their differences, all the more because King Peter was not responsible for what had occurred before the war when he was still a minor. But Hadsel correctly noted that the resolution of the Yugoslav question was closely linked to the mutual relations of the Great Powers and their struggle for the creation of spheres of interest.

In trying to find a solution to these weighty issues, Hadsel seriously considered the idea of a Balkan federation. He remarked that it could be achieved only on a democratic basis as a substitute for the dictatorial regimes that had previously existed in the Balkan states. To achieve that goal, the Great Powers would also have to renounce their traditional political competition for the domination of the Balkans. Hadsel noted that American policy toward the Balkans had not yet been defined. The statement of the American government on 5 February 1944, however, showed that it wanted stability in the Middle East because of oil sources on the Arabian peninsula.

In his study Hadsel worked with voluminous material about contemporary events in Yugoslavia and probably also in consultation with the responsible American politicians. These sources give his work importance. Hadsel recognized that the partisan movement and the socialist revolution in Yugoslavia had far better prospects than did the chetniks and the restoration of prewar conditions. Most important, Hadsel's study showed that public opinion in America and American politicians were on the side of the national war of liberation by March 1944.[24]

7

WILHELMINA AND FRANKLIN D. ROOSEVELT: A WARTIME RELATIONSHIP

Albert E. Kersten

On 16 June 1942 Queen Wilhelmina embarked in London on an airplane of the British king's for a flight to Shannon Airport in Ireland, where she transferred with her company to an American Catalina flying boat that President Roosevelt had sent to transport her to Canada. In July the two heads of state met at Roosevelt's estate at Hyde Park, and in August the queen made an official visit to Washington. On that occasion she addressed the American Congress. After visits to New York and Boston she returned to Canada for an official visit, and by the end of August she was back in London. In July 1943 she met President Roosevelt for the second time privately at Hyde Park.

These two occasions mark the only direct contact between the American president and the Dutch queen. Although, they were contemporaries, clear reasons for direct relations were not very pressing. Of course, to their countries both individuals were important national leaders during the war, but this did not build a basis for mutual relations. Nevertheless, one has to admit that during the war years a special relationship developed between Franklin Delano Roosevelt and Queen Wilhelmina. The initiative for this relationship sprang from Roosevelt in November 1939, and it was developed after the German invasion of the Netherlands in May 1940, after the queen and her cabinet had established themselves in exile in Great Britain. It is difficult to give the relationship flesh and blood, because only a small amount of reliable firsthand information is available, consisting mainly of their correspondence.[1]

The relationship could be divided into three sections. The first concerned the personal, family relationship, which refers to Roosevelt's care for and interests in the personal well-being of the queen and her family, especially Princess Juliana and her two daughters, who were living in Canada during the war years, and Prince Bernhard, who visited the president on several occasions. The second element of the relationship concerned the personal contacts between Franklin Roosevelt and Queen Wilhelmina, in which they appreciated each other as statespersons and exchanged views on the war situation. The last element concerns their contacts on international affairs, mainly on issues related to the situation in occupied Europe, especially Holland, and postwar arrangements on international security and the treatment of Germany.

This division of the relationship clarifies that the emphasis had to be put on the official aspects of their contacts and on their special nature. One should keep in mind that, contrary to the other contemporaries discussed during this conference, Queen Wilhelmina did not represent a state that was one of the main actors during the Second World War. The relations between the United States and the Netherlands reflected their international position of respectively great and small power. Despite the cordiality of the relationship between the president and the queen and their respective officials, one should keep in mind that to the United States, the main power in the alliance against Germany and Japan, the Netherlands were relatively unimportant for the Allied war effort. Until the defeat of the Netherlands forces in the Indies, the Dutch contribution to the war was of some importance; it provided strategic raw materials such as rubber, tin, bauxite, and oil and played a part in the Far Eastern defense. After March 1942 the merchant navy was the main Dutch asset for the war effort.[2]

This view on the Dutch position in the Allied international power structure during World War II certainly does not match the contemporary opinions. The Dutch foreign minister, Eelco Van Kleffens, voiced the views of the Dutch community when he described the international position of the Netherlands as ranking a little bit lower than the leading great powers, but far superior to the small states without any overseas territory.[3] Certainly, Queen Wilhelmina held the same views; she even critized Van Kleffens when he developed a scheme for a network of regional security organizations under the aegis of the United States and Great Britain. In her opinion this scheme incorrectly reflected the view that the kingdom of the Netherlands was "just a small country."[4] This overstatement of the Dutch international position by the government-in-exile—an overstatement that was congruent with prewar views on the importance of Dutch neutrality for the international balance of power—carried with it certain expectations regarding the influence of the Dutch government on Allied wartime and postwar affairs. In general these expectations have remained unfulfilled despite the efforts of the Dutch cabinet and especially its minister for foreign affairs, Van Kleffens, to gain equal treatment for the Netherlands.

To Queen Wilhelmina, direct relations with the Western wartime leaders were important, although she did not intensify these relations. She preferred to live in isolation outside London and met only once a year the British prime minister, Winston Churchill, at 10 Downing Street. Meetings with the leaders of the other governments-in-exile in London also were of low frequency or incidental.[5] Therefore, it is more remarkable that Queen Wilhelmina put such effort in the relationship with President Roosevelt. Already in 1941 the queen had planned a visit to the United States, and it was her intention to make a third visit to the president in 1944.

One more introductory observation on Queen Wilhelmina has to be made. Her constitutional position was quite different from President Roosevelt's. According to the constitution, she was head of state, commander of the armed forces, and chief of the foreign relations and of the colonial territories. In fact, these constitutional powers had been restricted by a preceding article that gave political responsibility to the cabinet ministers. Under regular constitutional conditions the cabinet was controlled by the Estates General. However, during the London exile this constitutional balance had been disturbed by the absence of elected representatives of the Dutch people. Instead of the constitutional triangle, a dual system was in operation. In practice it gave the queen a stronger position than the cabinet. Nevertheless, when Queen Wilhelmina and president Roosevelt discussed political affairs, it was a somewhat unbalanced conversation: such discussions were within the president's constitutional duties. But despite the fact that Queen Wilhelmina's power was less restrained in exile that it had been at home, she still had to leave political discussions to her ministers.

Thus there was much out of balance between the official positions of Roosevelt and Queen Wilhelmina. Roosevelt represented the major Allied power and was constitutionally entitled to the conduct of international relations. Queen Wilhelmina lacked the constitutional powers for international negotiations and governed a small power that regarded itself as an international force ranking not far behind the Great Powers. In practice these circumstances did influence the relationship, but they were not the decisive factors in shaping it.

THE PERSONAL RELATIONSHIP

Franklin Delano Roosevelt sent his first personal and unofficial message to Queen Wilhelmina shortly after the November crisis of 1939 and its imminent threat of a German invasion in the Netherlands. He offered Princess Juliana and her children a place "completely safe against airplane raids" in his vicinity in Washington or Hyde Park.[6] In showing interest for the well-being of the queen's family, Roosevelt certainly touched a sensitive spot. Queen Wilhelmina herself could not look back at a very happy childhood. She had been educated and trained for the throne, especially after the death of her father, King William III, in 1890. Her marriage to Hendrik of Mecklenburg-Schwerin had not been a harmonious one; her difficult personality had contributed to that result. Her dedication to state affairs as her personal duty never slackened, for she regarded it as her holy duty. However, after the marriage of Princess Juliana to Prince Bernhard of Lippe-Biesterfeld in 1937 and the birth of the princesses Beatrix and Irene in 1938 and 1939, the queen's life had been enriched by a family life that she greatly enjoyed.[7] According to the American envoy in The Hague, George A. Gordon, who transmitted Roosevelt's November message, the president's attention for the personal well-being of the queen's only daughter's family "was deeply appreciated." During the interview with Gordon Queen Wilhelmina

> had difficulty in mastering her emotions: she expressed herself more freely than [was] her wont, and referred most appreciatively to what she qualified as the spontaneity and kindness of your offer. In fact at one point she said "I really cannot find worlds to express myself" which coming from Queen Wilhelmina, I think may be taken as an unmistakable indication of her very genuine appreciation of your message.[8]

On 19 December 1939 Roosevelt repeated his offer for accommodation at the White House or at his estate on the Hudson River. In her answer, written in her rigid English in longhand, the queen expressed her deep appreciation for Roosevelt's offer but indicated that in case "the worst should happen," the princess and her family would move to a safe harbor in southern Europe, and they expected to be safe there as long as the fighting continued.[9] When in May war came to the Netherlands, Princess Juliana and her family evacuated to Great Britain[10] and proceeded later that month on board the Dutch warship *Sumatra* to Canada. Thus Roosevelt's offer for transport and shelter of 19 December 1939 and his new proposal of 18 May 1940 to send a ship to Ireland to take the queen and her family to the United States were not accepted.[11]

Roosevelt's interest in the well-being of the Dutch royal family did not disappear. In December 1940 Princess Juliana spent a few days at the White House. She repeated her visit with Prince Bernhard in June, and it was to him that Roosevelt suggested that the queen should come to the United States to discuss the rebuilding of Europe and the reconstruction of the world. Princess Juliana and Prince Bernhard entered into a personal correspondence with Franklin Roosevelt, who also occasionally received letters from Princess Beatrix addressed to "Uncle Franklin." In 1942 he assisted Princess Juliana in finding a suitable house in Lee, Massachusetts, to spend the summer. Queen Wilhelmina's transfer to Canada was prepared after presidential instructions under strict security arrangements. During her stay at Hyde Park, Roosevelt took the queen on a visit to the Delanos who lived farther north on the Hudson,[12] a kindly gesture that the queen had some problem savoring. According to Van Kleffens she did not talk much, and sat "a bit pitiful, . . . a bit stoical and a bit out of place amidst of the loudly speaking Americans with their Scotch and rye and ice tea."[13] When by the end of 1942 Queen Wilhelmina intended to go to Canada on the occasion of the birth of her third grandchild, Roosevelt tried to discourage her from doing so because in his opinion the northern air passage was "not by any means a safe one."[14] The personal friendship of the two families was underlined by the choice of Roosevelt as godfather to the newly born Princess Margriet.

It is very difficult, if not impossible, to discover the core of the relationship between Roosevelt and the Dutch royal family during the Second World War. One could say Roosevelt's personal attention to the royal family was nothing more than part of the sphere of relations between heads of state. However, the attention he gave to Princess Juliana and Prince Bernhard exceeded this formal relationship. From Roosevelt's utterances to intimates of his entourage, it is evident that he greatly appreciated Queen Wilhelmina's courage and dedication. According to his son James, Queen Wilhelmina was "one of the few living persons of whom he was slightly in awe."[15] Roosevelt's private secretary William Hassett revealed that Roosevelt used to call the Queen "'Minie' and made her like it."[16]

These indications of mutual appreciation are not of great assistance if one wants to learn of their personal contacts as president and queen. For at that point another dimension entered the relationship that brought into the front line both individuals as "politician" and "stateswoman." One can deduce it already from the ways in which they dealt with their mutual correspondence. Roosevelt started the correspondence in November 1939 on a personal basis, but he did not forget to consult his secretary of state as to whether he could do so.[17] Despite their personal style and nature, Roosevelt handled the letters of Queen Wilhelmina as official correspondence by asking the advice of his assistants or cabinet members before replying. Wilhelmina on the contrary regarded her relationship with the American president as a personal affair in which her ministers should not be involved. She corresponded with the president without consulting the prime minister or the minister for foreign affairs probably until April 1942. She had decided to visit Princess Juliana in Canada and the president during the summer of 1942 without informing her cabinet. She entrusted Prince Bernhard with the preparations for the journey, but the British Foreign Office alerted the Dutch cabinet. When the prime minister gently reminded the queen that when visiting foreign heads of state she had to be accompanied by a cabinet minister, she consented to Van Kleffens's presence despite her anger over this interference.[18] This incident placed the conversations and correspondence of Queen Wilhelmina with Roosevelt in the proper constitutional setting and in the following years they were conducted in this manner. On several occasions it was the cabinet that took the initiative for a royal letter to the White House in order to bring an important issue to the attention of the president, thus trying to bypass the Washington bureaucracy.

DISCUSSIONS OF THE INTERNATIONAL SITUATION IN 1942 AND 1943

In August 1941 Queen Wilhelmina had greatly appreciated Roosevelt's invitation to discuss international affairs with him at Hyde Park. However, she postponed the visit because she expected important changes to occur soon in Germany due to internal collapse.[19] When in June 1942 she met Roosevelt, the position of her kingdom had changed considerably. The Netherlands Indies had been occupied by Japan, and the Dutch contribution to the Allied war effort had greatly diminished. Wilhelmina had meticulously prepared her conversations with the president at Hyde Park on 11 and 12 July, but as she confided to Van Kleffens at his arrival at the Roosevelt mansion, she had been disappointed by the president's attitude. In her opinion she had not conducted a single sincere conversation with Roosevelt, although he had invited her to discuss the "future peace." Roosevelt was "a man who continuously [told] anecdotes," who hardly let his conversation partner speak.[20] To Queen Wilhelmina, who was accustomed to leading the conversation herself, it must have been a strange experience. When Roosevelt continued this pattern of conversational behavior in the next round, the queen did not hide her disappointment. Later that day she "most politely" urged Roosevelt to listen to Van Kleffens's concept for regional security organizations as the basis of postwar international security. Roosevelt did so without showing much enthusiasm.[21] Although no information is available on the other conversations between Roosevelt and Wilhelmina, there is no reason to believe that the president changed his usual conduct.

The results of the meetings between Queen Wilhelmina and President Roosevelt in 1942 and 1943 were of some importance to the Dutch government, because it gathered firsthand information on Roosevelt's views on postwar international affairs. Roosevelt talked about his views on an international trusteeship for disputed areas and for strategically important zones that had been abused by the enemy. Germany, Japan, and Italy had to be disarmed and the smaller powers, among whom he probably classified the Netherlands, should be charged with the control of any clandestine rearmament of these three nations. According to Roosevelt, the Great Powers should police the international community after the war. Regarding international economic relations, he was in favor of international cartels for raw materials such as had been created in the 1930s for tin, rubber, sugar and tea.[22] In 1943 the conversations concerned more specific issues, such as the membership of the Central Committee of the United Nations Relief and Rehabilitation Administration, food for the occupied territories in Europe before the termination of hostilities, the publication of a general warning to Germany and Japan on the destruction of lives and properties in the occupied countries, and finally the conditions for the surrender of Italy. The structure of the United Nations Organization was the sole postwar subject they discussed.[23]

At first sight the conversations between the queen and the president were rather superficial. Roosevelt probably did not long for an intensive discussion of international and postwar affairs with Queen Wilhelmina, and he restricted the conversations to a one-way communication of his own opinions and ideas. So one could conclude that this experience had to be rather frustrating for Queen Wilhelmina, who had come to the New World to discuss world affairs with Roosevelt as an equal. From the little information available on their conversations, bilateral issues seem not to have been discussed. However, despite her promise to the prime minister to discuss political issues with Roosevelt only with her minister of foreign affairs in attendance, the queen ignored these restrictions in regard to the future of the Netherlands East Indies. On this subject as well as on the issue of postwar political reform and the German policies in occupied Holland she had prepared a speaking note. It stated that the Netherlands East Indies should be administered in an efficient way without regard to traditional petty party politics. The queen denied every allegation of economic exploitation of the Indies by the Netherlands. The benefits of its industrial development had been reinvested, and "how could we submit to the fact that others deprive it?"[24]

These general statements reflect reactions to the American mood against colonialism and concern on the future of the Indies. The Dutch cabinet had also developed a scheme for the future of the Indies, but it had not convinced Queen Wilhelmina at all. Up to 1942 her personal relationship with the Indies had been a peculiar one. She had never visited the Indian archipelago, as she admitted to Harry Hopkins with some embarrassment early in 1941. The reasons had mainly been of a personal nature: She disliked the long journey by sea, was afraid of the humid warmth, and was scared to death of infections.[25] As to the future of the Indies, her views were rather conservative. In January 1942 she agreed to an official statement regarding an imperial conference to be held after the war to discuss the structure of the kingdom, but the prospect of Indonesian independence was absolutely not on her mind. In this respect she shared the opinion of the cabinet; however, contrary to her ministers, she did not sufficiently understand the importance of the anticolonialist mood of American public opinion leaders who queried why American soldiers should die to restore European colonial empires in the Far East. When in May 1942 the appointment of an Indonesian as minister without portfolio in the cabinet was proposed to counteract Japanese propaganda and American public opinion, Queen Wilhelmina initially opposed it for very formal reasons.[26] She demonstrated the same attitude toward the proposal of Prime Minister Pieter Gerbrandy, the recently appointed minister for the colonies, H. J. van Mook, and Foreign Minister Van Kleffens for drafting a scheme on the future structure of the kingdom, again because of strong anti-colonialist tendencies in the United States. Van Kleffens had submitted this proposal to the queen shortly after her arrival in Canada; soon he was informed that she would not feel committed by the draft and its publication, but regarded herself "absolutely free" concerning any future decision.[27]

Queen Wilhelmina discussed this vital issue for the Netherlands with Roosevelt twice, as the president told General Douglas MacArthur a year later. He explained to her that a clear Dutch policy toward the Indies and a public statement on it were necessary to improving public opinion in the United States as well as to the war effort in the Indies and for the future peace. The queen promised to consult her ministers on this "momentous question." Later, during her visit on 7 August 1942, the queen explained to Roosevelt that due to the differences in the level of development, a uniform policy for the Indies as a whole was unrealistic. She expected that Java could gain an autonomous status within a reasonable number of years (between fifteen and fifty), but for the most backward areas every cipher would be "sheer speculation."[28]

From these records it is unclear whether Roosevelt tried to convince Queen Wilhelmina of the need for a change in her government's policy toward the Indies. Even if their talks were just an exchange of views, they had a great impact on her future attitude. In her speech to the American Congress on 6 August, she had limited herself to a description of the principles and the development of the "place of the overseas territories in the framework of the Kingdom."[29] Soon after her return to London, she discussed with van Mook a declaration of the future framework of the kingdom and proved to be less reluctant. One year after the Japanese attack on Pearl Harbor, Queen Wilhelmina made a radio speech to the Indies that promised in general terms autonomy to "Greater Netherlands under the tropics."[30] In fact, this speech addressed American public opinion and constituted the implementation of Roosevelt's advice of July.

Roosevelt probably aired his opinions on the future of the East Indies in a very restrained way to Queen Wilhelmina. Basically he was of the opinion that Dutch rule could not be restored in the Indies and that the territory should be administered by an international authority in which the Netherlands would participate. Later on this concept was embodied in the plans of the Postwar Foreign Policy Advisory Committee of the Department of State.[31] Roosevelt never aired this strong opinion on the future of the Netherlands Indies to any Dutch diplomat or cabinet minister. All those who spoke with him on this issue believed that the president endorsed the restoration of the Dutch administration in the Indies. Therefore, to the Dutch it remained obscure what Roosevelt precisely had in mind.

OCCUPIED HOLLAND AND THE PSYCHOLOGICAL IMPACT OF NAZISM

After general references on the situation in occupied Holland in their 1941 and early 1942 correspondence, Queen Wilhelmina and President Roosevelt's mutual concern on the deterioration of general conditions and the harassment of the population by the German authorities increased. From November 1942 onward this subject came up in every letter. It concerned not only the bad living conditions and the severe regime that the Germans had forced on Holland and the other occupied countries, but also the damage this occupation policy would cause to the general well-being in the long term. At first Queen Wilhelmina was very much affected by the hardening of German occupation policies "into a real reign of terror." Especially she was worried about the many hostages taken by the Germans "from amongst the best and ablest of citizens."[32] In March 1943 her perspective was still darker. The Nazis had hardened the lives of the people in Holland by evacuating most of the coastal area and destroying all its buildings. Several hundreds of thousands of Dutch people had been "abducted to Germany as slaves," and the main industrial and agricultural sources of the country's prosperity were destroyed. In addition to this material destruction, a program for breaking the nation's spirit was in progress, a program aiming at the merging of the population of the Netherlands with the German Reich, "wiping out our national heritage and civilization." The longer the Germans continued this annihilation of the Netherlands as a nation, the more difficult it would be to restore the basic values after Allied victory.[33]

It is not surprising that Queen Wilhelmina regarded Roosevelt's radio address of 12 February 1943 on punishment of the Nazis as an appropriate opportunity to draw his attention to the dangers of Nazi ideology. She was in favor of a very harsh policy toward the Nazis after the war, and she wanted to have Roosevelt on her side. It was not "sufficient to punish a few wrong-doers and simply leave the others alone," she wrote to him. "The Nazi-poison has infected the minds of *all* Nazis, and the young ones are beyond re-education which will be necessary for *other* Germans." After the Allied victory the Nazis would remain a danger to world peace and the queen invited Roosevelt to think of ways to neutralize this danger. She herself preferred exiling all Nazis to "some remote region," but in any case "stern measures [seemed] unavoidable."[34]

Roosevelt did not respond. In May 1943 the queen wrote the president again, now at the instigation of the cabinet. She expressed her great concern regarding the deportation and exploitation of a considerable number of the Dutch working force in the German war industries. These people and the members of the armed forces who had recently been called back as prisoners of war to Germany could be abused as hostages in case of Allied operations against Germany. She asked Roosevelt whether anything could be done to stop or at least mitigate the German behavior toward these people. During her visit to Hyde Park in June 1943 the issue was discussed. Roosevelt promised—in due time and after consultation with Churchill—to warn Germany (and Japan) against the destruction of lives and property in occupied territories and the mistreatment of deported persons in Germany.[35] Roosevelt also consented to the immediate delivery of some food to occupied Holland before the end of hostilities, and he promised to make a renewed effort for Churchill's agreement.

Food for occupied Holland and the treatment of Nazis after the war remained the prime subjects of the correspondence between Roosevelt and Queen Wilhelmina during the last two years of the war. On the treatment of Nazis agreement existed between them, but it was typical for Roosevelt that after a very general description of his viewpoint, he did not enter into a private exchange of views with the queen on the subject, but referred to the European Consultative Commission in London as the proper channel for expressing Dutch opinions regarding the liquidation of the Nazi party and the treatment of its members.[36]

Regarding food for occupied Holland, Roosevelt showed more attention. Of course, he was not the sole authority in the Allied camp who demonstrated great concern about the situation in occupied Holland after September 1944. However, it should be noted that he instructed a number of his intimate assistants who went to Europe—for instance Stanley Hornbeck, Judge Samuel Rosenman, and Louis B. Wehle—to give special attention to the Dutch situation.[37]

CONCLUSIONS

Wilhelmina's relationship with her fellow head of state Franklin Delano Roosevelt was a special one, certainly to herself. She admired him greatly, something she felt for very few men in her life. Instead of being the average Dutch politician, the American president impressed her with his personality. In her memoirs, *Lonely But Not Alone*, she wrote that her admiration had been growing most by listening to Roosevelt's fireside chats at 3:00 a.m. at Stubbings, her home in exile near London, and by his statecraft, initially as sympathizer with the Allied cause, later on as ally in the war. When she met him in June 1942 she had been impressed by his strong personality, his willpower and tenacious perseverance. Meeting him assured her "that he would never yield or abandon a just cause and that fighting for it he would persevere to the very end."[38] Maybe Queen Wilhelmina was also flattered by the down-to-earth way in which Roosevelt treated her—not just as the Queen of the Netherlands, but as a woman governing and caring for an occupied country in exile. His natural superior behavior did melt down her icy and stubborn attitude, which had impeded good contact with many other individuals. Van Kleffens and William Hassett confirm this impression. All in all, to her personally, it was more important than any other war experience.

What about Franklin Roosevelt? He explained his attitude to Stanley K. Hornbeck after Hornbeck's appointment as ambassador to the Netherlands in November 1944. Roosevelt described the history of his contacts with the royal family since November 1939. He referred to Queen Wilhelmina as "a grand and an amazing person." However, he had started the conversation by noting that in the past the Dutch court had been the most formal court in Europe. "He did not know how they would be in the future."[39] Did Roosevelt expect that their contacts might have changed Queen Wilhelmina?

The relationship between Franklin D. Roosevelt and Queen Wilhelmina was most fruitful in the personal arena. In the realm of state affairs, both personalities were too experienced to enter into adventurous operations. Roosevelt deliberately kept Wilhelmina out of the Great Powers issues, and this clearly disappointed the Dutch queen.

8

THE OSLO STATES AND FRANKLIN D. ROOSEVELT

Ger van Roon

Shortly after the outbreak of the Second World War in 1939, someone suggested that President Roosevelt could be the savior of the world by restoring world peace after the Polish defeat. Roosevelt answered: "The people of the United States would not support any move for peace initiated by this government that would consolidate or make possible a survival of a regime of force and of aggression."[1]

Four months later as the Soviet Union's attack on Finland intensified Roosevelt's concern but reports revealed that House leaders opposed a loan to Finland, Roosevelt declared in the Congress:

> There is without doubt in the United States a great desire for some action to assist Finland to finance the purchase of agricultural surpluses and manufactured products, not including implements of war. There is at the same time undoubted opposition to the creation of precedents that might lead to large credits to nations in Europe, either belligerents or neutral. No one desires a return to such a status.[2]

Interest in the 1930s has largely concentrated either on the depression and its effects on the domestic situation of particular countries or on the origins of the Second World War, focusing mainly on Germany. This rather disjointed approach has resulted in quite separate and therefore unconnected views on both themes. Also the literature on international relations about this period has been influenced by this compartmentalized and too linear approach. Many authors in this field, but not Paul Kennedy,[3] reject any approaches connected with economic evolutions or changes. In this respect there is sometimes also a tendency to neglect the influence of domestic factors. In my opinion much attention must be paid to the interaction of domestic and international factors.

The Group of the Oslo States,[4] at the moment a fast forgotten term, was founded in the shadow of the League of Nations. They included Belgium, Denmark, Luxembourg, the Netherlands, Norway, and Sweden; later Finland too. These countries with their about 10 percent of world turnover of trade and about 30 million inhabitants hoped to be an alternative; in a time of depression and protectionism they strove for a reduction of tariff barriers; with their tradition of neutralism and from their position as small states they worked in a time of rearmament and preparation for war for concerted action for peace and for preventive diplomacy.

The theme of the Oslo states is an interesting subject. It relates quite different fields of research from the 1930s such as the League of Nations, the depression, appeasement, neutralism, the Third Reich, the Second World War. Let me explain this in a few words. The economic and political cooperation of the Oslo states rose in the shadow of the League of Nations. And until 1940 the Oslo states played their role in the League, sometimes a prominent role. Under the pressure of the depression they opted for cooperation. During the first years the economic aspect of their cooperation dominated; later the political aspect became more important. In the fight between protectionism and freer trade and at economic conferences such as the World Economic Conference of 1933 in London, these states attacked the tariff problem.

The Oslo states were physically small. However, their importance in foreign trade was greater than that of France and about the same as Germany. Without the support of one of the Great Powers, the effect of their endeavors was restrictive. They worked together in a coalition of the smaller states of Northern and Western Europe. When viewed in the short term, their cooperation did a great deal for the rapprochement between the Scandinavian states and between the later Benelux states. When viewed in the long term, their coalition was an early case of international cooperation in the history of European understanding and integration. Several leading Oslo politicians, including Paul-Henri Spaak, Halvard Lange, and Joseph Bech, belonged to the founding fathers of the Western European integration after World War II. Until the outbreak of the war the coexistence of the Great Powers was considered to be an important aim. Great Britain, preoccupied with its domestic situation and problems, needed peace. Its politics of "appeasement" was supported by the great majority of the Oslo states. In an opening speech for a meeting of experts of the Oslo states in March 1937, the Dutch prime minister, Hendrik Colijn, used the term "economic appeasement" very consciously. Before and during the so-called phony war between Hitler's defeat of Poland in September 1939 and his invasion of Norway and Denmark in April 1940, many proposals for mediation were offered by politicians and inhabitants of Oslo countries.

In the mid-1930s, when it became more and more clear that the League gave no basis for security, the Oslo states embarked on a course of isolation. They rejected the system of automatic and obligatory sanctions and declared themselves neutral. The aggressive and expansionistic foreign politics and foreign trade politics of the Third Reich threatened the Oslo countries. From the beginning of the Second World War, especially from 1938 on, the Oslo states worked for a localization and a quick end of the war. They planned common steps and common measures. From August 1939 they had a permanent staff center in Brussels. In the history of the cooperation of the Oslo states seven periods can be discerned: (1) The Convention of Oslo (1930); (2) The Convention of Ouchy (1932); (3) Finland's accession to the Oslo alliance (1933); (4) growing political cooperation (1935-36); (5) Trade Agreement of The Hague (1937); (6) Conference of Copenhagen (1938); and (7) Conference of Brussels (1939).

After his election in 1933, President Roosevelt continued to pursue the protectionist policies of his predecessors to enable him to introduce his New Deal. For this reason too, the dollar had been devalued. This decision, however, was contrary to the recommendations of the preparatory committee of the League's World Economic Conference in London. Shocked by this event, the Dutch chairman of the committee, Leonardus J.A. Trip, wrote to his prime minister

> I think there can be little doubt that the monetary chaos which reigns in the world today and which has been compounded very considerably by the decision of the American administration, is one of the principle obstacles to trade, and that there can be no question of an improvement in international trade, until the world's leading powers, particularly the British Empire and the United States, have once again committed themselves to an international monetary system based on gold.[5]

At the same time, however, Roosevelt was willing to throw his influence into the discussions at the Geneva Disarmament Conference. In a message to all heads of major states, Roosevelt declared that there could be only two reasons for continued armament after the terrible lessons of the First World War and suggested a three-step plan to build a road to a more secure world.

In the letter introducing his message to Congress, Roosevelt said the elimination of offensive weapons would "make the little Nation relatively more secure against the great Nation."[6] The heads of state of the Oslo countries were enthusiastic about Roosevelt's proposal. King Haakon of Norway wired Roosevelt that "my Government quite agrees with your appeal."[7] King Christian of Denmark said that his "Government entirely shares the hopes expressed in your message."[8] King Gustav of Sweden answered: "I sincerely participate in your hopes that at this moment all Nations join in concerted action for political and economic peace."[9] King Albert of Belgium noted that his "country has suffered too much from a war endured through the necessity of defending its independence and its territory and of respecting its international obligations, not to earnestly wish that every effort be made with a view to consolidate peace and assuring absolute respect for the guarantee pacts to which it has given its adherence."[10] Queen Wilhelmina of the Netherlands declared that "substantial disarmament is now imperatively necessary, for continued armaments lead to competition . . . to inevitable war." She added: "The Netherlands are ready to take with the other Nations of the world the four steps that you propose."[11]

Roosevelt's proposal also found support among politicians and the press in the Oslo states. The Swedish press even believed that "the unexpectedly conciliatory tone of Chancellor Hitler's speech was attributed largely to the fact that the President had taken the stand he had."[12] Colijn, who was about to become the Netherlands' prime minister, said to the American envoy: "The President's appeal to the heads of state was very fine. I hope it will be successful, but I am afraid the applause the message received throughout the world, does not mean that everyone is ready to accept Mr. Roosevelt's proposals."[13] On 22 May Roosevelt replied through Elmer Davis in Geneva. Davis announced that "we are willing to consult the other states in case of a threat to peace, with a view to averting conflict."[14] Davis's promise, however, fell victim to domestic political action and became "tangled" in the Senate debate.[15]

Some common effort of the United States and the Oslo states was a response to the problem of the Jewish refugees from Germany. In September 1933 the Netherlands' foreign minister, Andries C.D. De Graeff, took the initiative for a solution to this problem at an international level. On 10 October a resolution to create a refugee commission passed the League of Nations; on the following day the Netherlands, Belgium, Denmark, Sweden, and the United States took their place among the states represented in this commission. Though Cordell Hull said that the United States should neither take part in the selection of a high commissioner nor suggest nor approve any American for this position, an American, James McDonald, was the unanimous choice for this post.

For the Oslo states the American neutrality laws had different implications. These states had never felt totally secure in a League of Nations without the United States. They feared the League would become a tool of the Great Powers. As a result of changes in the legislation affecting American neutrality, interest grew in the United States in how neutral European states had fared during the First World War. After the League failed in 1935 and 1936, as the former neutral states took the lead in a return of Europe's smaller states to neutrality, American policy had some similarities with that of the states of the Oslo alliance. Both wanted not to be bound by collective security obligations or to the strict neutrality of former times. Both accentuated their neutrality with increases in their defensive measures. Trade negotiations also took place and agreements were concluded between the United States and Norway, Belgium, Finland, and the Netherlands.[16] On both sides of the Atlantic there seemed to be a feeling that closer links should be established between the Oslo group and the United States.

Secretary of State Hull was impressed by the results of the Trade Agreement of The Hague in May 1937. In a talk with the Norwegian envoy, he declared that his trade policy and the policy of the Oslo states were "fundamentally related" in their aim of removing trade barriers.[17] But Roosevelt and Hull were pessimistic about the political situation in Europe. They saw Germany as "the great stumbling block to a return to normal relations" because of Germany's trade politics and because of its "political domination" of the rest of Europe.[18]

In early 1937 there were fears of new hostilities in the Far East, and Hull made a long statement setting out his deep concern about the escalation of force in the world. He assured that the United States would support every effort to solve world conflicts by peaceful means.[19] All of the Oslo states expressed their support for this statement. The Swedish foreign minister, Sandler, suggested cooperation through the League of Nations with nonmembers and pleaded for a fresh initiative to monitor the manufacture and sale of armaments at the national level.[20] The Netherlands' prime minister, Colijn, identified elements of his own policies in Hull's statement. He considered the content to be important, because it did not take the side of either vested interests or new aspirations. He hoped that the United States would mediate in the attempt to solve existing problems.[21]

One of the politicians from the Oslo countries who visited the United States that year was the Belgian prime minister, P. Van Zeeland. The governments of Britain and France had asked him to investigate the possibilities of improving international economic relations as part of their policy of "economic appeasement." As president of the Assembly of the League of Nations, in June 1936 Van Zeeland had alluded in his closing speech to the fears of a new war. To prevent war, he said, it was not enough to use political means; the Great Powers should make joint efforts to bring about economic recovery and so ensure that a war did not break out.[22] In Washington Van Zeeland met Roosevelt on several occasions and had repeated talks with Hull. Their discussions elicited the view from the American side that Europe should put its own house in order rather than wait for the United States to take the lead. The latter would be interested only in consultations within a broader framework, when the great European powers had agreed on a specific plan of action.[23] Nevertheless, Van Zeeland was convinced that the government in Washington was interested in what he was trying to achieve.[24] He considered that there was a real chance of cooperation between the United States and Europe.[25] Van Zeeland published his findings in January 1938 and proposed that cooperation should be established among Britain, France, and the United States with Germany and Italy. The American press, however, wrote that Van Zeeland's proposals were doomed from the outset, as they overlooked numerous political issues.[26]

During this period the U.S. government watched developments in Europe with concern. While Anthony Eden remained foreign secretary, Washington and London consulted one another regularly.[27] Roosevelt was, however, reluctant to commit himself. The U.S. economy was in recession and Roosevelt was not certain that he could rely on the support of public opinion.[28] He had talked of a boycott and other measures after a Japanese aircraft attacked an American gunboat on 12 December 1937, but he did nothing. Roosevelt wished to avoid a war rather than risk starting one. In early 1938 he considered involving nine smaller states, including Sweden, the Netherlands, and Belgium, in an international code of conduct on disarmament and equal economic opportunities for all countries. This plan, which was originally an idea of Sumner Welles, Under Secretary of State, was intended to support rapprochement between Britain and Germany, and would also reduce the tension in the Far East.[29] Britain let it be known that for the time being it would simply protest to the Japanese government and considered an American peace initiative to be premature. Moreover, it was also on the point of recognizing the Italian conquest of Abyssinia, which shocked Roosevelt, who was not happy with the "new realism" in Europe.[30]

In the majority of the Oslo states the feeling was growing that the United States could still save the situation and that in the event of a new conflict in Europe, the Oslo states would have to seek American support. The U.S.

envoy to Stockholm, Fred Dearning, reported that Sweden was seeking closer relations with the United States.[31] After the German annexation of Austria, he wrote that the whole of Scandinavia was dissociating itself from Germany and the Soviet Union and moving closer to the United States and Britain.[32] In Belgium the king's equerry, Raoul van Overstraeten, was concerned about food supplies in wartime and wished to form a "pool" with the Scandinavian states and the Netherlands. Such a plan would require the cooperation of the United States. Van Overstraeten suggested to King Leopold that Spaak, his Foreign Minister, should send a special envoy to Washington.[33]

The mounting tension in Europe in 1938 brought the United States and the Oslo states closer together. At certain moments it even seemed as if some form of cooperation had begun, although this never amounted to a common policy. It was Hitler's aggression against Czechoslovakia that heralded the first phase of cooperation between the United States and the Oslo group. When the crisis began, Roosevelt, who received conflicting advice from his envoys, at first wished to intervene and help Czechoslovakia, in the same way that he had supported Spain. He was, however, restrained by Hull, and in the end no action was taken. Nevertheless, Hull's deputy, George Messersmith, warned that if things continued in the same way, states such as Denmark, Belgium, and the Netherlands would be next on the list after the Eastern European countries.[34] Roosevelt considered a war unnecessary, and for this reason he called upon the governments concerned to continue negotiating and appealed to Mussolini to act as mediator. The American envoys to neutral states were instructed to inquire whether the heads of state of those countries would be willing to join in a peace appeal by Roosevelt to Hitler. Before replying Queen Wilhelmina consulted King Leopold and the Netherlands government contacted the governments of Switzerland, Belgium, Denmark, and Sweden by telephone to ascertain their views.[35] As it transpired, the Swiss government had already taken the required action independently, the Danish government was agreeable to some form of joint step, and the King of Sweden had contacted Hitler the previous day. Queen Wilhelmina let it be known that she was willing to take the action required of her, but that she considered it to be inappropriate after Munich.[36] Nevertheless, the American envoy to The Hague, George Anderson Gordon, did not appear unduly put out, and reported that if the international tension were to increase again, he expected that the Danish and Netherlands' governments, and possibly the Belgian government too, would be willing to cooperate with the United States.[37]

In December 1938 alarming reports from Europe led Roosevelt to believe that there was an acute danger of war. In his State of the Union address on 4 January 1939, he spoke of "storm warning signs from Europe."[38] A few days before Hitler was due to open the new "Reichstag," Roosevelt summoned the Netherlands' envoy, Alexander Loudon, and had a long talk with him. The same night the envoy sent a coded telegram to The Hague, which read as follows:

> President summoned me to him today in order to transmit following warning to Dutch government. President disturbed at reports from three separate sources, that Germany and Italy have signed offensive and defensive pact, and are engaged in getting Japan to join in. Germany has decided to turn towards the West. In one of the various plans, none of which feature Belgium, possibility is raised that Germany will provoke a conflict with the Netherlands in course of the next few months, probably at about the same that Italy submits official territorial demands to France.[39]

The need to regulate food supplies in wartime led to the start of some cooperation between Belgium and the United States. The matter was also raised at a meeting of the Oslo states.[40] Because a first visit of the Belgian special envoy, Prince de Ligne, produced some positive results,[41] after the alarming reports in December, it was decided that De Ligne should pay another visit to the United States. On his return at the end of March 1939 De Ligne reported that the United States had agreed to support the neutrality of Belgium as long as itself remained neutral. Hull had even alluded to the possibility of American intervention if Belgium's borders were violated.[42] The American press referred to the result of the early elections in Belgium as a triumph for democracy. In a talk with the American chargé d'affaires, the Luxembourg foreign minister, Joseph Bech, recalled the long-standing ties between his country and the United States.[43] Furthermore, American warships paid an official visit to Amsterdam, and the American Chamber of Commerce in The Hague pleaded for an extension of trade and cooperation between the Netherlands and the United States.

Mussolini followed Hitler's occupation of Prague with a coup of his own when on 7 April 1939 Italy added Albania to its list of conquests. Roosevelt, seeking to make a contribution to European peace, asked Hitler and Mussolini whether they were willing to spare a number of smaller states, including the seven Oslo states.[44] Roosevelt volunteered to transmit the answers to the smaller states. The German government, however, immediately asked the governments of the states in question if they felt threatened by Germany. Not altogether surprisingly, they replied that they did not. Jan Patijn, the Netherlands' foreign minister, was not particularly happy with Roosevelt's request to Hitler and Mussolini and told the Belgian envoy that in his opinion it had been intended merely to pacify American public opinion.[45] Several of the American envoys to the Oslo states reported that they preferred not to say anything about Roosevelt's statement. The depression and the undermining effects of German expansionism had combined to deprive the Oslo states of what little room to maneuver they had left.

The crisis in August 1939 came as no surprise to the Oslo states. On 22 August 1939 the foreign ministers of the states gathered at Brussels on the invitation of the Belgian government. In the presence of the foreign ministers King Leopold of Belgium read out an appeal on behalf of the heads of state on the evening of 23 August 1939. The appeal was broadcast by radio and the text had been sent to all diplomatic missions in Brussels a few hours earlier. After outlining the dangers that were looming, King Leopold appealed to the opposing parties to respect one another's rights and those of other states and to find a peaceful solution to the dispute that had arisen. He also called upon the other heads of state to support the appeal. Already on 20 August 1939 the American Assistant Secretary of State, George Messersmith, had received a telegram from Brussels, asking for the support of the U.S. government and the U.S. press for the appeal.[46] Roosevelt answered on 25 August with the following message:

> I have read with the utmost measure of satisfaction Your Majesty's address of August 23 and the appeal for the maintenance of peace made therein in the name of the powers of the Oslo group. Your Majesty expressed the hope that other heads of state might join their voices with yours in the same desire for the peace and security of their peoples. I take this occasion to assure you that the people of the United States and their government wholeheartedly share the hopes and the aspirations so eloquently expressed by Your Majesty.[47]

In a message to King Victor Emanuel III of Italy, Roosevelt, however, referred to the American peace proposal made four months earlier. To the amazement of the Belgian ambassador, Roosevelt appealed the following day to President Ignace Moscicki of Poland and—on two separate occasions—to Hitler to cooperate in finding a peaceful solution to the conflict, and offered his mediation.[48] In the summer of 1939 there were still some 9,400,000 people in the United States unemployed, and many Americans were very much opposed to the idea of their country becoming involved in another war.[49] Despite this, in August 1939 Roosevelt received the Belgian ambassador and the Netherlands' envoy to discuss the possibility of a safe shipping route across the Atlantic to Antwerp and Rotterdam for vessels sailing under neutral flags.[50] This meeting may also have been a consequence of Belgium's efforts to realize its plans for safeguarding supplies in wartime, plans to which the Netherlands had become a party. The new Netherlands' foreign minister, Eelco N. van Kleffens, telegraphed the following message to Washington:

> President's offer discussed today at meeting of Belgian and Netherlands delegations, at which deep gratitude once again expressed for line taken by President. Meeting considered, it would not be possible to make definite proposals until belligerents announce, what measure they will take, but would nonetheless greatly appreciate hearing any suggestion, which the President might make.[51]

As far as the plan for a "neutral zone" in the Atlantic was concerned, the American attitude changed in accordance with the mood of the country and the public's perception of the war. Whereas the United States had at first suggested both Antwerp and Rotterdam as neutral ports, it later opted for Antwerp alone, possibly at Britain's instigation. Similarly, whereas it stated originally that it would discuss the matter of the neutral zone with Britain, it later informed Belgium and the Netherlands that they would have to arrange this directly with Britain.[52]

Nevertheless, the U.S. government wished to cooperate with the states of the Oslo group. On 28 September 1939 the American envoys to the Oslo states handed over to the governments concerned a memorandum, stating that the delay in introducing a neutral zone was a consequence of the problems concerning the neutrality legislation, but that the government of the United States would submit further proposals to the representatives of the Oslo states in Washington very soon.[53] The following day most of these representatives were summoned to the State Department for a meeting with John D. Hickerson, the chairman of the commission for trade with neutral countries. Hickerson told them that he was in favor of an exchange of confidential information between his government and that of the seven Oslo states and an extension of mutual trade relations. He also stated that the U.S. government was of the opinion that trade between the neutrals should be disrupted as little as possible by the war, and had informed the British government of that fact.[54]

The contacts between the United States and the Oslo states in October and November 1939 evolved around three issues in particular: plans for cooperation, the consequences of the war at sea for the neutral states, and the risk that the war would escalate. In late September the U.S. government had informed the Oslo states that it would be willing to exchange confidential information and to cooperate in matters of trade. Favorable replies to this offer were sent shortly afterward by Sweden and Belgium and later by Denmark as well. The Netherlands' reply was not to be received for a long time.[55] Suggestions by Sweden and Belgium that the United States should assume the leadership of a "neutral bloc" went too far for the latter's liking. The U.S. government had to consider isolationist tendencies among the population, although the country was less neutral and more anti-German than several of the Oslo states. The establishment of a neutral zone across the Atlantic to Antwerp and Rotterdam created more problems than Roosevelt had anticipated and met with adverse reactions from the British. Nonetheless, questions in this field were discussed further. When Alexander Loudon called on Roosevelt on 18 October, the latter stated that he and the army commanders were concerned about the large German troop concentrations near the Netherlands' and Belgian borders, and asked Loudon to inquire of The Hague whether these reports could be corroborated.[56] The Netherlands' government confirmed the truth of the reports, but added that Germany had provided assurances that the measures were not directed against the Netherlands. Nonetheless, the Netherlands' government said that it would appreciate it if the president could indicate his concern through the American diplomatic representative in Berlin and ask for an explanation.

On 11 October 1939 President Roosevelt sent a telegram to President Mikhail Kalinin of the Soviet Union requesting that it should not make any demands on Finland, which would be prejudicial to the relations between the two states and represent a violation of Finland's independence. Roosevelt also sent a telegram to King Gustav of Sweden in which he indicated his interest in the forthcoming conference of heads of state of the Scandinavian countries in Stockholm, evidently hoping that it would serve to strengthen Scandinavian unity.[57] By expressing his interest in Finland so openly, Roosevelt did, however, create certain expectations among the Scandinavian states, which thanked him for his intervention. The Belgian ambassador in Washington, Baron Hervé De Gruben, even went so far as to describe the steps as "an American intervention in the political problems of Europe,"[58] which it was not intended to be.

Rather unexpectedly, the United States launched a major peace offensive in February 1940 amid a great deal of publicity.[59] Its first step was to contact forty-six neutral states to exchange views on how peace could be promoted after the war by means of disarmament and international economic stability. Shortly afterward it was announced that Sumner Welles, the American Under

Secretary of State, would visit Europe. Both steps were intended to pave the way for the reestablishment of peace and were preceded by the appointment of a special American envoy to the Vatican. All the signs were favorable, and the time seemed right. The war had evidently simmered down. The United States was experiencing increasing inconvenience from the war at sea, and a successful bid for peace would strengthen Roosevelt's position in the elections.

On 10 February 1940 the press reported that according to a statement issued by Cordell Hull, the American Secretary of State, informal discussions had begun with the governments of neutral states, since all of them wished for the reestablishment of world peace. Hull added that the belligerents could participate insofar as the discussions concerned international economic questions and disarmament. The purpose of the discussions was to assess the possibilities. In preparation for the discussions Hull summoned the ambassadors and envoys of forty-six neutral states to the State Department, and between 10 and 16 February the American representatives in the same states handed over an aide-memoire, in which the American government explained the plan in more detail. Christian Günther, the new Swedish foreign minister, expressed great interest and undertook to submit the plan to the cabinet. At the same time he pointed out to the American envoy that exchange of views on these matters had also taken place between the Oslo states.[60] The foreign ministers of the other Oslo states also welcomed the American initiative. In the Belgian reply, Spaak wrote that the Belgian people had witnessed the transformation of their country into a battlefield during the First World War and wished nothing better than a lasting peace.[61] However, after the return of Welles from his journey through Europe, Roosevelt announced at a press conference that no further steps could be expected of the United States.[62] In this way the peace offensive, which had been launched so conspiciously little more than a month before and which had attracted so much public interest, ended as abruptly and as unexpectedly as it had begun. This episode led some of the European diplomats in Washington to wonder whether there were any constant factors at all in American foreign policy or whether it was largely determined by chance events and off-the-cuff decisions.[63]

Despite the establishment of closer relations between the United States and the Oslo states before and after the outbreak of the Second World War, there was no real cooperation between them. The last days before the German attack on Belgium, Luxembourg and the Netherlands demonstrated this all too clearly. Joseph Bech, Luxembourg's foreign minister, sent on 7 May 1940 a rather belated reply to the American government's letter of mid-February. Whether he was hoping for a new American peace initiative or wished in this way to draw attention to the perilous position of his country is uncertain. In any event, he pointed out that his government had always supported attempts to achieve a just and lasting peace, and that it believed that such a peace should be based on law and respect for treaties and not upon brute force. He indicated that the Luxembourg government would gladly cooperate in any such endeavors and believed that in the circumstances it would be better if the peace were to be prepared by a statesman of stature rather than by an international conference.[64] On 10 May 1940, the day the German offensive began, King Leopold made a last appeal to the United States. In a telegram to Roosevelt he stated that he did so "in the secure knowledge that you will support with all your moral authority the attempts which we are now making, with resolve and determination, to preserve our independence."[65] The president cabled back that the offensive had shocked the American people, but, as in the case of the Spanish Civil War, he did not send in the marines. The Netherlands' government made no special efforts to contact Washington in the days before the German offensive. By July 1940 Sweden and Finland were the only two Oslo states that had not fallen victim to German aggression, and the hopes of a peace conference that both the United States and the Oslo states had entertained were now dispelled.

Whether the Oslo states as a group could have escaped this fate if they had cooperated more closely is a moot point. With the support of the United States they could have extended their mutual cooperation and strengthened their independence, and this perhaps might have prevented them from having to defer increasingly to the wishes and demands of the Third Reich. Then perhaps Hitler might have been induced to drop his invasion plans against them. As it turned out, the invasion of Scandinavia and the Low Countries helped convince both Americans and Europeans that true neutrality was no longer a real protection for a policy of independence in the twentieth century.

9

LATIN AMERICA AND FRANKLIN D. ROOSEVELT

Henry Raymont

INTRODUCTION

It is a great pleasure as well as a high honor to be invited to the Roosevelt Study Center to speak on Roosevelt and Latin America. I understand that it is the first time that Roosevelt's Latin American policy has been considered at Middelburg. The omission is not really surprising. Latin America is not a subject that has generally commanded wide scholarly interest in Europe any more than in the United States. Even at the Franklin D. Roosevelt Library, the official home of the president's papers at Hyde Park in New York State, the amount of research that has been conducted over the last four decades on Roosevelt's approach toward hemisphere affairs, what became known as the Good Neighbor policy, has been minimal.

I would be less than candid, then, if I did not express my feeling that the recognition of the Latin American component in the Roosevelt presidency seems "a trifle belated," as a distinguished United States historian once said in this very forum when he noted that for all the interest shown in his country about European topics, "It cannot be said that the United States has occupied a corresponding place in the European consciousness."[1]

From my vantage point, there is a touch of poetic justice in this. In striking contrast to the Latin American specialist, for the general historian in the United States, Roosevelt's Good Neighbor policy seems to have held no lasting fascination. Clearly it was never subjected to anything like the pervasive critical analyses these scholars have devoted, and continue to devote, to other international aspects of the Roosevelt presidency—his efforts to overcome isolationist sentiments at home, his leadership in the war against the Axis and in the complicated planning for the establishment of a postwar world order. For example, the popular historian Charles Beard in 1946 wrote a two-volume study, *American Foreign Policy in the Making, 1932-1940*, without once mentioning the Good Neighbor policy.

I must at the outset confess to a personal bias: I grew up in Latin America and for me, like for so many of my generation, Roosevelt was a hero and the Good Neighbor the watchword of our time. I will not forget the thrill of standing on my tall father's shoulders to watch FDR's arrival at the Congress building in Buenos Aires. We had arrived in Argentina only a few weeks earlier as refugees from Nazi Germany. His visit reassured us that democracy would prevail in the world.

On a sunny Monday, 30 November 1936, more than 1 million Argentines took to the streets of Buenos Aires to welcome Franklin D. Roosevelt, the first U.S. president to visit their country. The day had been declared a national holiday. People were in a festive mood, eager to catch a glimpse of the man who had been extolled by their government and press as the leading advocate of democracy in the world and the devoted friend of Latin America. Roosevelt, riding in an open car next to President Augustin P. Justo, looked completely at home; always the veteran campaigner, he waved and flashed his famous smile at the cheering crowds. *The New York Times* told its readers next morning, in a dispatch from Buenos Aires, that the reception was "in every way the largest and most jubilant that country has ever extended to anyone."

The outpouring of friendship from the hemisphere's southernmost nation was highly significant. Argentina had traditionally cast itself as Washington's relentless rival for leadership in the hemisphere. The multitudinous reception was surely a measure of the magnitude of change in inter-American relations that had occurred even before Roosevelt's first term had ended.

The president, fresh from the triumph of his reelection, had decided to make the long ocean voyage to address the opening session of the Inter-American Conference for the Maintenance of Peace. Having proposed the meeting in January 1936, he now wished to make a personal appearance to underscore his continued dedication to hemisphere solidarity in a world threatened by war. His effort was well rewarded.

Within days the conference adopted his proposal calling for consultation in the event that the peace of the American republics was threatened. It was the first step toward a collective security arrangement with the United States, an action contemporary observers agreed would have been inconceivable but for Roosevelt's personal popularity and the trust engendered by the Good Neighbor policy. To fully appreciate Roosevelt's impact south of the border it needs to be recalled that until he took office in 1933, the gulf between the United States and Latin America was perhaps deeper than at any time since the war with Mexico almost a century earlier.

There existed then an unrelenting hostility toward anything that remotely suggested U.S. intervention or hegemony. This mood reflected the accumulated resentment over what Latin Americans considered to have been three decades of odious U.S. policies—Theodore Roosevelt's "Big Stick," the continuing military occupations in Central America and the Caribbean, Taft's "Dollar Diplomacy," Hoover's discriminatory tariffs, and the devastating effects on the region's economy when the stock market crashed in 1929 and with it the Republican illusions of indefinite prosperity. As Secretary of State Cordell Hull put it, "Our inheritance of ill-will was grim."[2]

Even before completing his first years in office, President Roosevelt had moved to consolidate a secure inter-American order, transformed adverse Latin American attitudes toward the United States, and won overwhelming support for these policies from Congress and the people. Thus the new chapter in inter-American relations began, remarkably, even while the main energies of the new occupant of the White House were directed to the formidable task of leading his convulsed country out of the Great Depression. Before the year was over, Roosevelt had managed to give his inaugural address pledge to adopt a "policy of the good neighbor" to all the nations of the world, a special meaning for the neighbors of the hemisphere.

In quick succession, he had withdrawn the last marines from Nicaragua, signed an executive agreement to remove the marines from Haiti, begun negotiations to end the United States' protectorate over Panama and to renounce Washington's rights to intervene in the internal affairs of Cuba. On a multilateral level, in December he had sent Hull to Montevideo to sign an Inter-American convention that proclaimed that "No State has the right to intervene in the internal affairs of another." The convention was promptly ratified by the Senate, thus practically abrogating Theodore Roosevelt's corollary to the Monroe Doctrine that in the past had served as justification for the United States to act as the hemisphere's policeman.

Thus at Buenos Aires, three years later, culminated a new and momentous chapter for the Western Hemisphere, replacing the unilateral Monroeism and "Big Stick" policy that had proved so disruptive to inter-American relations and domestic politics. So was the Buenos Aires conference the great landmark in the relations between the two parts of the hemisphere; so was the principle of equality fastened onto Pan Americanism; and so the colossus of the North finally became the Good Neighbor, *de jure* as well as *de facto*.

For generations to come, Roosevelt's triumphal visit to Buenos Aires became the symbol of the constructive transformation the Good Neighbor policy had brought to inter-American relations—just as for a generation later the violence that greeted Vice President Richard M. Nixon in Lima and Caracas in 1958 symbolized its unraveling.

It is no exaggeration, I believe, to suggest here that Roosevelt's new approach toward Latin America was the most distinguished foreign policy achievement of his first two terms in office. Indeed, no other U.S. president in the present century, with the exception of John F. Kennedy, has had so much influence on hemisphere events, has had so much firsthand experience in Latin American affairs, has been on such warm terms with Latin American heads of state and their peoples. No other was able to impart confidence and respect with such a magisterial air of cultivation and political intelligence.

And yet in the United States astonishingly little is remembered about FDR's extraordinary contribution to inter-American relations. By contrast, the image of Roosevelt and his Good Neighbor policy has remained firmly fixed in the Latin American collective memory.

Indeed, the Roosevelt presidency set new standards for United States-Latin American relations, eventually to become a paradigm of harmony and cooperation against which all subsequent U.S. administrations would be measured. Certainly to millions in the hemisphere Roosevelt represented what was most enlightened, generous, and affirmative about the United States.

This chapter therefore obviously dissents from the often-stated belief that during his first term Roosevelt paid scant attention to foreign affairs and that even the Good Neighbor policy did not loom large until totalitarianism had cast its shadows over Europe in the late 1930s. Quite the contrary, I would argue that practically from the day he took office in March 1933, through his second term in 1940, Latin America occupied a major place in the Roosevelt administration's foreign policy agenda. Moreover, I hope to show that Roosevelt's Good Neighbor policy was based on a coherent vision and a broad understanding of the historical forces that unite the New World as well as on considerable firsthand experience in the region.

It is the purpose, then, of this chapter to call renewed attention to the neglected segment of Roosevelt historiography relating to his unique contributions to hemisphere affairs. It shall focus on the Latin American perception of the Roosevelt era by describing briefly three elements that, in my opinion, most effectively accounted for the success of his approach toward Latin America: (1) the Good Neighbor policy, (2) the New Deal, and (3) his leadership.

It will also attempt to trace the policy's origins and characterize its novelty and subsequent decline, and then to re-evaluate the Good Neighbor in the light of what may be if not wisdom, at least a measure of perspective.

CONFIDENCE IN THE GOOD NEIGHBOR

By the time the Buenos Aires conference was held late in 1936, the degree of confidence that Roosevelt's policies had inspired in Latin America knew no modern parallel. Just by looking at the record, one finds that in no time at all, relatively speaking, he had largely succeeded in overcoming the legacy of distrust and animosity left by its predecessors. Whatever may have been his ultimate motives, Roosevelt was perceived as bringing Latin America out of the ghetto into the forum. With consummate tact and no lack of personal charm and political ingenuity, he set about to present his own extension of the Bolivarean message—that as long as the Latin American republics lacked unity they would remain marginal and remote to the forces forging the world's future. In alliance with the United States, they could help alter balance of power in favor of freedom and democracy in major international councils. They had never heard such a message before. The message was as important psychologically as it was politically.

For years Latin Americans had resented being treated essentially as the object of U.S. and European economic interests, each competing for raw materials and markets to place their manufactured goods. Suddenly there had appeared a U.S. leader seemingly willing to revive the notion of the Founding Fathers that the New World had common roots and a common destiny in history.

Indeed, the friendliness Roosevelt encountered during his 1936 trip to the South American capitals—for he visited Rio de Janeiro and Montevideo as well as Buenos Aires—had been foreshadowed by the approving response the heads of state of the neighbor republics had given his proposal for the Buenos Aires conference. President Alfonso Lopez Pumarejo of Colombia, one of the hemisphere's most respected democratic leaders, spoke for most of them in a message welcoming the idea of the conference.

> We Colombians understand the policy now developed by the President of the United States to be a radical and favorable modification of the policy which formerly aroused uneasiness and mistrust among the Latin American peoples .

> . . Since the beginning of your Excellency's Government a fundamental change of direction has been effected which all the American peoples justly value and which is a new cause of sympathy and of prestige for the United States.[3]

Like Roosevelt, Lopez and other democrats in Latin America sought to lead their peoples in founding a new society within which the principles of freedom, equality, and social justice enshrined in their constitutions would be translated into reality and not compromised by powerful oligarchies capable of having universal suffrage manipulated by special interests.

The morning of Roosevelt's arrival in the Argentine capital, the influential newspaper *La Nacion* summed up Latin America's high expectations for the conference.

> A new epoch is about to begin, and our continent—which has none of those tenacious hates nor that insurmountable spirit of revenge that exists in other continents—is preparing to assume its destined role as monitor in the world community. Even if this objective is not immediately attainable, even if conditions in Europe and Asia are such as to prevent the acceptance of the Americas's message of peace, nothing can detract from the historical importance of these meetings of the next few days to implement President Roosevelt's initiative.[4]

The editorial captured two essential features reflecting the impact of the Good Neighbor policy. Foremost was a recognition of the importance Roosevelt attached to U.S. ties with Latin America.

Judging from the record of his accomplishments, this cannot be exaggerated. A second and related feature was the widespread impression created in Latin America that through the new partnership the region was both sharing in Roosevelt's progressive New Deal politics emanating from Washington while at the same time gaining a more significant role in international affairs. These features were of great importance to the self-esteem of a proud people who before the advent of the Roosevelt era had widely perceived themselves as marginal to U.S. concerns, if not as victims of "Yankee imperialism."

To be sure, both the domestic and international contexts undoubtedly contributed to the new policy. Clearly the nation's economic distress and isolationist tendencies prevented Roosevelt from following an activist foreign policy in Europe and Asia; on the other hand, there was no opposition to building closer ties with Latin America or to organizing a regional system in the interest of hemispheric security. In fact, each convention, each treaty submitted to Congress binding the nation more closely to the other American republics was approved by the Senate without a dissenting vote.

THE NEW DEAL

Important as the implementation of the Good Neighbor policy was, there is much evidence that Roosevelt ultimately won Latin America's confidence and admiration in other, and at least equally significant, ways—his domestic policies and the style of his leadership. He was, after all, the architect of the New Deal, the revolutionary domestic program that pulled his nation out of the Great Depression and gave a new sense of direction to one of the major transformations of a modern democratic and industrial society.

For once the political, economic, and social problems a U.S. president was confronting at home were familiar to those most of the rest of the hemisphere had been struggling with since independence: poverty, hunger, unemployment, the rational management of financial and economic resources by the state. He thus kindled hopes among the Latin American democracies that their own halting efforts to bring reform to the region and change in the status quo had found an inspiring and powerful ally and a practical model.

Quick to personalize, Latin Americans saw Roosevelt fight economic paralysis and social injustice in the same indomitable way he had fought to overcome the infirmity of his paralyzed legs, with resolute willpower. For them the president and the New Deal represented the victory of ideas over matter, of action over inaction, of change against the status quo of experimentation over rigidity.

To be sure, years of suspicion were not easily dispelled. Not all Latin Americans rushed to embrace Roosevelt's policy. "The Good Neighbor Policy," wrote Mexican historian Alfonso Aguilar, a Marxist, "because of its very nature, contained insoluble contradictions. While on the one hand, it showed respect, previously nonexistent, for the Latin American nations, on the other hand, it manifested itself as an effort to further subordinate them to United States economic needs."[5]

Nonetheless, even this doctrinaire critic of the United States went on to acknowledge that under Roosevelt's presidency, "a promising outlook for improved relations seemed to be in view."

More representative of the Latin American mainstream was the assessment of Victor Andrade, who was Bolivia's ambassador to the United States for almost two decades and later foreign minister, in his 1976 memoir, *My Mission for Revolutionary Bolivia.* "Franklin Roosevelt deserves full credit for repudiating the Big Stick policy formulated by his cousin Theodore. In doing so he swept aside a century of fear and distrust which had divided Latin America and the United States. In a sense, by the Good Neighbor policy, the

United States established itself as champion to liberate the masses from need, oppression and slavery."[6]

A new kind of dialogue with the preeminent power of the American continent was emerging. When in the United States, the richest country in the world, nearly 20 million people were facing starvation in the early months of 1933, Latin Americans had every right to recognize a convergence of problems. But even that recognition required political leadership before such a new dialogue was made possible.

SYMPATHETIC LEADERSHIP

Beyond the practical rectifications to which Roosevelt subjected Washington's domestic and Latin American policy, perhaps the greatest impact on Latin Americans was the magnetic force of his leadership qualities, his outgoing optimism, so typical of the New World spirit, his uncanny ability to project human warmth and understanding and at once be politically effective. He seemed uniquely endowed, as it were, with the gift of genuine sympathy, the kind of universal intuition one associates with a great artist, capable of transcending diverse cultures and social conditions. Along with his penchant for applying lessons of history and personal experience, it helped guide much of his action. The emphatic use of such themes as that of "a sympathetic appreciation of the other's point of view" in his speeches perhaps suggests a clue for the insights that led to such successful policies.

Not surprisingly, then, in the Latin American hagiography Roosevelt occupies a place unmatched by any other foreign leader. Avenues, schools, and thousands of babies were named after him. Textbooks and the popular literature treat his presidency almost invariably in reverential terms. To this day, mention Franklin Roosevelt to politicians and scholars anywhere from Mexico to Argentina and the name at once evokes a gilded age and the old watchwords of the Good Neighbor: hemispheric solidarity, peace and prosperity, economic and social progress, mutual respect—above all, mutual respect. It is as if in Latin America's collective memory they have remained as living symbols of the Roosevelt era—one of those rare moments in inter-American history when the "sister republics" were truly regarded as part of an "American family"—not as stepchildren or country cousins.

A common criticism of Roosevelt's foreign policy has been that it was often the result of improvisation, indecision, or even a shallow understanding of world affairs. In point of fact, at any rate where Latin America was concerned, this assessment is spectacularly false. I would argue instead that Roosevelt was not only keenly involved and informed, but also remarkably consistent in his views about the Western Hemisphere—at any rate after 1917.

To be sure, something deeper must have been at work to account for the swift turnaround from outspoken hostility to admiration Roosevelt achieved for the United States across the hemisphere—something like a coherent conception of the world and the place of U.S. relations with Latin America in it. There is ample evidence to suggest that Roosevelt possessed such a conception and deliberately set about building his policy around it. Indeed, it can be safely contended that from the moment he took office, Roosevelt was determined to dispel the suspicions and misunderstandings that had brought Washington's relations with the other hemisphere republics to the verge of collapse and to transform a wary, languishing Pan American movement into an effective continental alliance based on mutual respect and the recognition of the New World's shared goals of renovation and revolution, of freedom, democracy, and social justice.

There is also abundant evidence to show that Roosevelt devoted more attention to Latin America than is generally realized, that the interest stemmed from travel in the region, and that the concepts that went into the Good Neighbor policy, far from being something novel for him, had been stirring, at least incipiently, since the time he became acquainted with Latin American diplomacy during service in the Wilson administration as assistant secretary of the navy. This would become the more sharply delineated if contrasted to his cautious and often shifting positions toward Europe and Asia once he occupied the White House. It was hardly by accident that he made his first trip abroad as president, in 1934, to Colombia and Panama.

"One of the distinguishing characteristics of a great man is that his active intervention makes what seemed highly improbable in fact happen," writes Isaiah Berlin. It is surely difficult to deny that the friendly relations Roosevelt forged through the Good Neighbor policy and other actions was of this improbable and surprising kind. Foremost, Roosevelt's determination to respect the autonomy of America's neighbors, so antithetical in spirit and practice to the policy of his predecessors—and of his own early beliefs—requires further consideration.

In terms of his intellectual growth, what makes this shift the more remarkable is that while Roosevelt, the patrician Democrat from Dutchess County, served as assistant secretary of the navy in the Wilson cabinet, he had been imbued with the rambunctious interventionism so characteristic of that age. While his chief, Navy Secretary Josephus Daniels, a southern pacifist, grudgingly signed Wilson's order in 1914 to occupy the port of Veracruz in retaliation for the arrest of some U.S. Navy personnel who allegedly had violated Mexican laws, Roosevelt told the press that "sooner or later the United States government must go down there and clear up the Mexican mess," adding that "the best time is right now."[7]

Yet between 1917 and the mid-1920s Roosevelt had made a complete turnaround, from being an ardent admirer of Theodore Roosevelt's interventionism to being an equally fierce advocate of nonintervention, scrupulous respect for the sovereignty of the neighbor republics and diplomacy based on equal rights before the law.

The shift foreshadowed the more pragmatic approach that would mark the Roosevelt presidency both in domestic and foreign affairs, as aptly characterized by Arthur M. Schlesinger, Jr., "when contradicted by facts, realism set in and he adjusted his attitudes with wonderful dexterity as and when circumstances required it."[8]

Indeed, by the mid-1920s Roosevelt firmly believed that interventionism not only was wrong, but that it had long outlived its usefulness as had protectionism; he was therefore determined to persuade the Democratic party that these irritants needed to be removed and U.S. diplomacy mobilized to secure hemisphere unity. All this found its first reasoned conceptual expression as a policy recommendation to the Democratic party in a landmark article, "Our Foreign Policy: A Democratic View," in the July 1928 issue of the quarterly publication of the Council on Foreign Relations of New York, *Foreign Affairs*. Significantly, of its thirteen pages more than half were dedicated to a discussion of United States-Latin American relations. In fact, the article practically constituted a blueprint of what Roosevelt's Latin American policy would look like after his own election. Thus four years before he came to the White House, Roosevelt had already recognized the critical problems of inter-American relations and envisioned a solution: The United States should abandon tutelage for collective action.

In place of the old antagonisms that benefited no one, he proposed the development of political and economic cooperation that would unite the Western Hemisphere. He thus demonstrated the ability to develop a conceptual framework, congruent with what he perceived to be the national interests, from which the Good Neighbor policy would flow naturally.

Commenting on the *Foreign Affairs* article, Antonio Gomez Robledo, one of Mexico's leading diplomatic historians known for his acerbic criticism of U.S. foreign policy, observed with great perspicacity in a book published in 1958: "Noble words from that generous spirit written before he aspired formally to the highest office and when the world was not yet plunged into the economic and political crisis that would impel the United States to seek a more cordial understanding with Latin America on other levels. Words that simply revealed the felicitous internal evolution of the president's mind."[9]

I believe that few U.S. historians, except for Frank Freidel, have shown a comparable insight into the "felicitous internal evolution" of Roosevelt's approach. Most tend to go along with the pragmatic notion that casts the Good Neighbor as paving the way to a wartime alliance. In retrospect it did just that—only between 1919 and 1928, when the policy was first conceived, it was peace and not a wartime alliance that Roosevelt sought to consolidate.

Just now, half a century after the halcyon days of the Good Neighbor, the old verities about New World solidarity have become blurred, if not faded altogether. Few seem to remember anymore that for a decade of Roosevelt's presidency close relations with the other American republics and a relentless nurturing of the inter-American system were critical elements of U.S. foreign policy, even in the midst of World War II. Moreover, for a decade after the president's death, the spirit of the Good Neighbor policy continued to stoke the embers of United States-Latin American relations so that the legacy of goodwill he left behind assured the support of most major U.S. postwar policies. It is a chapter of the Roosevelt era that risks being forgotten by his compatriots.

This is one reason why I must repeat how much I appreciate this *apertura al Sud* created by the Roosevelt Study Center by incorporating Latin America into your vision, just as I am sure Roosevelt would have wanted it.

I also wish to express here my gratitude to the Franklin and Eleanor Roosevelt Institute for providing support for a research project I have begun in Mexico to re-create the resonance of the Roosevelt era through oral history interviews and the assembling of documentary materials for Hyde Park.

I would like here to share some of the results of this pilot project by quoting excerpts of two of these interviews. The first is with Dr. Josue Saenz, a distinguished Mexican economist and director of statistics from 1940 to 1945 of the Ministry of Economy. Like most of those interviewed, he identifies Roosevelt's affirmative reaction to the ascent of Lazaro Cardenas, Mexico's populist president, in 1934 and, more specifically, to the nationalization in 1938 of the foreign oil companies as the turning point in modern United States-Mexican relations.

> You may recall the Mexican expropriation of the oil, which was the first major expropriation in the world, was carried out by Cardenas in 1938. Article 27 of the Constitution of 1917 specified the national or public ownership of nonrenewable natural resources. Still, it was impossible for the Mexican government to establish effective control.

> At that time our political clout was negligible and the United States was not only a powerful neighbor, but at that time big oil and big government were very much working together . . . .
>
> When FDR came to office instead of a pro-business climate in the United States there began a pro-government climate. So Cardenas felt he could expropriate the oil companies without fear of economic reprisals by the United States government.

Saenz then went on to comment on the quality of people attracted by the Roosevelt administration.

> There was a tremendous change that was immediately noticed in Mexico. And it was felt that there was a tremendous difference between a man like Secretary of State Kellogg and Cordell Hull; a tremendous difference between Henry Wallace and the previous Secretary of Agriculture; and, of course, between Coolidge and Hoover, on the one hand, and Roosevelt, on the other. Coolidge and Hoover focused on a very narrow range of problems in the United States; FDR, having the world vision—the Good Neighbor policy being one part of it. It was a tremendous change.[10]

The second interview I will summarize for you is with Carlos Fuentes, the Mexican novelist, who had met Roosevelt as a schoolboy in Washington, where his father was political counselor at the Mexican embassy during the late thirties.

> During the Roosevelt years the United States finally came to terms with the Mexican Revolution, instead of Satanizing it, harassing it, creating unnecessary problems, creating a reliable villain in Mexico, a spook of its own fabrication, as it happened during the Coolidge and Harding years, most notably. The United States decided to understand what was happening South of the border. I think the impulse came from Roosevelt; he was aided by many other people.
>
> He found obstacles in other members of his cabinet but finally he understood, he realized that it was in the interest of the United States to understand what was happening in order to have not a reliable villain but a reliable friend on it southern border.
>
> Roosevelt was a statesman who could see far; he understood that the interest of the United States was to have friends and allies during the Second World War and that the condition for the national security of the United States in Latin America was to respect internal movements, internal policies in each and every one of those countries. . . .[11]

THE GOOD NEIGHBOR'S RELEVANCE TODAY

Though the Roosevelt era with its Good Neighbor policy has failed to win similar public or even scholarly attention in the United States in recent years, it shall, we may be sure, regain just recognition someday.

One need only consider the similarity between the dismal state in which United States-Latin America relations were the day Franklin D. Roosevelt took office and the day Ronald Reagan left it. This parallel alone should give the most entrenched *Realpolitiker* in Washington pause to think about the practical and strategic merits of a moral, intelligent, and historically coherent foreign policy. Yet by now in the United States and probably in Europe, the Good Neighbor policy barely rates an aside, a bit of folklore that vaguely recalls a moment of seraphic hemispheric harmony for reasons that no longer seem to be very important to the authors. However, as I have attempted to show, in Latin America the Roosevelt era is a chapter nobody wants to forget.

I cannot resist the temptation in the presence of so many distinguished historians from both sides of the Atlantic to consider with you this simple but fundamental question: Why is Latin America such an impenetrable, elusive subject? Perhaps because beneath what critics at home and abroad have routinely deplored as neglect or indifference stand larger and more intractable conceptual problems that must be examined before a reasonable explanation can be found.

In order to understand current Latin American attitudes and preoccupations and the policies they reflect, perhaps we must better understand the cultural and historical forces that have shaped them. From 1776 on the United States was always a presence in Latin America—spiritually, politically, and, increasingly, materially—although its presence made itself felt in different ways at different times.

Indeed, much of the hemisphere's history might be written in terms of a quest for self-identity. It is a quest that moreover has not taken place as a soliloquy but in the form of a constant dialogue with the United States. As the Mexican poet Octavio Paz put it: "The United States image is always present among us, even when it ignores us and turns its back on us; its shadow covers the entire continent."[12]

The stark contrast between the friendship and cooperation Roosevelt evoked among the other American republics and the distrust and stress that preceded and followed his presidency lends itself all too easily to exaggerations of the romance he brought to inter-American relations. It must be acknowledged, for example, that signs of exhaustion and internal conflict became apparent already in 1943, two years before Roosevelt's death, notably following the resignation of Sumner Welles, his longtime friend and a key architect of the Good Neighbor policy, as Under Secretary of State. And as is wont in a democracy there were occasional contradictions and failings, as with the intractable dilemma of how to deal with dictatorships and violations of civil liberties while observing the principle of nonintervent-ion in the internal affairs of the members of the American family.

Yet it might also be contended with much plausibility that the Roosevelt era was unlike any other in our century. At no other time was so much top-level attention focused on relations with Latin America. Not until then, or since, did hemispheric affairs occupy such a prominent place in the scheme of U.S. foreign policy. And, most certainly, at no other time did the United States attain higher prestige, genuine understanding, and friendship across the political spectrum of Latin America, both among governments and the vast masses of people.

This is sufficient reason for attempting another critical look at the Roosevelt era and its Good Neighbor policy or, on a wider canvas, at the perennial predicament that confronts Latin America in its quest for a sustained role in its relations with the United States and the international community in general. Today we must appreciate, for example, that the ideal of hemispheric solidarity continues to exert a not-negligible appeal—even though by now much of the thrust seems directed at Latin American separatism—especially in an era of economic interdependence that no country can hope to face in isolation. Many more questions arise and require examination: Was this creative explosion during the Roosevelt era just a historical oddity? Or was it rooted in a long tradition, a shared New World past? Or, to put it another way: Does the Western Hemisphere constitute a true cultural configuration with its own history? And if such a configuration exists, how can it be defined?

These are the kind of issues worthy of further discussion, for there are no easy answers. Yet certainly they are critical to forging a nuanced policy toward a region that has come to feel once more that it is marginal to U.S. interests, and that we cannot afford to alienate beyond a certain safety point. I believe that the Bush administration, notwithstanding the foolhardy invasion of Panama, may be slowly becoming aware of this.

To meet the challenge of the decade of the 1990s the United States must clearly look beyond the immediate differences and abandon the policy of confrontation that marked the Reagan era. What is needed is a rethinking and renovation of foreign policy priorities similar to those effected by Roosevelt in 1933 and Kennedy in 1961, based on a broad regrasping of first principles as they were envisioned by the Founding Fathers and the leaders of Latin

American independence—that the American republics share not only a geographic continent or what today might be called a geopolitical space, but also the values and beliefs of New World siblings in a freer, more just, and more democratic life.

10

CHIANG KAI-SHEK AND FRANKLIN D. ROOSEVELT*

Hsi-sheng Ch'i

An impressive body of literature on U.S.-China relations in World War II has been produced in the last four decades. While this literature contains many excellent studies on a variety of subjects, it also suffers from two rather conspicuous shortcomings. First, it relies heavily on English-language sources, and second, it tends to define issues and assess results from a predominantly American perspective.

One reflection of these shortcomings is the lack of in-depth analysis of the dynamics of the interpersonal relationship between Franklin D. Roosevelt and Chiang Kai-shek from the Chinese perspective. Since FDR and Chiang played dominant, and often exclusive, roles in shaping their respective country's political, military, and diplomatic strategies, it is only reasonable to assume that the ways they perceived of and interacted with each other must have had a major impact on U.S.-China relations during the war. In fact, of all Allied leaders, FDR and Chiang had the longest relations, dating back to the outbreak of the Sino-Japanese War in 1937.

This chapter represents only a preliminary effort to examine the relations between FDR and Chiang by drawing on the Chinese-language materials that have become available in recent years. The length of this chapter necessarily precludes detailed discussion on any specific policy in U.S.-China relations, but addresses two issues affecting the relationship between Chiang and FDR. The first issue is how Chiang perceived FDR. The second issue is why Chiang relied so much on personal diplomacy and how he actually conducted it. It is hoped that this chapter may stimulate scholars to rethink the validity of some of the conventional wisdoms in the literature on U.S.-China relations and explore new directions of research.

CHIANG'S PERCEPTIONS OF FDR AND THE UNITED STATES

Probably the most remarkable feature of China's wartime diplomacy was Chiang's perception of FDR as the only friendly foreign leader and the United States as the only trustworthy ally. The warmth and appreciation with which Chiang regarded FDR and the United States stood in stark contrast to his hostility toward the British leaders and government, who were also China's allies and actually began giving aid to China before the Americans did.

Basically, Chiang regarded British attitudes toward China as being shaped by prejudices "they had acquired in China twenty years ago." The many violent disagreements between the two countries left Chiang with the u - shakable conviction that the British were immoral, cowardly, incompetent, and untrustworthy. Throughout the war Chiang constantly complained about the British leaders' putative arrogance and disrespect for China's international position,[1] and suggested that China would not even accept British aid as long as its attitude toward China remained unchanged.[2] The depth of Chiang's anger at Churchill was best exemplified by his rejection of Churchill's invitation for Mme. Chiang to visit Great Britain as an extension of her highly successful tour of the United States. Chiang warned his wife that she might fall prey to either Churchill's tricks or insults if she went to London.[3] Chiang was utterly convinced that Churchill and his government felt only malevolence toward China.

China also had many quarrels with the United States over loans, Lend Lease, military strategies and campaigns, reforms within the Chinese government, relations between the Kuomintang and the Chinese Communist Party, and China's foreign policies. Furthermore, although the United States and China shared the common goal of defeating Japan, they were separated by enormous gaps between their political cultures, institutional frameworks, and national interests. It is therefore all the more remarkable that their relations were not nearly as acrimonious as Sino-British relations during the same period.

At least three factors can be cited to explain the difference in Chiang's attitudes toward the United States and Great Britain—his perception of FDR as a person and a leader, his perception of the dependability of the United

States as a military ally, and his perception of the desirability of the United States as a long-term partner in international politics.

Chiang's favorable impressions of FDR as a person and a leader were formed at an early stage of the Sino-Japanese War. Chiang was moved by FDR's numerous messages expressing admiration for the bravery of Chinese soldiers and his willingness to do everything possible to help China resist Japan's aggression.[4] Chiang also learned that FDR had a genuine affection for China's culture and people because of his ancestors' long business association with China.[5] It is important to note that Chiang formed his favorable impressions about FDR long before he considered the United States an important factor in China's diplomatic strategy, or Roosevelt as having the power to give China meaningful assistance.[6] In fact, Chiang felt genuinely grateful toward FDR for the modest scale of support that he gave to China and told FDR that he "understood" why the president was unable to do more.[7]

After the war in Europe broke out, China's position in Asia became even more isolated. FDR's decisions to grant loans to China and to recognize only Chiang's government further convinced Chiang that only Roosevelt showed "true friendship during hard times" and that "the U.S. is China's true friend whenever China is in trouble."[8] In the spring of 1941, Chiang declared to Lauchlin Currie, Roosevelt's envoy, that he regarded FDR as the "greatest man in the world."[9]

Two subsequent events further solidified FDR's image in Chiang's mind. The first was Roosevelt's decision in May 1941 to initiate negotiations with China toward the renunciation after the war of America's unequal treaties with China. As it turned out, FDR not only abrogated these unequal treaties ahead of the original timetable but put pressure on the British to follow suit. To Chiang, the new U.S.-China treaty (which became effective on 20 May 1943) was conclusive evidence of FDR's acknowledgment of China's contribution to the war and acceptance of the country as an equal member in the international community.[10] The second event was FDR's insistence, over the objections of both Great Britain and the Soviet Union, that China be invited to sign the Four Power Agreement in Moscow on 30 October 1943, thus conferring upon China the status of a major power. Afterward Chiang felt moved to praise Roosevelt's conduct as "an expression of the highest level of morality."[11] Chiang's trust in and respect for FDR had become so firmly established by this time that not even the Stilwell crisis of 1944 or the Yalta agreement of 1945 were able to shake it.

When FDR died in 1945, Chiang's immediate urge was to journey to Washington to attend the funeral even though he had previously vowed not to go to the capital of a Western country to meet its leader.[12] Although this trip did not materialize, mourning services were held throughout Nationalist China in Roosevelt's honor. A more lasting tribute to FDR was paid by Chiang several years later, after his Nationalist government was driven to the island of Taiwan, when he named the longest and broadest boulevard in the capital city of Taipei after Roosevelt. To this date, FDR remains the only head of a foreign state to be accorded the honor of having a street in Nationalist China named after him.

Chiang's perception of the United States as a viable ally also evolved over a number of years. To be sure, Chiang had long regarded the United States as the only country that had treated China fairly in modern history while all other countries had exploited it. To Chiang, France, Great Britain, and the Soviet Union all lacked sincerity in their dealings with China. "Only the U.S. has a traditional commitment to peace and justice. Therefore, only the U.S. is our best friend."[13] Yet Chiang entertained little expectation of receiving assistance from the United States during the initial stage of the Sino-Japanese War because the main thrust of his diplomatic strategy was to provoke the traditional colonial powers (such as France and Great Britain) into a joint intervention, or to use the League of Nations as a forum to bring sanctions against Japan.

The first significant indication of Chiang's appreciation of the potential of the United States in the East Asian power equation was his appointment of the noted scholar, Dr. Hu Shih, to become China's ambassador to the United States in September 1938.[14] Although both Germany and Italy were attempting to mediate for peace in China at this juncture, Chiang informed FDR that he regarded the United States as the only leader for peace.[15]

During the next year or so, Ambassador Hu sent Chiang numerous cables interpreting for him U.S. foreign policy and FDR's personal inclinations. Chiang was told that although FDR and other U.S. leaders had a sound understanding of the menace posed by Japan, their options were severely limited by the isolationalist public opinion and the Neutrality Act.[16] While Hu predicted that U.S. policies would eventually turn hostile toward Japan, he advised Chiang that the most realistic course of action for China for the time being was "to persevere in war and wait for change to occur" (*k'u ch'eng tai pien*). In other words, there was little China could do to influence U.S. policies, and its expectations regarding U.S. assistance should be kept as low as possible.[17]

But by 1939 Chiang was no longer content with such a passive recommendation and began to view the United States as having the potential to play a more active role in pushing Great Britain, the Soviet Union, and France into a grand alliance against Japan. This effort was intensified as Chiang became more worried that the outbreak of the war in Europe could compel France and Great Britain to appease Japan even more in Asia.[18] Concomitantly, Chiang also saw the possibility of tapping America's enormous economic resources to help China carry on its fight against Japan.

Chiang made a major move in his diplomatic offensive to win support from the United States when he dispatched T. V. Soong, his brother-in-law, to Washington in June 1940 as his special personal envoy.[19] Soong's stay was extended indefinitely, and his presence in Washington brought a sharp change to the style of Chinese diplomacy in the United States. Whereas Ambassador Hu Shih, a prominent scholar and philosopher, had preferred a low-key approach to his hosts, Soong was a consummate operator of the backroom style of politics and made strenuous efforts to ingratiate himself to key operatives in the executive and legislative branches of the American government, with a particular emphasis on winning FDR's personal attention to China's needs. Soong's presence in Washington not only greatly heightened the importance of the mutual perceptions between FDR and Chiang, but elevated the importance of personal diplomacy in U.S.-China relations. FDR was approached more frequently and more aggressively by Chiang to grant commercial loans to enable China to purchase certain urgently needed commodities.

The international developments in 1940 also sharpened Chiang's awareness of the growing importance of a close relationship between the United States and Chiang. By October Chiang began to propose for the first time that the United States join China (and Great Britain) in a common struggle against both Japan's aggression and the communist threat to peace in Asia and the world.[20] In his "Proposal for US-British-Chinese Cooperation," Chiang asked the United States to make large loans to support China's currency, to supply China with 500 to 1,000 warplanes, to send military and economic delegations to China, and to plan for full-scale military cooperation in case of war between either the United States or Great Britain and Japan.[21]

Although FDR declined to enter into such a cooperative scheme at this time, Chiang and his associates were greatly elated by the president's Fireside Chat of 29 December 1940 in which he tied the fate of the United States, China and Great Britain together and affirmed the U.S. intention to serve as the arsenal for the democracies, including giving China military supplies.[22] Chiang saw this speech as an evidence of his influence over FDR and as the signal of the beginning of a close "strategic relationship" with the United States.

Soon after Chiang's wish was fulfilled by the attack against Pearl Harbor, he told FDR in unequivocal language that "China's foreign policy is to follow the American leadership in both military and political areas. Whatever [international arrangements] the U.S. declines to join, we will not join. Whatever [international arrangements] the U.S. decides to join, we also must join. We assume that the U.S. policy toward China is predicated on the same principle." In other words, Chiang was willing to defer completely to FDR's leadership insofar as China's international relations were concerned. "To put it simply, this is China's foreign policy."[23] This attitude basically underlay Chiang's policy toward the United States until the end of the war.

Chiang's trust in the goodwill of FDR and the dependability of the United States also encouraged him to envision a more ambitious long-term relationship with the latter. Chiang made his first overture to FDR concerning the desirability of cooperation between China and the United States in February 1941. He argued that the United States was the only country capable of helping China after the war, and that only after China became developed could it prevent the spread of communism. The basis of Chiang's argument was the complementarity between these two countries since China had rich resources and a large population but was economically poor while the United States was rich and highly industrialized but needed markets for export and investment.[24] Shortly after Pearl Harbor, Chiang suggested to FDR that "the U.S. and China are the two Pacific countries with the closest bonds of common interest," and that it would make perfect sense for both countries to enter into an alliance for the future.[25] By early 1943 Chiang's hope for a long-term U.S.-China alliance became more crystallized. Chiang was now convinced that the center of world politics would gradually move to the Pacific and that only long-term cooperation between the United States and China could maintain peace and stability in Asia and prevent Japan from becoming a threat again in another twenty years.[26]

From this discussion of Chiang's perceptions, it is clear that the United States occupied a unique place in Chiang's Kai-shek's wartime strategy, but central to this strategy was the figure of FDR. By far the most important aspect of Chiang's wartime policy toward the United States was his emphatic, and often exclusive, effort to cultivate a personal relationship with Roosevelt.

CHIANG'S APPROACHES TO FDR

To be sure, the cultivation of a cordial personal relationship with other leaders is a normal part of diplomacy. FDR gave added weight to personal diplomacy by relying on a small group of individuals to serve as his eyes and ears in China. However, FDR picked his agents primarily for their talents and ability to enhance the cooperation between the United States and China. FDR's agents had either expertise on China, professional and administrative abilities, diplomatic skills, or sound political judgment. None of them were related to FDR's family or had close personal ties to the Chiang family.

In contrast, Chiang exercised great care to assemble a far more elaborate network of people specifically for the purpose of cultivating and maintaining a highly personalized relation with FDR. Broadly speaking, Chiang built his network with at least three considerations in mind.

The most critical consideration was that the inner circle consist of people in whom Chiang could have absolute trust—that is, his own family members. His brother-in-law, T. V. Soong, served as his special representative in Washington from 1940 to 1943, and his other brother-in-law, H. H. K'ung, was given the same responsibilities during 1944-45. All important messages and sensitive negotiations between the two governments were conducted by these two men, often directly with FDR or members of the White House staff.

The role of Chiang's wife is of particular interest in this connection. She was present at nearly all meetings between her husband and top American officials stationed in or visiting China. She played a key role in interpreting for Chiang the meaning of American politics and in helping him draft his personal messages to FDR. When she traveled abroad, she became a vital instrument in China's diplomatic arsenal. In late 1942 Mme. Chiang accepted an invitation from FDR to visit the United States. Even though the purpose of her trip was to receive medical treatment for an old injury, Chiang recognized the potential to engage in personal diplomacy and informed FDR, "I ask that you speak with her as frankly as if you were speaking to me directly. I am confident that my wife's visit will increase the personal friendship between you and me and expand our two countries' relations."[27]

As it turned out, Mme. Chiang maximized the impact of personal diplomacy at the highest level, developing very warm relationships with both the president and Mrs. Roosevelt.[28] In spite of her status as a private citizen, she plunged into intense negotiations with FDR over a wide spectrum of issues that fundamentally affected the relationship between the two countries.[29] During the many months of negotiation, the Chinese embassy in Washington and the foreign ministry in Chungking were both kept on the sideline. Since Soong had lost his influence around Washington by this time, Mme. Chiang urgently cabled Chiang to dispatch her elder sister to Washington as a personal reinforcement. She even attempted to make a deal with FDR concerning the Burma campaign without Chiang's prior authorization.

A second consideration in Chiang's effort to build a network was his perceived need to have an American designated by FDR as the latter's personal liaison to China, preferably on a regular basis. Chiang offered to give this person the title of his political advisor, but FDR and Chiang obviously had different expectations of what his duties were from the very outset. The Americans assumed that they should send a man with Asian expertise and the right political instincts to steer Chiang in the direction of internal reform, but Chiang's expectation was that "the political advisor must be fully aware of President Roosevelt's inclinations so that he can serve as a perfect intermediary between President Roosevelt and me."[30]

The primacy of this expectation became obvious during May-June 1941, for example, when Owen Lattimore was recommended by FDR as the political advisor. Before accepting him, Chiang was basically interested only in Lattimore's relations with FDR. When told by Soong from Washington that Lattimore might not know FDR personally, Chiang replied that the reason why he wanted the president to recommend a political advisor was that he wanted to establish direct personal contact through this person.[31] Lattimore's appointment was finalized only after he had assured Chiang that he indeed knew FDR personally and after a separate letter from FDR certified to Chiang that Lattimore's basic political attitudes were similar to FDR's own.[32]

Chiang's purpose for receiving a political advisor from FDR became clear once Lattimore was installed on the job. Basically, Chiang treated Lattimore as the president's ear through whom he could transmit his views and demands directly to the president.[33] In fact, Chiang left little room for Lattimore to exercise his own discretion on what and how to report to the president but asked that Lattimore's draft letters be submitted for his final perusal before they were sent off to the president.[34] By asking to read and approve Lattimore's letters before they were sent, Chiang sought to gain full control over their contents. And by using Lattimore's pen to make his points, Chiang also hoped to cash in on Lattimore's credibility with FDR and persuade the president to accept them as if they had been made by Lattimore. Even if FDR rejected them, there would be no blow to Chiang's dignity because the intermediary had actually made the suggestions. This style of operations fitted well into the traditional pattern of how intermediaries were utilized in Chinese politics.

When Chiang realized that Lattimore could not deliver what he had wanted, the advisor was sent home. Later, in the summer of 1944 when Chiang's relations with General Joseph Stilwell, the president's top military representative in China, became impossible to continue because of Stilwell's contempt for him, he again asked the visiting American vice president, Henry Wallace, to urge FDR "to send a personal envoy in whom he has complete confidence to China and to work with me all the time, to manage the important issues in the military, political and economic areas."[35] When General Patrick Hurley arrived at Chungking later, Chiang and his associates made tremendous efforts to cooperate with him and valued Hurley as the most effective conduit to the president.

A third consideration in Chiang's mind was to build a supporting cast of Americans and Chinese who possessed their own access to the president and had the ability to buttress the messages and demands that Chiang sought to convey to him. During the war years, a substantial group of such people were identified and cultivated by the Chinese government. This group included former members of the White House staff, the Federal Power Commission, the Army Air Force, China missionaries, and businessmen with links to major industrial corporations.[36]

Chiang's ultimate instrument of personal diplomacy was face-to-face contact with FDR. Although the idea was first broached soon after Pearl Harbor and explored on several other occasions, Chiang's nationalism posed a serious obstacle because he did not want to journey to Washington to visit FDR lest he be perceived as a vassal paying homage to his lord. Finally, in November 1943, arrangements were made for the two leaders to meet at a neutral site—the Cairo Conference. Chiang went home greatly satisfied since he had extensive exchanges of views with FDR in private sessions and wa particularly elated by his wife's success in extracting a verbal commitment from FDR to grant China a $1 billion loan. Chiang probably also felt his strong emphasis on personal diplomacy was vindicated when Roosevelt wrote to tell him afterward that "I have gained a fuller understanding of the problems of your great nation and especially that I have gained a real friend with the leader of that nation."[37] Although the loan commitment was later withdrawn because of the objections of Henry Morgenthau, Chiang probably remained convinced that the president was his only hope of getting the loan in the first place.

As the crisis in U.S.-China relations intensified in the midst of Japan's Ichigo campaign and Stilwell's increasingly gloomy reports to Washington and stronger pressure on China in the summer of 1944, Chiang was driven to place even greater importance on maintaining a direct line to FDR. To achieve this objective, Chiang decided to send to Washington H. H. K'ung, his other brother-in-law. He introduced K'ung to FDR as "the person in whom I have complete trust and who commands comprehensive knowledge about China's political, economic, and fiscal conditions."[38] Chiang told the president that K'ung was uniquely qualified to promote friendship and cooperation between them, and that K'ung was not only authorized to transmit all messages from him to FDR but to negotiate and make commitments on his behalf.[39] At this juncture, General Hurley was also dispatched by FDR first as his personal envoy and then as U.S. ambassador to China. Together, these two men became the most important links between Chiang and FDR until the end of the latter's life.

REASONS FOR CHIANG'S APPROACHES TOWARD FDR

Why did Chiang put such an exclusive emphasis on developing a personal relationship with the American president through private channels? Several considerations are obviously pertinent to this question.

To begin with, Chiang's own leadership style in domestic politics exhibited a persistent tendency to take personal charge over things or delegate authority only to members of his immediate entourage. In dealing with his domestic political counterparts, Chiang also put a premium on the cultivation of private contacts and direct access. Such a leadership style was in tune with China's political culture, but Chiang evidently believed that it could be equally extended to the realm of foreign relations. As Chiang once told FDR, "private contacts will greatly improve our mutual understanding and friendship."[40] Chiang's preference for the personal approach toward Roosevelt also was motivated at least partially by the belief that he needed to create the impression for domestic consumption that he was the only Chinese leader the American president would recognize and deal with.

Chiang had good reasons to believe that this approach dovetailed well with FDR's own style. For instance, Chiang learned from Lattimore that the president also preferred the quiet personal channels of communication because "the president does not want himself or you to be unnecessarily constrained by the complications that can be created if these issues are discussed through the open channels."[41]

Chiang's perception of FDR as a man with preference for private contacts was reinforced by the profuse praises that FDR heaped upon his envoys, in sharp contrast to the president's tendency to make disparaging remarks about career diplomats and his distrust of bureaucracies.[42] Thus, for instance, after Lauchlin Currie's return from his first trip to China, FDR told Chiang that he had depended heavily on Currie, consulted with him constantly regarding all political, economic, and military issues relating to China, and allowed him to exert quiet influence behind the scenes.[43] Later in the war, FDR described another envoy, Hurley, as not only a person with rich diplomatic experience and political perspective but also a strategist whose judgment he respected highly and said that the United States needed "more men like him."[44]

Nonetheless, Chiang had little need to cultivate FDR's personal goodwill as long as he entertained few expectations of U.S. aid. Between 1938 and 1940, Chiang's main objective regarding the United States was to get a few modest loans. Since Morgenthau, Secretary of the Treasury, already played an active role in shaping the U.S. government's policy of economic aid to China, Chiang did not see much reason to approach FDR directly.

The situation changed with the enactment of Lend Lease in 1941, when the focus of U.S.-China negotiation shifted from economic assistance to the issues of Lend Lease materials' acquisition, distribution, and utilization. Concomitantly, the authority to grant aid had been shifted from the Treasury Department to the White House. From this point on, it became increasingly important for Chiang to win over the president and his personal advisors.

From the Chinese perspective, however, the new situation was complicated by two additional factors. First, Chiang realized that the president would normally rely on his own military experts for assessment of China's military needs and recommendations on the amount of U.S. assistance to be granted. Yet, from early on in his efforts to secure American aid, Chiang sensed that many people in the U.S. military harbored unfriendly attitudes toward his government. Chiang's meetings in October 1941 with the head of the American Military Mission sent to China (AMMISCA), General John A. Magruder, gave him a strong impression that the U.S. delegation lacked appreciation of the conditions in China and did not have any concrete plans to assist the country.[45]

As the war went on, Chiang was provided with more reports of the unfriendly attitudes of people in the U.S. army.[46] He became convinced that the U.S. army's unfriendly attitudes had been caused by their uncritical consumption of the Chinese communists' propaganda.[47] Chiang's frictions with General Stilwell, his American chief of staff from 1942 to 1944, only made the situation worse. Under these circumstances, Chiang was virtually driven to the conclusion that his only chance of receiving favorable consideration by the U.S. government was to neutralize the U.S. military and make direct appeals to the American president.

A second factor that propelled Chiang to seek greater direct access to FDR was the exclusion of China from practically all top-level Allied military councils. Chiang was particularly offended by the Allies' decision to deny China representation in the Combined Chiefs of Staff and the Munitions Assignment Board, which were charged with the responsibility of mapping strategies and making allocations. China's exclusion from these bodies meant that the strategies and military needs of the China theater were to be decided by Anglo-American planners alone, an arrangement that was utterly unacceptable from the Chinese point of view. Chiang bitterly complained about the exclusion as a form of racial discrimination and believed that only access to the American president could compensate for this severe handicap.

Chiang's assumption of the efficacy of personal diplomacy toward FDR was reinforced both by the advice he received and his own observation. Chiang was told by his nation's good friends in the U.S. government that China's needs would be met more promptly if he only pressed FDR hard enough.[48] Chiang also saw how effective FDR could be in cutting through the bureaucratic red tape to deliver concrete results. In late November 1940, for instance, when FDR, at Chiang's urgent request, instructed Morgenthau to put together "a stabilization loan of fifty million dollars to the Chinese in the next 24 hours," the Treasury Department lost no time in complying with the president's order.[49]

Therefore, Chiang gave personal diplomacy such a preeminent role because, in his view, the president had practically become the only one in the U.S. government who was both sympathetic to China's cause and capable of satisfying China's needs.

A COST-EFFECTIVENESS ANALYSIS

How effective was this diplomatic style in dealing with FDR? We can answer this question by first examining the costs that such a style produced.

Probably the most negative effect of this style was the demoralization of the regular foreign service in both countries. Soong's arrival at Washington in June 1940 caused Ambassador Hu Shih and his staff to become increasingly sidelined. The situation became more anomalous when Soong was named China's foreign minister but stayed on in Washington. Many Chinese leaders in Chungking became very upset by these arrangements, and Sun Fo, the son of Sun Yat-Sen, and an important leader of the Kuomintang, even ridiculed Soong as "a government in exile" on U.S. soil. Hu Shih eventually became so disgruntled that he resigned from the post. Although his successor, Wei Tao-ming, was a Soong favorite, the Chinese embassy's normal functions in the United States were never fully restored. Soong's eagerness to practice personal diplomacy also made General Hsiung Shih-hui, head of the Chinese Military Mission to the United States, feel completely isolated and useless at his Washington post since nobody in the U.S. government bothered to deal with him.

The U.S. embassy in Chungking suffered from a similar decline. After 1940, Chiang basically stopped discussing important issues with the American ambassador or using him as the channel to transmit messages to the U.S. government. The situation was not improved even after General Hurley became the U.S. ambassador, since he obviously continued to define his own role first and foremost as the personal conduit between the two Allied leaders and only marginally as the head of the U.S. diplomatic mission in China. Hurley kept most embassy staff in the dark about negotiations between FDR and Chiang and decided neither to seek nor to listen to the opinions of his subordinates. Their relations became so strained that the embassy staff finally staged a "revolt" and created a major crisis in the State Department with long-term ramifications for America's Asian policy.

A closely related cost of this diplomatic style was the alienation of powerful bureaucrats in the host country. This posed a lesser danger for the United States because most of FDR's envoys went to China only for short visits (Currie, Nelson) and dealt only with the Chiangs. But General Stilwell, who stayed in China for over two years, managed to make himself intensely disliked by many leaders in the Chungking government not merely because his reform proposals allegedly threatened their interest, but because his propensity to invoke the president's name proved too overbearing for them.

The problem with Chiang's envoy in the United States was far more serious. When Soong first arrived in Washington, his aggressive style was so refreshingly un-Chinese that it initially impressed his American hosts. But they soon became upset by what they perceived to be Soong's manipulativeness and by his attempt to monopolize all communications between the Chinese government and American cabinet officers. They also resented Soong's indulgence in high-pressured tactics to pry Lend Lease materials from the federal departments and his tendency to routinely go to the president for personal intervention whenever he encountered resistance at the level of federal departments. Even erstwhile supporters of China's cause eventually found Soong unpleasant to work with.[50]

The Chinese style also created practical difficulties. Most Chinese requests for economic loans or Lend Lease materials were made without detailed explanation of why these items were needed or how they were to be utilized. Chiang's expectation was for the United States to make a commitment to one big splashy loan or major arms delivery to help China gain international prestige or shore up the sagging morale of its people even though the actual delivery might be delayed or not made at all. Such thinking naturally ran counter to the modus operandi at either the War or Treasury Department. When Soong went over the heads of Marshall or Morgenthau to seek FDR's endorsement, the president was sometimes swayed to grant his requests, only to be told by his own subordinates why he should not have done so. In time, all the parties in the host country who ever worked with Soong felt that they had been tricked by him.

This style of operations offended so many officials that Currie felt compelled to bring it to Chiang's attention during his second visit to Chungking in 1942. By late that year when Mme. Chiang visited the United States, Soong had already turned into a *persona non grata* in Washington, and FDR no longer wanted to negotiate with him. Although Soong was replaced by K'ung in 1944, the Chinese operating style remained basically unchanged.

Still another risk of excessive reliance on personal diplomacy was the temptation it offered the intermediaries to exceed their roles to engage in self-enrichment or self-aggrandizement. Certainly the personal judgments and temperaments of Currie, Soong, and Hurley all left their marks on the mutual perceptions between Chiang and FDR. This was quite normal.

But there were other possibilities for an intermediary to exploit his position to serve personal interest. Lattimore seemed to have labored hard to exaggerate his own influence over the American president and American public opinion in Chiang's eyes. It has long been speculated that Soong and K'ung abused their privileged information to make huge financial profit . Stilwell suspected his ouster to have been brought about as much by how Hurley reported and interpreted the situation to FDR as by Chiang's insistence. There were also suggestions that Hurley utilized his powers as a special envoy to capture the ambassadorship. All these speculations point to the potential hazards of putting too much weight on personal channels to conduct states' foreign policies.

On the positive side, however, the reliance on a few chosen intermediaries to conduct diplomacy yielded several important advantages. One advantage was that it increased the pace and candor of the communication flow. The strict confidentiality of the exchanges enabled the principals to explore sensitive topics without committing themselves to irrevocable positions. Thus, for example, the issue of whether the Allies should defeat Japan or Germany first was discussed in private exchanges between Chiang and FDR. After their meeting at Cairo, Chiang finally yielded to FDR's advocacy of defeating Germany before Japan without revealing it to his own countrymen.[51]

Direct diplomacy also enabled the principals to speak with a degree of bluntness that would otherwise have caused serious damage to relations between their countries. FDR's gloomy assessment of conditions in the

China theater and his many appeals to Chiang to avert a civil war with the Communists all might have been rejected by the Chinese had they been conveyed through the normal diplomatic channels. Chiang found these messages tolerable only because they had come directly from FDR.

The weight of a personal envoy or letter could create great pressure upon the other leader to take prompt or reciprocal actions. When frictions were caused by acts committed on lower levels of bureaucracies, the principals could repair them by personal intercession. Thus, for instance, U.S.-China relations reached a major crisis after the U.S. government transferred its 10th Air Force, which was assigned to support the China-Burma-India Theater, from India to the Near East in 1942 without prior notification to the Chungking government. But Chiang finally softened his stand after FDR wrote him a personal letter and sent Wendell Willkie to China as a peacemaker.[52]

For Chiang, a special benefit of personal diplomacy was the exposure it gave him to frank reports and harsh assessments from the intermediaries. A serious problem in Chinese politics was the lack of people who dared to tell Chiang the truth about anything. This problem was probably least serious with respect to U.S.-China relations since nearly all the intermediaries between Chiang and FDR had given Chiang very frank views on the deficiencies of the Chinese government or the root causes of difficulties in relations between the two countries.[53]

The two leaders' mutual perceptions definitely made a major contribution toward stabilizing U.S.-China relations. FDR's faith in China's latent greatness in future world politics gave him the capacity to treat its current weaknesses and incompetence with greater tolerance. Roosevelt considered himself to possess far greater political sophistication than his generals, and concluded that the support for Chiang must remain as the symbol and centerpiece of his China policy. As he explained to Marshall, it would be counterproductive to attempt to demand strict obedience from Chiang, a man who had struggled to become the "undisputed leader of 400,000,000 people" and who had created in China "what it took us a couple of centuries to attain," and that one could not "speak sternly to a man like that or exact commitments from him as we might do from the Sultan of Morocco."[54]

On the other hand, Chiang's genuine trust in FDR as a true friend of China and his respect for Roosevelt as a world leader with great vision and ability also tempered his highly nationalistic (or xenophobic) approach toward foreigners. Even in mid-1944 as his relationship with Stilwell continued to deteriorate, Chiang confined his anger to Stilwell and continued to profess his complete acceptance of FDR's leadership in international political, economic, and military affairs.[55] While Chiang was prepared to risk the total suspension of U.S. aid in September-October 1944 over his insistence that Stilwell be recalled, he never put any blame on FDR personally. In fact, FDR's willingness to recall Stilwell made Chiang feel that the most serious obstacle in U.S.-China wartime cooperation had been removed. Afterward, Chiang considered relations between the two countries to have become better than during any previous period and expressed gratitude to FDR for having sent him three capable envoys in Hurley, Nelson, and Wedemeyer.[56]

Chiang himself cogently summed up his complex feelings toward FDR. When he heard the news of FDR's death, he wrote in his diary dated 13 April 1945:

> in spite of FDR's appeasement of the USSR and his partiality toward the CCP [Chinese Communist Party], he at least observed certain limits and had his principles. He was not a hegemonist who relied on power. Hereafter, however, I am worried that the U.S. government may become vulnerable to the manipulation by the British, may deviate from its principles and may not behave as independently as under FDR. FDR's death should make us more wary about handling Sino-Soviet relations in the future.[57]

FDR's last message regarding China was brought to Chiang posthumously. On 24 April 1945 Hurley told Chiang that Roosevelt had instructed him in their last meeting to enlist the assistance of Great Britain and the Soviet Union to help China to become an independent, free, democratic, and unified country.[58] Even though the details of the Yalta secret deal were to be revealed to him and caused him much pain in the ensuing months, Chiang probably remembered FDR best for the latter's genuine compassion for, and grand vision about, China's future. Given our current knowledge about the complexity of China's domestic politics and the priorities of America's global strategy, the highly personalized relationship between FDR and Chiang probably produced as many positive results to the wartime alliance as could realistically be expected.

Part III

FDR'S FOES

11

HITLER'S PERCEPTION OF FRANKLIN D. ROOSEVELT AND THE UNITED STATES OF AMERICA

Detlef Junker

Despite an almost insuperable mountain of monographs devoted to all aspects of world politics in the years 1933 to 1945 in general, and relations between the Third Reich and the United States in particular,[1] it remains difficult for the historian to reconstruct Hitler's image of America and explain his policy toward that country. While this chapter will concern itself with Hitler's *perceptions* of Roosevelt and the United States, by way of introduction I would like to recall that it continues to be far from easy to arrive at unambiguous answers even to seemingly obvious questions raised by Hitler's U.S. policy. For example:

- Given American isolationism in the 1930s and U.S. neutrality legislation, was Hitler hoping the United States could safely be ignored as a factor in his foreign policy in the long term as well? Was he expecting to push through the central points of his political program—that is, "Lebensraum" (living space) in the East, destruction of the Jews, and hegemony over Europe from the Atlantic seaboard to the Urals—with the tacit consent of Great Britain, and all of this *without* forcing the United States out of its self-imposed isolationism?
- Was he pinning his hopes on achieving victory in a European Blitzkrieg before the United States could intervene?

- Assuming that Hitler did have a plan for world domination, the last step of which was war between a Europe ruled by national socialism and the United States, between the New World and a resurgent Old World, what sort of war was this to be? A war to attack the United States in the Western Hemisphere or to keep it from intervening in European affairs?
- Was this war to culminate in an invasion of the United States, or was it meant to obtain by military means what Hitler had failed to achieve through the Three Power Pact of 1940 (that is, to contain the United States in the Western Hemisphere and force it to acknowledge the National Socialist racial and economic order in Europe)?
- Why did Hitler declare war on the United States after the Japanese attack on Pearl Harbor in the face of England's refusal to conclude a peace treaty on Hitler's terms and although the German armies were bogged in the mud outside Moscow?

My topic, the reconstruction of Hitler's perception of the American president and the American people, is obviously but one aspect among others, but one means—hopefully fruitful—of shedding light upon these very complex questions.

Speaking generally, it may be said that Hitler's perception of Roosevelt and the United States was inherently circumscribed by his ideological dogmatism. This inability to take in any objective reality beyond his own fixed prejudices manifested itself with respect to Roosevelt and America as well. In his role as ideologue and programmatic thinker, he claimed that war and the violent competition of races and peoples for limited living space constituted the eternal purpose of world history and set its agenda. In keeping with this theory, Hitler, fanatical autodidact that he was, absorbed only those items of information about the United States that coincided with his own prejudgments. Although Hitler did concern himself with aspects of American culture, politics, and the economy, he was fundamentally unable to change his perspective and see the world from the American point of view. Drawing on the theories of Sigmund Freud and Jean Piaget, I would suggest that in his emotional and cognitive-social development Hitler never succeeded in developing those patterns of perception and insight that enable a realistic interaction with one's environment.

Apart from limitations of a fundamental and dogmatic nature, there existed other, objective, obstacles to Hitler's gaining a realistic understanding of Roosevelt and America. Hitler spoke no English, had never been to an Anglo-Saxon country, and regarded all democratic traditions as ipso facto

Jewish, internationalist, and as such a crime against humanity. His worldview was Eurocentric, fixated on the European theater and military land power. He never developed an even remotely adequate notion of the possibilities inherent worldwide in Anglo-Saxon seapower. In addition, Hitler personally hated water and sea. On land, he wrote in 1928, he was a hero, at sea a coward.[2]

The historian attempting an unambiguous verdict about Hitler's image of America and Roosevelt is faced with the problem of a lack of detailed statements by Hitler himself on the subject. It is only in his "Second" or "Secret Book," written in 1928 and published in 1961, that we find a more detailed exposition of his views about America; only in his address of 11 December 1941, on the occasion of the Declaration of War on the United States, that he presents us with, as it were, his perception of Roosevelt. Of course, there is also the passage in Hermann Rauschning's *Hitler Speaks*, the authenticity of which is, however, dubious on external and controversial on internal grounds. Hence I do not propose to use it as a possible source.

Finally, a reconstruction of Hitler's image of the United States is further complicated by the fact that Hitler's attitude was ambivalent throughout. Alternating between admiration and contempt, Hitler's views never coalesced into a realistic or permanent picture of the United States. As we will see, a very similar situation applies with regard to his views on Roosevelt.

Very few expressions of Hitler's opinions concerning the United States prior to his writing of the "Secret Book" have come down to us. For the period before 1924 there exist a few hate-filled tirades against Woodrow Wilson who, as a bought agent of bourgeois capitalism, a puppet of Jewish arms dealers and the Jewish press, forced an isolationist America into war against Germany. In the same sources Hitler declares America in general, and New York in particular, to be a hotbed of world Jewry. Accompanying these sentiments are standard commonplaces, widespread in the Europe of the time, deriding American materialism.

If one checks *Mein Kampf* for references to America, one notices that the United States plays no role at all in Hitler's program, which is centered on Europe, or in his thinking about possible allies for Germany; agitation against the Dawes Plan is notably absent, and the differences between National Socialist ideology and American democracy are either too obvious or too irrelevant to be mentioned. On the other hand, the few times the United States does appear, the tenor of the remarks is one of consistent admiration. According to Hitler, the Germanic race is master of the United States thanks to a sound racial and immigration policy, albeit constantly threatened by the Jewish bacillus. For Hitler the United States was the very model of a state organized according to the principles of race and space. Given its favorable ratio of population to living space—the decisive criterion in Hitler's ideology—the United States was the archetype of a world power, destined to replace the British Empire.[3]

In his "Second Book" these assumptions become even more prominent. The United States appears as the prototypical world power: characterized by adequate living space, a correct racial policy enforced through immigration laws, a large domestic market, a high standard of living, extraordinary productivity, and technical innovativeness by mobility and mass production.[4] It has even been suggested by one of the younger generation of Hitler scholars, Rainer Zitelmann, that Hitler's ultimate goal was not an anti-modernist agrarian utopia but a highly industrialized economy modelled on that of the United States. While Hitler may have been contemptuous of American society and culture, he was fascinated by the country's economic and technical development, according to Zitelmann.[5]

However, in the "Second Book" the United States appeared not only as the prototype of a world power and the model for a National Socialist organization of living space, but also—at the same time—as a danger and challenge to Europe and Germany.

Hitler criticized what he referred to as the "incredible naivety of bourgeois nationalists" who thought that such a challenge could be met in the context of an open world economy and free world trade. He also attacked the Pan-European Movement of his time for harboring the illusion that American hegemony could be countered adequately by founding a "United States of Europe." Conflict with the United States was inevitable, as there was no such thing as the peaceful coexistence of rival states in Hitler's worldview, and could only be waged successfully by a racially regenerated Europe under German leadership. Only a Europe so united would be in a position to "stand up to North America in the future" according to Hitler. "And it is the responsibility of the National Socialist Movement to prepare our Fatherland for this task to its utmost capacity."[6]

These oft-quoted words, written in 1928, may be interpreted as Hitler's anticipating a future some time after a National Socialist subjugation of Europe. They may well be read as anticipating at least a trade war between the United States and a Europe run by Hitler and no longer guided by the rules of a free market or free trade; they might even be read as anticipating a full-scale war between the United States and Nazi Europe.

Such a reading would establish a certain continuity with similar remarks made by Hitler in the years 1940 and 1941. In those years he repeatedly spoke of an impending conflict between the economic policies of Europe dominated by national socialism and the United States, occasionally even of a future war between Europe and the United States, a war that would have to be fought out after his death by the next generation. England remained the wished-for ally throughout in his visions of future conflict with the United States.[7]

This hypothesis of a relative consistency in Hitler's perception of America—that is, of the United States as an important world power, at one and the same time a shining example and threat—does not, however, bear very close scrutiny. The contrast between it and Hitler's actual conduct of foreign policy in the period from 1933 to the summer of 1940 is too striking. Up to the signing of the Munich Agreement, Hitler had ignored the United States completely; up to the invasion of Poland, he continued by and large to do the same. In no foreign policy decision of those years did Hitler show any consideration for American interests. In key documents, such as the Four-Year Economic Plan of the Hossbach Memorandum, America is not even mentioned. The remark Göring made to Ambassador William C. Bullitt in November 1937 was therefore not without some justification, namely, that Germany had good relations with some countries, bad relations with others, and no relations whatever with the United States.[8] On becoming chancellor, Hitler could regard U.S. goodwill as useful but relatively insignificant. Up to 1936 President Roosevelt received cordial treatment both from Hitler and the state-directed press. Only after Roosevelt's famous "Quarantine speech" of October 1937, whose anti-Nazi intentions Hitler recognized clearly, did Hitler's attitude toward America change. The longer the shadow grew that Roosevelt cast over the Atlantic, the more pressing became Hitler's need to reexamine his perceptions of Roosevelt and the United States. And the picture that emerged—of the potential enemy posing a threat to Hitler's claim to domination over Europe—was considerably different from that of the years before 1933.

Almost all historians, when seeking to explain this break, assume that the Great Depression, coupled with American isolationism and neutrality legislation, led to a rapid loss of America's significance in Hitler's eyes.[9] This is a plausible hypothesis, although to my knowledge not a single direct statement by Hitler himself explicitly supporting it has been preserved. Assuming this hypothesis to be correct, it would appear that Hitler was confident of being able to pursue his foreign policy goals in Europe without regard to U.S. reactions. In the light of this interpretation, Hitler's perception of America, when scrutinized closely, turns out to be a reflection of America's objective position at any given moment. He regarded the United States as a power to be reckoned with when it was actually or potentially involved in European affairs, as weak when it was not.

In the period from 1933 to 1936 Roosevelt, the New Deal, and the United States generally were treated cordially by Hitler and the Nazi press—despite massive and mounting criticism of the terror then beginning in Germany in the American media.[10] If one sets aside the dubious recollections of a Hermann Rauschning or a "Putzi" Hanfstaengel, there is no evidence of any critical remark by Hitler about Roosevelt or the United States.[11] Speaking to Louis P. Lochner of the Associated Press on 24 February 1933, Hitler described his government's attitude to the United States as one of "sincere friendship."[12] Hitler's response to Roosevelt's call for disarmament of 16 May 1933, was also couched in friendly if platitudinous terms.[13] On 14 March 1934 Hitler sent a message to Roosevelt through Ambassador William E. Dodd in which he congratulated him on his "heroic efforts on behalf of the American people." The German people, he continued, were watching the president's successful struggle against the economic crisis with interest and admiration. What follows may be taken as revealing the official interpretation accorded Roosevelt and his New Deal in the first year of Nazi rule:

> The Chancellor is in accord with the President in the view that the virtue of duty, readiness for sacrifice, and discipline should dominate the entire people. These moral demands which the President places before every individual citizen of the United States, are also the quintessence of the German State philosophy which finds its expression in the slogan "The Public Weal Transcends the Interests of the Individual."[14]

Roosevelt, so went the basic tenor of the German press in those years, was confronted by a similarly revolutionary challenge as that facing Hitler and Mussolini; he too was a kind of Führer, using dictatorial measures to intervene in the economy; he too had realized that the era of unfettered individualism and parliamentarianism had had its day. Parallels were drawn between Roosevelt and Hitler as individuals as well as between the tasks confronting them. Roosevelt's book *Looking Forward* appeared in German translation only months after publication in 1933 and met with a warm reception in National Socialist Germany. The party organ of the NSDAP, the *Völkischer Beobachter,* commented: "Many statements could have been written by a National Socialist. In any case, one can assume that Roosevelt has a good deal of understanding for National Socialist thought."[15]

As has been mentioned, this assessment of Roosevelt was revised after the Quarantine Speech at the latest. Hitler had already taken the speech seriously in October 1937. In his address to the Reichstag on 11 December 1941, he declared that Roosevelt had systematically begun to incite American public opinion against Germany in 1937, Roosevelt's speech of 5 October of that year being especially "despicable." Hitler was particularly incensed by Roosevelt's statement that 90 percent of the world's population was being threatened by 10 percent. This, he declared, was proof positive that Roosevelt did not count the Russians among the aggressors.[16]

Following this speech an almost pathological hate built up in Hitler that repeatedly vented itself in public: for example, in his memorable address to the Greater German Reichstag on 30 January 1939 in which he announced annihilation of the Jews in case of a world war; in his sarcastic reply to the president's appeal for peace in the Reichstag on 28 April 1939; and in his war speech of 11 December 1941. Hitler's public utterances concerning Roosevelt tally substantially with those nonpublic ones that have come down to us. Running like a thread throughout, manifesting itself in the speech accompanying the Declaration of War, and corroborated by entries in the diaries of Joseph Goebbels, is one question: Why did Roosevelt drive the United States into a, from Hitler's point of view, futile war with Germany?

As of 1937 Hitler sought to explain Roosevelt's foreign policy as a reaction to the failure of his economic policies: The president's foreign policy was a domestically motivated flight into war. Unable to get the unemployed off the streets or to stop the decline of the American economy, war was Roosevelt's last resort. At the close of 1937 Hitler—but also, for example, Goebbels—noted the renewed rise in the number of people unemployed in the United States to 11 million.[17] In the speech delivered on 30 January 1939, Hitler compared the failure of the United States—despite natural advantages such as space and plentiful raw material—to solve its social problems with the Third Reich's success in eliminating unemployment.[18] According to the protocol of a meeting with Mussolini on 2 June 1941, Hitler declared that

> If one analyzed the personality of Roosevelt, one came to the conclusion that he was consumed by hatred of the Duce and the Führer, because these two European statesmen had succeeded in solving problems which had defeated him. Despite his brain trust, despite the gigantic debt which he had burdened the United States, he had not achieved anything. Unemployment was still running at 11 to 12 million in America, and the misery in that country, especially in New York, remained great. His actions were, thus, clearly motivated by jealousy of the Duce and the Führer, and dictated by the hatred born of his own failure.[19]

The contrast between the alleged "tremendous upsurge of life, the economy, culture, art, etc." under the Third Reich on the one hand and the unemployment, public debt, speculation, ruined economy, and the failure of the New Deal on the other was also a central idea of Hitler's war speech. Roosevelt, according to Hitler, knew that he had failed in times of peace; therefore his only alternative lay in diverting public attention from domestic to foreign affairs.[20]

More important to Hitler and far more typical for him than the charge that Roosevelt was driving the United States into war for domestic reasons was his conviction that FDR was not acting independently, but as a puppet and agent of international Jewry, of Jewish capitalism, of Jewish bankers and Wall Street gangsters. This accusation ran like a thread through all his private and public statements from 1937 to his so-called political testament of 1945. It is well known[21] that in Hitler's dogmatic, Manichean teleology of history, the element of total negation, the satanic and evil principle, is embodied in the Jews, because they—being a people without living space for two thousand years—threaten to ruin and destroy the purpose of history. Since Hitler saw his own mission within the context of world history as leading the Germanic race and the German people into the final battle against the Jews, any state that denied his claim to power, any politician who opposed him, became ipso facto an agent of "international Jewry"—Roosevelt and the United States included. The fact that America was engaging in anti-German policies was in itself apparently enough to prove to Hitler that Germanic and German elements in the United States had been poisoned and corrupted by the Jews. In support of this connection, suffice it to quote a few sentences from his war speech: One had to consider, according to Hitler "that the spirits this man has summoned to his aid, or rather who summoned him, belong to those elements who, as Jews, can have a vested interest solely in destruction and never order." "It was the Jew in all his satanic malice who gathered around this man [Roosevelt], but of whom this man also wanted to make use." "We know the power behind Roosevelt; it is the eternal Jew, who thinks the time is ripe for carrying out on us that which we had to see and experience with horror in Soviet-Russia."[22]

Goebbels's diaries as well are filled with invective against Roosevelt, the "servant of Jewry and slave of capitalism," "the evil genius of American politics."[23] In his war speech Hitler himself referred to Roosevelt as a "hypocrite," "forger," and "warmonger." He continued: "That he [Roosevelt] calls me a gangster is all the more irrelevant as this term is American and not European in origin, probably due to the lack of such elements here. But quite apart from that, I cannot be insulted by Mr. Roosevelt at all, for I consider him—much as I do Woodrow Wilson—to be mentally ill."[24] As far back as 16 April 1939, Marshal Göring had remarked to Mussolini that in view of Roosevelt's public appeal of 14 April one might gain the impression that the president was suffering from "the beginnings of a brain disorder." In this appeal Roosevelt had called on Hitler to guarantee the territorial integrity of thirty-one states in Europe and the Near East. As this list included countries such as Palestine and Syria, which were under British or French sovereignty, the duce was moved to comment that "Roosevelt seemed to be having problems with his geography."[25]

Roosevelt, arrogant and hypocritical, who sermonized about peace while himself warmongering; who accused Germany of aggression while committing one breach of international law after another—this too was a constant feature of Hitler's image of Roosevelt in those years. What particularly infuriated Hitler evidently was Roosevelt's strategy of accusing the Nazis of aspiring to world dominion and even wanting to attack the United States on the one hand, while on the other himself infringing the Monroe Doctrine and meddling in European concerns. Roosevelt, declared Hitler in his war speech, no more had the right to interfere in inner-European affairs than the German head of state had the right to pass judgment on conditions i America.[26] He gave repeated assurances, publicly and privately, that the propaganda being spread in the United States about an alleged German plan to invade the Western Hemisphere was laughable and absurd. Such an assertion, Hitler stated in the Reichstag on 30 January 1939, could only be improved on by the prediction that, following this invasion, "we intend to occupy the full moon."[27] In a conversation with John Cudahy, a former American ambassador to Belgium and avowed isolationist, which took place on 25 May 1941, Hitler had the following to say when asked about the problems of a German invasion of the Western Hemisphere:

> The Führer responded that there was no reason to comment on this question militarily, as it was not only childish, but absolutely absurd. The leading war-mongers in America were quite aware of the impossibility of a German invasion. They made this accusation knowing it to be false, so as to draw America more easily into war; in the belief that American involvement in the war would benefit their business interests. He [the Führer] was of the opinion that they were deceiving themselves on that point. America's participation in the Great War had not brought it any commercial advantages either. These assertions of a German invasion were not worthy of serious discussion. To declare that Europe wanted to conquer America was tantamount to asserting that America wanted to conquer the moon.[28]

It was only this negative and hate-filled perception of Roosevelt, in particular his characterization as a puppet of Jewish capitalism, that enabled Hitler to answer a question he had posed himself and that he put before the German people in his war speech: the question, in fact, of why Roosevelt—like Wilson before him—had become a fanatical enemy of Germany. On the very day that Hitler declared war on the United States, he reaffirmed his belief that no real conflict of interests existed between Germany and the United States. According to Hitler, Germany was perhaps the only Great Power never to have possessed colonies either in North or South America. Furthermore, the United States had drawn only benefit from the immigration of millions of Germans, and, he continued, the German Reich had never adopted a hostile attitude toward the United States. Regarding the outbreak of World War I, Hitler drew attention to the conclusions of the Nye Committee, according to which capitalist interests in the United States had brought about that country's entry into the conflict. Nor were there other territorial or political conflicts likely to affect the interests, let alone the existence, of the United States. The difference in the organization of the state was granted; this was, according to Hitler, in itself no reason for hostility, as long as one type of state did not try "to step outside its own natural sphere and intervene in others."[29]

Comparing Hitler's statements about Roosevelt and the United States from the period 1937 to 1941 with the monologues held in the Führer headquarters from 1941 to 1944 and the surprisingly detailed remarks on the United States to be read in his political testament of 1945, one finds that the years 1941 to 1945 saw no change or development in his thoughts on the topic. Only his hatred of Roosevelt grew; when the president appeared it was always as a mentally ill criminal and con man, a pawn of the Jews. Criticism of U.S. culture and the American way of life also became more prominent. A remark Hitler made on 7 January 1942 is most revealing:

> Ancient Rome was a colossal, serious state. Great ideas inspired the Romans. This is not true of England today. Yet I prefer an Englishman to an American a thousand times over. To the Japanese we have no inner affinity. Their culture and way of life are too different from ours. However, it is against Americanism that I feel a hatred and abhorrence of the most profound kind. One is closer to any European state. America was in its whole intellectual and spiritual attitude a society dominated by Niggers and Jews.[30]

On 24 February 1945 Hitler once again took up the central idea of his war speech, while at the same time holding fast onto his racist worldview and anti-Semitic obsessions. The war with America, Hitler dictated for posterity, was a tragic chain of events, as nonsensical as it was against all reason. But an unfortunate historical accident had decreed that his own assumption of power should coincide with the very moment in which "the chosen representative of world Jewry, Roosevelt, took over the helm at the White House." In Hitler's eyes this war was senseless, for "Germany makes no demands of the United States, and it has nothing whatever to fear from Germany. All the conditions for peaceful coexistence exist, each state in its own sphere. But everything is being fouled up by the Jew, who has chosen the United States as his mightiest bulwark. That and that alone spoils and poisons everything."[31]

By way of conclusion, I would like to stray a little beyond the formal confines of my topic—Hitler's perception of Roosevelt and the United States—and turn once more to the years of 1940 and 1941, the two years that were decisive in terms of Hitler's policy toward America.

As we have seen, there existed for Hitler no genuine grounds for conflict between the two states, because in his worldview the natural and legitimate sphere of influence of the German Reich lay in Europe, while that of the United States lay in the Western Hemisphere. Hitler had always considered the global definition of American national interest by Roosevelt and the Internationalists as impertinent and presumptuous. What Hitler wanted from the United States was what he had always wanted from Great Britain: to be all wed carte blanche in Europe. Consequently, the overriding objective of Hitler's U.S. policies from the summer of 1940 up to the Declaration of War consisted in keeping the United States, with Japan's help, out of the European theater, while refusing to let himself be deterred from his conquest of continental Europe by any U.S. intervention. After 3 September 1939 the United States was also a crucial factor in Hitler's repeated attempts to force England into recognizing his "New Order" in Europe and accepting peace on his terms. By July 1940, however, Hitler was forced to recognize that England was not going to make peace and that American support played no minor part in this decision; as a result, the United States moved more and more to center stage in his strategy of a global "Blitzkrieg." Roosevelt was putting Hitler under pressure, making him run out of time. The Führer had to "solve" his problems in continental Europe before the United States was in a position, politically and militarily, to intervene in Europe directly. Hence deterring the United States took on a pivotal role in Hitler's global strategy form the summer of 1940. Two of his statements, made one year apart in July of 1940 and 1941, express the dilemma very plainly: "England is pinning its hopes on Russia and the United States. If the Russian hope is eliminated, America is eliminated as well, because the dropping away of Russia means a tremendous increase in the status of Japan in the Far East" (July 31, 1940). "If we can keep the United States out of the war at all, then only by destroying Russia and then only if Japan and Germany act unambiguously and with cold determination" (July, 14, 1941).[32]

To sum up, if we distill the foregoing, the following essential point emerges: As of the summer of 1940 Hitler no longer thought of the United States without also thinking of Japan. Without Japan the United States could neither be deterred from entering the war in Europe—and this was for Hitler the purpose of the Three Power Pact signed on 27 September 1940—nor was it possible to wage, let alone win, a war against the United States. In my opinion, this basic fact holds the key to answering the question—a question much debated among scholars and one to which only hypothetical answers are possible, given the nature of the source materials—of why Germany declared war on the United States on 11 December 1941, four days after the Japanese attack on Pearl Harbor. This decision remains a puzzling one because it does not appear to make any sense—even in the only language Hitler claimed to understand, that of power. Neither the British Empire nor the Soviet Union had as yet been defeated. To declare war on the potentially most powerful country on earth under such circumstances must appear as megalomania, as a suicidal loss of any sense of reality, and as a dangerous gamble risking the very existence of the German Reich. If there is any sort of rational explanation for this act in terms of power politics, it must be sought in the Japanese alliance.

Without knowing of the impending Japanese attack on Pearl Harbor, Hitler had decided, by 4 December at the latest, to accede to Japanese demands for a mutual assistance pact among Germany, Japan, and Italy in case of a Japanese opening of hostilities against the United States, subject to the stipulation that the other two powers agreed to fight until a common victory had been achieved and not to seek a separate peace. This treaty was duly signed in Berlin on 11 December shortly before the German Declaration of War was handed over in Washington and before Hitler had delivered his speech to the Reichstag. Hitler seemed to have assumed that war with the United States was now inevitable, and that the only chance for the Third Reich to succeed in such a war and to keep the United States out of Europe lay in embroiling the United States in a two-front war waged simultaneously in Europe and Asia, in the Atlantic and the Pacific; for, as Hitler explained to Japan's Ambassador Hiroshi Oshima on 3 January 1942: "The Führer is of the opinion that England can be destroyed. What he did not know as yet, was how the United States might be defeated."[33]

12

MUSSOLINI AND FRANKLIN D. ROOSEVELT

Maurizio Vaudagna

Franklin D. Roosevelt and Benito Mussolini often expressed the wish to meet personally—an event that never happened however.[1] It was perhaps a lucky occurrence because they would have learned that, both in terms of political vision and personal style, "the two leaders—as historian John P. Diggins has remarked—never really understood one another."[2]

Their cultural background and their political purpose were deeply different. Roosevelt had nothing in common with the fascist values deeply rooted in Mussolini's vision: the notion of parliamentary democracy as an unending give-and-take on behalf of petty interests, the myth of the nation-in-arms, the expansionist mission of a vigorous people. Roosevelt's political culture was grounded in the idea that reform was the best way to save democracy, and he thought in terms of the Protestant ethic of public service.

Mussolini's background placed the Italian duce even further apart from Roosevelt and America. He was born in 1883 in a small village in central Italy. His father, an artisan of modest means and socialist leanings, had chosen young Mussolini's name, in the tradition of Jacobin and anarchistic imagery, in memory of Benito Juarez, the Mexican revolutionary leader and tyrannicide. Having grown up within the ranks of socialism, which Mussolini interpreted, however, with a notable tinge of irrationalism and antipositivist spirit, after World War I he was able to capitalize on the sense of uncertainty and fear shared by public employees, military officers, and small shopkeepers, a lower middle class to which Mussolini's mentality and life-style were particularly close.

Once in power, his private life was modeled after that of top public bureaucrats. He shared both conformist habits and double standards, and he was certainly a very far cry from the heroic imagery of the willpower and even more from a consumer-oriented and cosmopolitan "Americanization," in which, stressed Beniamino De Ritis, leading Americanist of *Il Corriere della Sera*, "women lived further and further from home and the fridge was the substitute of the kitchen."[3]

In international matters Mussolini was radically opposed to the Wilsonian ideal of a peaceful, liberal order among nations that, on the contrary, permeated Roosevelt's notion of the place of America in the world. By the 1930s the duce came to share a view of fascism as a higher order of the spirit based on individual self-sacrifice and abnegation and, as such, radically opposed to the meaningless lure of material affluence that in the 1920s and 1930s came increasingly to be identified with American Model T's and smiling movie stars.[4] Mussolini's frame of mind could hardly be more distant from the spirit of noblesse oblige, the civil religion of public service, and the enlightened rationalism of the "Country Squire in the White House."

Mussolini and Roosevelt had, however, something in common: They both had to face an economic emergency first, a war emergency afterward, and in the 1930s both came to lead social and economic "experiments" that attracted the attention of international public opinion. Both were also pragmatic politicians. Therefore, in spite of their presiding over different political orders, a fact that convinced Roosevelt to state that Mussolini and Stalin were "blood brothers,"[5] in 1933 and 1934 a feeling of sympathy and confidence developed between the American reformer and the Italian fascist, grounded not so much in the effort to understand each other's political philosophy as in the convergence of mutual interests. The initial understanding weakened as the armed confrontation between fascism and democracy emerged on the horizon. In Roosevelt's eyes, Mussolini came to be gradually transformed from the "admirable Italian gentleman" of 1933 into the "backstabber" of 1940.[6] The duce who in 1933 and 1934 had thought of Roosevelt as the fearless leader who moved America along the path of the corporatist economy—that is, "towards the economy of the twentieth century"[7]—in 1941 likened him to Sulla, the bloodthirsty Roman emperor, "a modest dilettante when compared to Roosevelt."[8] However, the spirit of understanding was not without consequence even later. Until the eve of Italy's entry into the war, Roosevelt tried to build a personal relationship with Mussolini as a way to distance the Italian dictator from Germany. In turn, until war propaganda came to prevail, the antidemocratic rhetoric of the duce was more moderate in tone when addressed to the United States than to Great Britain.

The needs of Italian foreign policy and, to a lesser extent, domestic consensus presided over the image of Roosevelt expounded by Mussolini and the fascist press. Changes in international relations between Italy and the United States brought about parallel changes in the picture of the New Deal, which in turn had to fit into the congratulatory self-celebration of the regime. As a result the fascist image of the American president went through two different stages. Italian-American relations had been basically very friendly from the mid-1920s until as late as 1935. In 1933 and 1934 Mussolini took part in the public discussion on the nature of the New Deal and wrote several very favorable articles. The interventionist state and the centralized political power that the Roosevelt experiment seemed to be building came to be interpreted as a breakaway from the liberal tradition and a move in the direction of the fascist example. In 1935 Italian relations with the United States worsened sharply because of the aggression against Ethiopia, and they would never return to the older harmony.[9] In Italy interest in the New Deal declined and Mussolini volunteered no further opinions in public. The fascist image of the American president changed: The Roosevelt experiment was considered a failure because the country was immature and the presidential leadership ineffective. America moved away from the path opened by fascism and fell back into the arms of "rugged individualism," which, however, amounted to chaos, social strife, and ultimately war. European antimodernism was at the root of the anti-American imagery expounded by fascist commentators between 1934 and 1938, a rationale that later merged with racism and anti-Semitism to frame the image of America in Italian war propaganda.[10]

Mussolini borrowed the images needed to paint the fascist picture of Roosevelt from two cultural traditions. On the one hand there was the polemic against "plutodemocracy," parliamentary institutions, and modern industrial life, of which the United States was an important part. This imagery was specifically fascist but, in the case of the United States, it merged with a long tradition of European stereotypes of America that had increasingly solidified since the eighteenth century. The European "dispute over the New World" was made up of diverse and contradictory images that, as had happened in the past with the myths of the Orient and Eldorado, had more to do with European hopes and fears than with American reality.[11] In the 1930s Italian elites had little information about America, were unfamiliar with its culture, spoke no English, even if the cosmopolitan upper middle class in the big cities had recently adapted American luxuries, and the regimented press attacked, in a craze of petty nationalist pride, the use of items and words such as "sandwich," "cocktail," "whiskey," and "jazz." Because real information was wanting, these images of America that were commonplace in Italy at the time were often nothing else but a sort of imaginary geography to express concepts such as dynamism, youth, and orientation to the future on the one hand or materialism, alienation, and mass regimentation on the other. What resulted was a set of two-sided, interchangeable stereotypes with opposite value implications: When America was said to be young, young meant either lively and courageous or inexperienced and rootless. Mussolini's vision of America was a combination of fascist irrationalism and traditional stereotypes that, depending on expediency, allowed him to resort either to the higher mission of the "young nations" shared by both Italy and the United States or to the disparaging European myth of America as a land short of history and culture.[12]

When Franklin D. Roosevelt took office in 1933, eleven years after the Italian "March on Rome," international relations between the United States and Italy were undergoing a period of transition. Since the mid-1920s Italy had pursued a policy of goodwill toward the United States and had promptly followed U.S. guidelines in matters of war debts, financial stabilization, disarmament, and international economic policy. By 1931 Foreign Minister Dino Grandi had framed a coherent policy based on the friendship with the Anglo-Saxon powers that had resulted in increasing international prestige, domestic stabilization, and a large influx of American investments.

In the early 1930s, however, the preconditions of Italian-American friendship were slowly vanishing. America was badly weakened by the depression. Its former position as the leading actor in international economic matters could not be sustained any longer. Hitler's access to power transformed the nature of fascism from a political order limited to Italy into the regime of a group of countries strongly established in the heart of Europe and apparently rapidly growing in number. The so-called Italian beggar imperialism, which fascism had inherited from the colonial spirit of late nineteenth century liberalism and which could nourish only limited territorial ambitions, was replaced by a forceful attack on the international order laid down by the Treaty of Versailles. Italian-American relations ceased to be mainly bilateral and slowly became a part of a larger confrontation between contrasting ways of life.

In the Italian domestic arena the regime was consolidating consensus and extolling the glories of the "Fascist Century." The monstrous celebrations of the ten-year anniversary of the seizure of power amplified the nationalist myth of the "Third Rome" and of the new empire. The "Fascist Revolution" claimed to have put into practice the requirements of the twentieth century that the depression had dramatically highlighted: a unified decision-making process; state regulation of the economy; the end of class struggle thanks to the corporatist order; the bond between the leader, the people, and the nation. In such a self-congratulatory atmosphere, whenever a new response to the depression was able to capture the attention of international public opinion, it was the duty of the commentators of fascism (and of its numerous admirers in the democratic ranks) to interpret the new experiment as an incomplete but hopeful attempt to follow in the line of Italian fascism. It comes to no surprise that in Italy the New Deal, which at the time enjoyed an enormous popularity, was bound to be treated accordingly.[13]

The interest in Roosevelt and the New Deal peaked in 1933-34. The duce's positive response was based on two lines of thought: The first was the notion of a Roosevelt dictatorship. According to this image, the American "duce" was concentrating absolute powers in his hands in order to be able to face the problems of the emergency. Second, the New Deal's statism and economic interventionism (especially the National Recovery Administration, the most important measure of industrial reconstruction), were building a new socioeconomic order somewhat similar to the Italian corporatist state.

In 1932 Roosevelt's election was not greeted by any particular enthusiasm. It was, on the contrary, mainly interpreted as a repudiation of Herbert Hoover in favor of a competitor whose political profile was still rather unclear. Fascist commentators mainly stressed his Wilsonian background. They hoped Roosevelt would weaken American isolationism and take the lead in seeking financial stabilization and the increase in international trade.

When, however, in his inaugural address in March 1933 Roosevelt vigorously vindicated strong leadership and wide-ranging executive powers to meet the depression, the atmosphere among fascist commentators suddenly changed. On 7 March 1933 *Il Popolo d'Italia*, the official daily of the Fascist party, devoted its front-page comment not to the German elections, which were opening the access to power for Hitler, but to the presidential speech, whose appeal in favor of centralized, discretionary powers was considered to be following the fascist example. In spring and summer 1933 the emergency legislation of the first "hundred days" marked the most centralizing and charismatic phase of the New Deal. Hitler's and Roosevelt's parallel successes were considered two different but convergent signs that the Italian example was of lasting, historic importance, and at the same time fascist commentators and observers drew an endless number of parallels between the New Deal and Mussolini's achievement.[14]

Both Roosevelt and the fascist leader wished to continue the cordial relations that had existed under President Herbert Hoover. In the spring of 1933 the exchange of courtesies was particularly warm. The new American ambassador, Breckinridge Long, a rather enthusiastic admirer of fascism and the corporatist state, delivered a copy of that very address which had sparked so much enthusiasm in Italian circles to the duce on behalf of the president. Mussolini replied that he would keep the present "as a token of your friendship" and that "relations between the United States and Italy had never been so cordial and friendly."[15] The Italian leader had not abandoned his old taste for journalism. His columns in *Il Popolo d'Italia* were meant to clarify the guidelines and the limits that public information was to follow. Partly because the American president was enjoying a very positive response from public opinion, in 1933 and 1934 Mussolini devoted careful attention to the New Deal. The American experiment allowed him to advance a number of insights as to where the political and social systems of the industrialized countries were heading.

In the first place Mussolini found parallels between Italy and the United States in Roosevelt's alleged wish to ignore Congress and the Constitution, "the ideological fossil from the eighteenth century." It was a theme that returned again and again in the fascist polemic against representative institutions. Fascist comments on the "cloudy American electoral campaign" of 1932 had sounded the theme of mass irrationalism, of the "phantom of the multitudinous and diverse crowd," manipulated by party machines and candidates who were unwilling to discuss any real issue beyond prohibition and beer.[16] The legislation of the first "hundred days" did include an exceptional delegation of power, and an article in the National Industrial Recovery Act (which was actually never enforced) allowed the president to stop production in any company if the national emergency so required. As a consequence the notion of a "Roosevelt dictatorship" emerged in fascist comments of the New Deal throughout the 1930s: It was a sign of sympathy in the first phase and a rebuttal of Roosevelt's criticisms of Italian authoritarian politics in the second.

"That of Roosevelt is a dictatorship"—argued Mussolini in *Il Popolo d'Italia* in June 1933—because "the American Congress has granted Roosevelt full powers." The same notion was repeated in the most detailed analysis the duce would write on the American experiment: a review of Roosevelt's book *Looking Forward*, which had just been published in Italian and "every page [of which] elicits the liveliest interest in the reader."[17] Mussolini portrayed a sort of American "duce" fighting against the obsolete political institutions of his country. FDR's leadership—argued Mussolini in another article of August 1933, "Between Two Civilizations"—was grounded in a unified command, in the model of the army, in heroic willpower. "Roosevelt's actions, moves and orders fall completely outside the guidelines of the will of parliament. There are no intermediaries between him and the nation. There is no parliament but a discipline cabinet office. There is no plurality of parties but one party only. One that will keep all discordant voices silent."[18]

The personalization of politics, which was common in all industrialized countries in the 1930s, allowed Mussolini to interpret the charismatic side of Roosevelt's leadership in the light of the fascist *Führerprinzip*: The unending dragging on of a political market basically identified with Congress was brought to a sudden stop by the willpower of the leader who embodied the principle of the nation and of *Macht*. While it was at the time an unwritten rule of American politics not to mention the president's handicap, the notion of a correspondence between the physical and spiritual qualities of the leader that Mussolini's style translated into the mimic of virility and determination was extended to Roosevelt as well. The duce repeatedly stressed Roosevelt's superior courage arising from the heroic effort to overcome his disease and embodied at the time in the burden of the lonely leadership of a country still unprepared for the changes to come. In Mussolini's eyes Roosevelt's taste for swimming was not so much a matter of therapy but amounted to a principle of physical effort somewhat parallel to the fascist parades in running or to images of the bare-chested duce threshing wheat in the open air. Roosevelt's conservationist cult of nature, which he so fondly recalled, was interpreted in turn in the light of the fascist ruralist myth, with the peasant mother as a symbol of the proletarian nation, the mythologies of land and blood, and the decadent nostalgia for naked bodies in primitive natural surroundings.[19]

All these themes emerged out of significant institutional changes and cultural debates. The growth of executive power was a common event in America as well as in European countries. New Deal planners criticized the burden of American individualism, while the principle of unified command elicited a great deal of interest in America as well as in Europe, where intellectuals of different political backgrounds were busy discussing the advantages of dictatorial leadership. In the first months of his presidency Roosevelt had frequently used the army metaphor, had asked for the relaxation of political strife, had framed the notion of emergency to legitimate legislation that did actually provide for an exceptional delegation of power. The point is that this process was a step in the modernization of liberal and parliamentary politics. Mussolini's interpretation in terms of a de facto

Italian-style dictatorship was a distortion and a propaganda device, possibly to be understood in the climate of these years, characterized by the triumphant "march of fascism" in contrast to the crisis of democracy.

In 1933 and 1934 the second area of interest in Mussolini's image of the New Deal was the parallel between Roosevelt's federal intervention in the economy and the Italian corporatist state, which in the early 1930s, amid the widely held sense that economic ideas had lost any credibility, came to be regarded with a lively interest by a large international audience, and appeared to be, as the British newspaper *The Observer* remarked, "the crowning originality of fascist achievement." As late as 1935 fascist intellectuals were eager to improve the regime's image at home and abroad by pretending that the most developed capitalist countries were following the Italian path.[20] Giuseppe Bottai, the most prominent theorist of the corporatist state and former minister of corporations, wrote a detailed article in *Foreign Affairs* in 1935 on the parallels and differences between the Italian corporatist institutions and the National Recovery Administration (NRA) codes of fair competition that established a federally licensed network of industrial consortiums to control production. When the Supreme Court declared the New Deal law of industrial reconstruction unconstitutional in 1935, fascist commentators of the American scene were unanimous in discerning a comeback of economic liberalism and a sign of individualist immaturity.[21]

The issue was no purely Italian matter. After a much talked about flight over the Atlantic Ocean, Italo Balbo, prestigious minister of aviation, reported to Mussolini about his meeting with Roosevelt, stressing that "the president had words of appreciation for the syndicalist organization of our country." Ambassador Long wrote to Hugh Johnson, administrator of the NRA, that the corporations were "along the lines of the codes which you have been wrestling with." A visit to the peninsula convinced Rexford G. Tugwell, a close advisor to the president and a leader of the New Deal planners, that Italy was a "compact and disciplined nation" . . . "doing many of the things which seem to me necessary." Comparative examinations of economic experiments in different countries, with the corporatist state in prominent position, were pursued by noted American economists such as Ernest Minor Patterson, president of the American Academy of Political and Social Sciences, and Lewis L. Lorwin of the Brookings Institution. The discussion swept through reviews and newspapers on both sides of the ocean, and Italian observers debated vigorously whether the New Deal was a sort of corporatist state in the making or whether the nature of the fascist state made the two systems incomparable in spite of superficial similarities.[22]

Once again Mussolini took part in the discussion, and his opinions set the guidelines every commentator was supposed to follow. The duce's most radical statement came in August 1934 as he reviewed a book written by Henry Agard Wallace: "America is on its way towards the corporatist economy," he stated bluntly. His more detailed analysis in reviewing *Looking Forward* was aimed at moderating the all-out enthusiasm of the most patriotic commentators. Mussolini resorted to a distinction he had developed in 1932 and that by then was a commonplace in the press. The difference with the United States was that Americans considered the crisis to be "in the system" (of laissez-faire capitalism) while the Italians thought of it as a crisis "of the system" that required "a step forward from one stage of civilization into the following." Fascism was "a real Revolution" that had "created the institutions needed to organically meet the problems which are affecting the United States, too." To be sure, Roosevelt was no longer "anchored to the dogmas of economic liberalism." But how much fascism was to be found in the New Deal? "In common with fascism," Mussolini argued, "is the notion that the state cannot but be interested in economic performance" . . . "the atmosphere around the theoretical and practical system [of the New Deal] is certainly akin to that of fascism, but it would be an exaggeration to look for more." Mussolini was very cautious: The follow-up to this article was that the press relegated the New Deal from a "revolution" to an "experiment" and a few well-known columnists calmed down their enthusiasm or even openly criticized their former statements.[23]

Why did the duce move so slowly? Just a few days before the Roosevelt's "bombshell message" had doomed the London Economic Conference to failure, much to the irritation of the "gold bloc" countries to which Italy also belonged. Italian foreign policy had shown long-term concern over financial stabilization whose failure came as a shadow over the formerly idyllic Italian-American relations.

On the other hand Italian self-celebration was the source of counterproductive effects within American government and public opinion. According to Luigi Barzini, a leading Italian columnist, after Balbo's triumphant flight over the ocean Americans were "no longer afraid of the word 'fascism'" and the Italian influence on the New Deal measures was openly admitted. The Italian government was not of the same opinion. Ambassador Augusto Rosso recalled that "when our press rushed to portray Roosevelt as Mussolini's disciple . . . I had the feeling that insisting on this theme was not a good idea, because . . . it seemed likely to me that the word 'fascism' would end up being used in party strife much to the damage of our interests." Republicans, notably former President Hoover, used to label the New Deal as a sort of fascist "regimentation," while populist and anti-monopolistic senators who were often favorable to different aspects of the New Deal, disparagingly branded the NRA as corporatist. The interest in avoiding incidents with the American government and public opinion prevailed over the wish for short-term propaganda gains. The press was still allowed to launch resonant and vacuous appeals to "Americans and Italians sharing common youthfulness, the vital drive of their race, the will and the fever for work." However, when Mussolini's article appeared in July 1933, the government's press service sent out an order that read: "It is not to be emphasized that Roosevelt's policy is fascist because these comments are immediately cabled to the United States and are used by his foes to attack him."[24]

The fascist interest in Roosevelt and the New Deal culminated in 1933 and 1934. Many in the 1930s were in search of "third ways," among them the New Deal and Italian fascism. What was meant varied to a great extent. In the New Deal the notion was that of a "middle way" between laissez faire and systematic public property. Fascists thought on the contrary in terms of a move away from both Washington and Moscow, from capitalist liberalism and class-oriented bolshevism into a new socioeconomic formation. Whatever the differences, however, the term was both obscure and attractive, and the fact that it was used in both countries made for additional common ground. After all, the Italian analysis of the New Deal amounted to a discussion on whether the Roosevelt experiment could be understood as a "third way" in the fascist meaning of the term.

The watershed of 1935 meant that the image of Roosevelt and the New Deal came to be increasingly determined by the tradition of elitist anti-Americanism, a trend that was to accelerate as the outbreak of the war approached. This is not to say that anti-Americanism was absent in the first phase. Disparaging contempt for American civilization was very much a component of the contradictory baggage of fascist ideas, and comprehensive denigrations of America had often emerged in the public debate of the 1920s and early 1930s. The attitude had been, however, more moderate, and anti-Americanism was used to analyze American society while the approach to Roosevelt and the New Deal utilized a different set of ideas.

Italian interest in the international arena continued to condition fascist attitudes toward America. In 1933 and 1934 the system of interdependence that had presided over the European situation of the 1920s was breaking down. Autarchy based on the expansion of the war industry was growing stronger in the dictatorial countries. When Germany and Japan withdrew from the League of Nations, the breakdown of the international system appeared evident and thunders of war began to be heard in the distance.

In 1935 Italy was busy in a colonial adventure that was bound to be inimical to French and British interests. The consequence was that the march which would bring Italy to the side of Nazi Germany started in Ethiopia. Relations with the United States quickly worsened, even if many ambiguities remained. America openly criticized the increasing aggressiveness of Italian fascism. In January 1936 Roosevelt mentioned the "twin spirits of autocracy and aggression."[25] Domestic isolationism, however, left the president little ground to counter the Fascists effectively, and, on the other hand, after 1937 Roosevelt still held on to the hope of convincing Mussolini to resume his old role of "Hitler's watchman" or of getting the duce out of his alliance with Germany. As a result the anti-Italian polemic took a more moderate tone, and the American president made several efforts to keep the personal relationship with Mussolini alive.

Italy also had very good reasons to try to moderate the new confrontational climate with the United States. The purpose of the Italian policy toward America was now the exact opposite of the pre-Ethiopian era. Internationalism, which would inevitably align America on the side of Britain, was to be restrained. Isolationism was the new partner because it allowed Italy to pursue its territorial expansion freely while in no way preventing fascism from benefiting from trade with the United States. The large deliveries of oil to Italy by American companies during the Ethiopian war had been a case in point. Roosevelt, on the contrary, and his popular New Deal were more and more identified with the democratic alternative to the "march of fascism."

From 1935 to 1938 the image of Roosevelt and the New Deal was slowly reversed compared to the pattern of 1933 to 1934, a trend that appeared to be still uncertain and contradictory as late as 1938, to turn then more radical and vulgar after 1939 and in the war propaganda. Mussolini did not volunteer opinions on American domestic affairs and until 1937 made several attempts to rebuild at least the façade of the old friendly relations. The press still approvingly reported the birth of the Social Security Act and the large public works appropriation, and timidly reaffirmed the notion that the welfare and public works policies of the fascist regime had inspired the American measures. A number of journalists were quietly happy with Roosevelt's electoral victory in 1936.

In spite of this, the old understanding had gone forever and nationalist, traditionalist anti-Americanism merged with the antimodernist and anti-bourgeois atmosphere of late fascism.[26] The official contempt for America was countered by persisting sympathies. For example, the cosmopolitan middle class, led by the duce's son, Arnoldo Mussolini, still had a craze for American movies, and the daily *La Stampa* from Torino tried to keep a more balanced posture in harmony with the pro-New Deal attitude of the Agnelli family. In general the criticism of America did not reach the radical tones used against Britain, at least until war propaganda took over.

Fascist anti-American images of Roosevelt and the New Deal consisted in a mirrorlike reversal of the previous attitudes, which often did not even need to change as long as a negative value implication was attached to them. So the partner preferred by fascist commentators was now Congress, which was supposed to put a brake on the administration's Wilsonian preferences while anti-British isolationist senators were often quoted in the Italian press. It goes without saying that all fascist columnists became "America Firsters" as the war approached.

The antiliberal polemic remained at the center of the stage in the post-1935 fascist image of America. In 1933 the hope was cherished that a vigorous, bold leadership would pressure a country burdened by liberalism but youthful and vital into making a move. In 1934, a year of transition in the fascist vision of the New Deal, Mussolini still cautiously recalled the comparison with fascism. "Judgement on this experiment," said the duce, "is to be suspended and we must wait."[27] From 1935 the opinion was advanced that all attempts at fascist-inspired modernization had failed and that the United States had reverted back into democratic chaos, feeding strife, disorder, and ultimately war. In that same year, as Italian-American relations were very strained, the Supreme Court ruled that the NRA, together with several other New Deal pieces of legislation, was unconstitutional, which in the eyes of Italian observers meant that the New Deal had crumbled.

A centerpiece of anti-American criticism was the notion that democracy was but a fake. Liberal institutions were instrumental in hiding the domination on the part of "magnates of industry and finance." The fall of the NRA announced the final parting of the ways between fascism and the New Deal, which coincided, however, with "the return of reactionary America."[28] Borrowing from the criticism of American acquisitive materialism, the United States was not described as a democracy but as a "plutocracy" in disguise or as opportunistic authoritarianism short of vigor and virtue and dedicated to deceiving and manipulating the citizenry.

The theme of the "Roosevelt dictatorship" was kept alive and took additional strength from its being aired in American public debate as well. Democratic electoral victories in 1934 and 1936 fed on the illusion that American politics was de facto moving toward a one-party system. More often, however, the issue was instrumental in denigrating Roosevelt's criticism and fascism. "How could that be done," *Il Corriere della Sera* asked in early 1936, by "the representative of a country where there is no real democracy but an autocracy that the president manages to dissimulate?"[29]

In the international arena the Italian role was described as part of a worldwide struggle between civilization and barbarism. If the United States turned its eyes away from the fascist model and opposed the mission of Italy in the world arena, the result was that America would fall backward into a more primitive stage of civilization. If, as Fascists claimed, Haile Selassie's Ethiopian empire was characterized by the shame of slavery, then the Ethiopian war ran parallel to the American Civil War while the U.S. administration was unable to pick up the emancipationist banner of Abraham Lincoln.[30] The struggle against the people that "deserves the merit of the discovery of America" coincided with the plunge of the United States into chaos and disorder, and the alleged victory of "rugged individualism" went hand in hand with a growing number of articles depicting the United States as a country of social anomie, full of thefts and kidnappings, and a land of hurricanes, floods, and earthquakes. Even more often fascist commentators described the social arena in the United States as that of a country ravaged by communism and social discord, as the widely reported San Francisco general strike of 1934 or the sit-ins of the automobile workers in early 1937 had demonstrated.

The fascist myth of the "duce" suggested that the responsibility for American decadence had to be attributed to Roosevelt's leadership, which, with the passing of time, would turn into the privileged target of an increasingly radical sense of contempt. Here again former attitudes were reversed. The American president started to be addressed as "il signor Roosevelt," which in Italian sounds sarcastic, condescending, and slightly contemptuous. While Roosevelt was depicted as bold and fearless in 1933, he then became confused "amateurish, lacking in plans and motivation," as Luigi Barzini, Jr., said in October 1936. "Not much is left of four years of effort . . . perhaps Roosevelt did not have the stature of a reformer."[31] War propaganda of 1941 stressed that American "plutocracy" . . . "is now seeking in war a surrogate for those experiments in which Roosevelt failed to cure the economy of the United States."[32]

After 1941 war propaganda became more and more vulgar and concentrated its attacks against the person of the president and his wife. A new reversal, a very disgusting one, was then effected: His paralysis was no longer portrayed as a challenge to his willpower but as the symptom of the president's and the nation's moral decay. Roosevelt was not "the heir to the anti-British spirit of Abraham Lincoln" but was insulted as an "infantile paralytic," a "megalomaniac from a psychiatric ward."[33] When Roosevelt launched the peace message of 15 April 1939, Mussolini stated in private conversations that it could have been conceived only by a man on the verge of mental illness and attacked by progressive paralysis.[34] Since the approval of the anti-Jewish laws of 1938, racism and anti-Semitism merged and both became the central feature of wartime anti-Americanism. Roosevelt was then defined a "Jew of Dutch extraction" and the "slave of the world Jewish-Masonic alliance."[35]

War propaganda had its roots in antimodernism, which was widespread in the European countries during the depression but had already existed since America made its massive appearance on the European scene at the end of the nineteenth century. Michela Nacci has argued that fascist anti-Americanism "was more radical, more malevolent in its attacks against Americans and ranged from irony to sarcasm."[36]

As the Italian military situation grew more hopeless, war propaganda grew correspondingly more radical and vulgar. However, the stereotype of a "Wilson's and Roosevelt's America which was shamefully rich . . . plutocratic and doctrinaire, greedy and fanatic, cynical and childish . . ."[37] was not believed by a population whose greatest majority had neither liked the German alliance nor welcomed the war. Many Italians, on the contrary, under the influence of relatives and acquaintances who had emigrated, thought of America as "the land of opportunity." After 1941, military defeats in Greece and Northern Africa made it impossible for Mussolini to enjoy any independent influence in the conduct of the war. "Mussolini's fate was sealed," thought Winston Churchill when America's entry into the war was announced.[38] By 1942 many groups inside the country knew that the war was lost and that continuation of the fighting would lead to ruin. At that point many Italians started to think that it was the United States which could utilize its Wilsonian tradition, its rich resources, its distance from European quarrels to putItaly back on its feet. [39]

13

FRANCO AND FRANKLIN D. ROOSEVELT

Javier Tusell

Apparently the question concerning the relationship between FDR and Franco can be stated in a very simple way: Their political ideals were radically antithetical, in a way more so than, say, those of Roosevelt and Mussolini. Although Franco was temporarily tempted by the appeal of fascism, he was in fact a conservative Catholic military dictator. He considered democratic liberalism, which he identified with Freemasonry, not just an unacceptable doctrine but one leading inexorably to communism. It could be argued that his political notions were predemocratic, while fascism was a postdemocratic doctrine. Roosevelt represented instead the attunement of the democratic ideal to the challenges that faced humanity in the difficult circumstances of the 1930s. Their worlds were consequently both antithetical and, above all, far removed from each other. It is not surprising then that there was never the least understanding between them.

But the matter has other revealing aspects. The relationship between both men is interesting because it leads to the problem of how the American president attempted to implement his ideals on global foreign policy with regard to a second-rate nation that only occasionally turned up among his basic interests. An investigation of relations between Spain and the United States from the time Franco began to play a relevant political role in the former will help specify Roosevelt's attitude toward a conflict that could affect world peace, his views on the options of neutrality versus intervention in an internal struggle where the future of one country's democracy was at stake, and his position regarding those who during World War II were, to say the least, benign to the Axis powers and to their continuance after 1945. Moreover, this relationship poses at heart some major issues, such as the relationship of means to ends, that have remained as problems in the foreign policy of all democracies.

ROOSEVELT AND THE SPANISH CIVIL WAR

Some commentators have interpreted American policy toward the Second Spanish Republic as resulting from a "malevolent neutrality" that would explain the republic's state of defenselessness when Franco's rebellion started in July 1936.[1] However, such a view does not seem fair. It is belied by the fact that in 1933 Claude G. Bowers, a militant Democrat, not a professional diplomat, and a friend of Roosevelt's who always identified the republic with his New Deal, was appointed ambassador to Spain. In his correspondence with the American president, he always showed a great admiration for Manuel Azaña and even found similarities between some Spanish Socialist leaders, such as Fernando de los Rios, and the American Democratic party. The former Spanish minister himself accepted such similarities, which explains his later appointment as ambassador to Washington. Bowers was not always well informed about the Spanish situation, and he insistently interpreted events with a partisan view. That would explain why he was frequently ignored by the State Department. However, as an important member of the Democratic party and someone who fully agreed with Roosevelt's fundamental aims, he was always heeded by the president.[2]

To understand Roosevelt's attitude toward the Spanish Civil War, both his sympathy for the republic and the state of affairs in the United States must be taken into account. The presumed passivity of the American president faced with the triumph of fascism in Spain must be seen not from the 1945 point of view but keeping in mind that the "appeasement" policy was, to some extent, shared by all democratic powers until 1939. Roosevelt was indeed, as we shall see, one of the democratic leaders who had stronger doubts about neutrality in the Spanish conflict. On the other hand, the determination to keep out of any European conflict was based not only on the resolutions of 1935 and 1936 but also on American general sentiment. Even Ernest Hemingway, who would later appear on the scene of the Spanish war, shared in this feeling. Furthermore, the years of the Spanish Civil War saw a great increase in the internal difficulties that confronted the president in Congress, which helped to paralyze his action in the Spanish conflict.[3]

All these facts help to explain Roosevelt's attitude concerning the Spanish Civil War.[4] In this respect, as well as in that of World War II, one must distinguish between the position of the American diplomats in Spain and that of the State Department and Roosevelt himself. The course of events must also be taken into account.

Bowers's position was from the beginning as supportive and enthusiastic as his attitude toward the republic had been. He never suggested direct intervention in Spain's internal affairs because that would have meant a great diversion from the current American foreign policy. But his sympathy for the cause of the Popular Front was always abundantly clear. He thought the Axis nations were at war with Spain's legitimate institutions. The rebellion, planned immediately after the 1936 elections (a statement Roosevelt underlined in the letter he got from Bowers), would take Spain back to the sixteenth century. There was no communist threat in Spain, democratic legality was observed. What is remarkable about this attitude is the extent to which it differed from that of the other representatives of democratic nations in Spain. Like the British and French ambassadors, Bowers spent the Civil War pe iod in French territory near the Spanish border. But he disagreed with their opposition to the Popular Front. Now he believed intervention to be a "sinister farce." On many occasions he felt outraged by the press, which he denounced for not reflecting the atrocities perpetrated by the right. When the Francoist authorities attempted to explain the reopening of the American consulate in Bilbao as a sign of recognition of the regime, Bowers insisted on keeping it closed. Bowers introduced the Spanish ambassador, de los Rios, to Roosevelt as a personal friend and, in January 1939, when the war was almost at its end and Franco's victory was evident, he described his regime as "hostile to the United States, to its leaders and its politics."[5] It might be argued that his position had no real bearing on the shaping of American foreign policy. However, such a view would ignore the fact that he was kept as ambassador even though his position diverged widely from that of the British and the French. And, when the war was over, he was even appointed to a new embassy, that of Chile, another nation with a Popular Front government. One must conclude, then, that he certainly influenced Roosevelt's attitude, as the correspondence between them proves.

In his memoirs Bowers suggests that Secretary of State Cordell Hull's attitude toward the Spanish Civil War was one of appeasement. Such a statement is of course an exaggeration, but there was in fact a significant difference of opinion between the two men. Hull himself remarks that Bowers did not seem to realize that no effort should be spared in order to avoid a general armed conflict. He also reminds us that the policy toward the Spanish struggle was also approved by isolationists, who saw in it an end to the risk of an American involvement in the European war, and internationalists, who were prepared to collaborate with the other democratic nations, mainly Great Britain. Hull writes that this policy was decided on with unaccustomed celerity and unanimity. He adds that, on the whole, the Spanish Civil War was not the cause of the outbreak of World War II.[6] All these statements are true. On the whole, it is safe to say that the attitude of the State Department was in agreement with the neutralist tenets of American foreign policy, seeking at the same time to align with British policies toward the Spanish Civil War.

Roosevelt's position concerning the Spanish Civil War and the new dictatorial regime under Franco moved, then, between these two fundamental poles. The policy of the United States was clearly closer to the neutralist option, but the notion remained that in a conflict in which a legal regime had been destroyed, partially due to the intervention of fascist powers, some mode of intervention would have been advisable. That would explain why Roosevelt's position, although decided at an early stage and on a general agreement, was on several occasions on the verge of being reversed and why, although maintained until the very end, it became so deeply unsatisfactory for the very person who advocated it.

Even before the State Department made clear its determination not to intervene in the Spanish conflict at the beginning of August 1936, the sale of fuel to the warships of the belligerent nations had already been discouraged.[7] The instructions of 7 August 1936 to the American diplomatic representatives avoided the term "neutrality" and made no mention of "civil war," but prescribed a strict abstention from any interference in the Spanish affairs. Thus Bowers was even urged not to attend those meetings sponsored by the resid nt diplomatic corps in Spain intended for the achievement of peace through mediati n.

At first, Roosevelt seems to have been deeply concerned about the "unfortunate and terrible Spanish tragedy," as Bowers wrote.[8] What worried him most, though, was its potential to precipitate a general European conflict. For this reason, the possibility of altering the current legislation was suggested at a time when the self-defeating effects of the nonintervention policy then being enforced by European democracies had not yet been perceived. Neutrality laws did not apply to internal national conflicts, so Roosevelt could only propose a "moral embargo" such as had been applied in the case of the Ethiopian conflict. Thus he described the sale of arms to the Republicans as "legal, but totally unpatriotic."

In January 1937, in order to fill a legal gap, the U.S. Senate and Congress voted for an embargo on the Spanish conflict with only one negative vote. They even vetoed sales through a third country. This decision became legally binding in May, also by a significant majority. The new neutrality act was firm and did not allow the president to act according to circumstances. It did not contemplate assisting a legal regime threatened by foreign subversion with the participation of other nations. At the time, Roosevelt did not wish to encourage a debate that would put his other reforms, such as the judicial reform, at risk. Neither was he inclined to request discretionary powers at a time when he was being charged with dictatorial attitudes.[8] Above all, he was not able to foresee the potential danger of such a neutrality in the Spanish case. He assured the socialist Norman Thomas, who supported the republic, that a policy seeking to discriminate between the parts in a civil conflict would be extremely dangerous. Other complaints arose from isolationist quarters: The progressive senator Gerald P. Nye declared himself in favor of an embargo on all arms trade except that which would benefit an American nation under attack from a non-American nation.

At first, the importance of these types of complaints was limited, but they became fiercer during the summer of 1937 when the intervention of Italy and Germany in favor of Franco became evident. Then both Thomas and Nye suggested that there was a state of war between Germany-Italy and the Spanish Republic, and they consequently requested an extension of the arms embargo to those nations. Thus the paradox arose that an internationalist such as Roosevelt would use noninterventionist arguments while an isolationist like Nye was more prepared to aid the Spanish Republic than the president himself.[10] But it was this latter attitude that caused Roosevelt's first doubts about the advisability of neutrality, as implemented so far. He subsequently requested Hull to write to the American ambassadors in Paris and London asking their opinion about the isolationist contention. Their answer was that from a technical point of view there was not a state of war between the republic and the fascist powers. Furthermore, it would have been necessary to apply an embargo on the Soviet Union and France as well. Roosevelt added these reasons to the argument that any extension of the embargo could endanger attempts at mediation.[11]

If by 1937 it had become apparent that American neutrality mostly benefited Franco, who had no difficulty in buying arms while the Republic was faced with the closing of the American market, the situation became even more evident in 1938. In May Nye proposed that the embargo on the Republican government be lifted. By then Roosevelt had realized the disadvantages of American neutrality but, at the same time, did not want the act of May 1937 repealed and still faced serious difficulties in domestic policy. He contemplated the solution of authorizing Bowers's presence on the Republican side as an indirect sign of solidarity with their cause. He also wrote him in August that he felt "dismayed" by the nonintervention policy of Great Britain and he trusted that "a bit later on, if the situation in Czechoslovakia does not end up in disaster, some kind of move is possible that will at least help to terminate the Spanish Civil War."[12]

In the final months of 1938 and the beginning of 1939, both Roosevelt and a great number of his advisors were aware that the attitude toward the Spanish Civil War had been a mistake that must be corrected. At the time the American president supported a negotiated agreement between the parties, through the mediation of the Vatican or some Latin American country, but this solution never materialized mainly because it had come too late. Franco's victory, which divided the opposition and created a clear material superiority, did not allow it. Besides, Roosevelt was still confronted by the same problems in domestic policy. Nevertheless, in November he submitted for consultation whether his right to lift the embargo on the republic could be sustained. Some of his advisors—Harold Ickes, for instance—supported this solution. But Hull's interpretation, according to which only Congress had the power to lift the embargo and any change would mean "a possibility of complications," prevailed.[13] By the end of 1938 at any rate, a lifting of the embargo would have meant a scant benefit for the Republican government, which lacked the money to buy arms.

Another factor that played a major role in the decision-making paralysis that overcame the American government with respect to the Spanish Civil War was the division about the conflict within American society itself.[14] In the final months of the war, American opinion clearly supported the republic, with only 14 percent supporting Franco. In liberal and intellectual circles the opposition to Franco was even more overwhelming. In the United States, however, as in the rest of the world, Franco enjoyed a great following among Catholics. Indeed this fact explains why Roosevelt avoided discussing the issue of the Spanish Civil War in the 1936 campaign, since it could alienate a part of the electorate.[15] From the end of 1937 onward, after the publication of the pastoral letter from the Spanish bishops supporting Franco, the great majority of the American Catholic media adhered to the military revolt. The journals *The Commonweal* and *The Catholic Worker*, where Dorothy Day wrote, took a more neutral position. Thus two bitter controversies developed, between Catholics on the one hand and Protestants and Jews on the other, which seemed to ignite a kind of religious confrontation uncommon in the United States. In fact, neither part was well informed about the situation in Spain, but Spain had become a cause of confrontation for the whole world. American Catholics, whose influence was not strong enough to change the general attitude of public opinion, did play an important role in stopping the embargo on the sale of arms to Spain from being revoked.[16]

By the final weeks of the civil war, Roosevelt was already convinced that his policy had been "a serious mistake," something he duly communicated to Bowers and the members of his cabinet. In his view the best policy would have been to veto only the transport of munition to the belligerent parties. His uneasiness concerning this matter is evident in his belated recognition of Franco. Only in February 1939, when Great Britain and France were about to establish relations with Spain, did Hull suggest to Roosevelt some contacts with Franco's representatives in Paris. The date set for the effective recognition of the victorious government emerging from the civil war was the same as that of the final victory. The day before, de los Rios, Republican ambassador to the United States, had formally bid farewell to Hull. On that same day, 1 April, Eleanor Roosevelt telegraphed her husband requesting that the State Department intervene in favor of those Republicans who still remained in Madrid. Her husband assured her that it would be done.[17] Bowers and those who sympathized with the Republican cause throughout the war also attempted to assist them, but in practice they hardly achieved anything.

WORLD WAR II

All the above must be kept in mind if Roosevelt and the U.S. attitude toward Spain and Franco during World War II is to be well understood. A revealing episode is worth mentioning here: When the first American ambassador in Franco's Spain, Alexander Weddell, was appointed, he asked Roosevelt whether he should bear any message from the president. Roosevelt replied that Franco should be reminded that FDR "did not like dictators."[18] Of course this message was not to be delivered exactly in those terms, but it reflected a basic attitude that must be considered when trying to understand the frequent tensions between both nations during World War II, many instances of which occurred against the will of the American diplomats in Spain themselves.

At this point, Spain's position during the conflict must be discussed. At first, notwithstanding the fact that Franco's ideological sympathies were always with Germany and Hitler, his ally throughout the civil war, Spain was clearly neutral. In the first stages of the war Franco was very close to Italy. He could not understand the agreement between Hitler and Stalin, and his interests were far removed from Poland. The situation changed dramatically, however, in the summer of 1940 with the defeat of France. Most of Spain's territorial claims concerned France, and now they could be asserted. Moreover, Italy too had become belligerent. Franco's Spain then chose to become a nonbelligerent friendly to Germany, a solution that could have been a first step to intervention in the war. In fact, Franco offered to intervene before Hitler had in any way pressed him. The "Spanish temptation" lasted for a few months only, however, until the end of 1940, and did not result in a belligerent standing. It is likely that the main reason was Hitler's scant and short-lived interest in a Mediterranean strategy, especially if it would mean alienating the support of Vichy France. Franco's inordinate claims, the disastrous state of Spain's economy, the inefficiency of the army, and deep discrepancies within the regime between conservative military sectors and the Fascist Falange are other factors that help explain Spain's marginal role in the conflict. Nevertheless, throughout the war Franco maintained an attitude clearly sympathetic to the Axis powers from the ideological point of view, and provided supply bases for their submarines and planes. On more than one occasion Franco's intervention in the war seemed imminent.[19] Great Britain's position concerning Spain's position remained unchanged. For Churchill, Spain's neutrality was always of the utmost importance. Although at one time he considered a military occupation of the Canary Islands and always deeply mistrusted Franco, he, together with the military command, thought it preferable to keep Spain out of the struggle, to diminish the risks involved in such an extremely complex situation. He thus arranged for two different types of devices to be used. The first and most important one was to open or close the way to foreign trade for a starving Spain depending on its behavior. Sir Samuel Hoare, the British ambassador to Spain, on the other hand worked at deepening the discontent among the Monarchist members of the military.

All this must be kept clearly in mind in explaining the position of Roosevelt's United States toward Franco's Spain during World War II.[20] As in the case of the civil war, there were important differences in points of detail between American diplomats and the State Department itself. One of the former, Willard Beaulac, has described Franco's situation as that of a "silent ally" who, together with the aid of Allied supplies, helped thwart the Axis powers' demands concerning Spain's participation in the war. This is an extreme case of sympathy for Franco, but as a general rule American diplomats in Spain were aware that it was possible to influence the Spanish position through foreign trade, as the British suggested. In contrast, a deep dislike for Franco and his regime prevailed in the United States, thus the tendency to impose clear-cut attitudes of neutrality on him or to condemn him to economic suffocation through restrictive means. Hull states in his memoirs that "we were never friendly to Franco's regime and I myself thought it harmful for Spain and the rest of the world." He also says, however, that his own dislike of Franco's behavior was minor compared to Hitler's frustration when Franco refused to enter the war.[21] Hull was in no way the most drastic of American leaders concerning Franco—indeed, he saw some positive aspects in maintaining Spanish neutrality, whereas Henry Wallace and Harold Ickes even favored an invasion of Spain prior to the landing in North Africa. Roosevelt's attitude to Franco was very likely influenced by these three views, but mainly by the latter two. The best proof lies in the late adherence of the United States to the British position and in those occasions in which differences arose between the leading American and Spanish diplomats, which were always greater than the disagreements between American and British diplomats.

The first American ambassador in Spain was Alexander Weddell.[22] Given Roosevelt's instructions to him, the establishment of close relations could not be expected. Even though commercial links between both countries were kept, there were, apart from political disagreements, economic conflicts derived from Spain's nationalization of the telephone company. The first attempt at rapprochement came from Franco, who in the first months of 1940 started negotiating loans from the United States, in view of the deteriorating state of the Spanish economy. Great Britain, having signed a commercial treaty with Franco's Spain at the beginning of March, convinced Weddell through Hoare, its ambassador in Spain, that this would open the way to allow both nations some influence over Spain's position. Weddell, however, found difficulties in persuading the State Department, where men like Sumner Welles, for instance, were opposed at first to lend any assistance to a nation that, they feared, was liable to enter the war on the opposite side. By September 1940, exactly when the danger of Spain abandoning its nonbelligerent standing was greater, the request for economic aid from Spanish leaders became almost desperate. Finally Weddell succeeded in persuading Washington, and in the first days of October Roosevelt agreed to the shipping of humanitarian aid, under management of the Red Cross, which Spain pledged not to reexport while also renouncing any intervention in World War II.[23]

Juan Beigbeder, the Spanish foreign minister, had used commercial relations as an argument to keep Spain from entering the war, but he was immediately replaced by Serrano Suñer. This and Franco's meeting with Hitler in Hendaye meant a worsening of diplomatic ties with the United States. In a stormy exchange held at the end of October, Weddell accused the Spanish government of allowing German censure in Spain, and Serrano declared his country's "solidarity" with the Axis powers.[24] The little publicity given to American aid (which, Weddell wrote, barely "scraped the surface" of necessity), the modification of the "status" of Tangiers after the Spanish military occupation, the attacks against the United States in the press, and the attempts at propagandist permeation in South America, mainly through the Council of Hispanity, are all facts that help explain the deterioration of relations in subsequent months. Spanish leaders would have liked to see a more isolationist candidate than Roosevelt win the 1940 elections, and occasionally precipitated demonstrations against Great Britain where the United States was included as well. Roosevelt himself did not abandon the idea of keeping some naval forces in Europe in order to put some pressure on the maintenance of Spanish neutrality. Only Churchill's pressure succeeded at the end of 1940 in making the American president reconsider the use of trade as a means to influence Spain's position. This policy was vividly described by Weddell as tending to keep Spain between the hammer of the German threat and the nail of hunger.

Nevertheless, throughout 1941 little progress was made. No matter how often he tried, Weddell could not meet with Franco because Serrano did not allow it, thinking it a prerogative of his office. Hull even held an extremely serious conversation with the Spanish ambassador in Washington, the most difficult in all his diplomatic career, according to his memoirs. In it he stated that in his opinion the attitude of the Spanish government belonged with that of the "most underdeveloped and uncivilized" countries, and he described Serrano's behavior as "extremely offensive."[25] The situation became more normal in the last months of 1941 as Serrano Suñer's political power diminished. But, since American intervention in the war took place at the end of 1941, the United States did not have a bureau in Spain capable of controlling the Spanish position through trade relations until the spring of 1942. Shortly before that, as evidence of the disintegrating state of relations between both countries, Weddell had even advised taking the Canary Islands by force, although pledging to return them.

In May 1942 Carlton J. H. Hayes arrived in Spain as the new American ambassador. He was a well-known historian, a liberal and a Catholic who had not supported Franco during the civil war and who could be considered to reflect Roosevelt's personal diplomacy, based on appointments directly answerable to him.[26] Hayes was able immediately to take advantage of the developments in Spanish domestic policy. Although caused by internal quarrels within the regime and not by any change in Franco's attitude to the war, the ministerial change of September 1942 meant the replacement of the Falangist Serrano with the conservative Catholic General Francisco Gomez Jordana. The change was interpreted by the new ambassador as a sign that

Francoist Spain was moving "slowly but certainly from the Falange to the Army and from the fiction of non-belligerence to the fact of real neutrality," as he wrote Roosevelt. Always a strong supporter of Jordana, he ended up supporting the Francoist regime as well. According to his memoirs, the Francoist regime was not a fascist dictatorship but a conservative coalition. His advisor, second embassy official Beaulac, was even more pro-Franco. Unlike Hoare, neither of them ever wanted to interfere in Spanish politics, and some of their public statements were criticized by the American left.

The turning point in Hayes's mission in Spain was the Allied landing in North Africa. Hayes helped persuade Roosevelt not to make the landing on Spanish territory. The military command, however, particularly Dwight Eisenhower, had a more important say in this matter, realizing as they did that an attack on Spanish possessions would bring about a diversion of resources and above all a serious loss of time. A few days before the landing Hayes reported that the British had assured Franco that he would not be the object of any attack. At their prompting, Hayes gave Franco a letter from Roosevelt at the exact time of the landing in which the president also assured him that the attack was not intended against Spain. While similar letters were handed over to Marshal Pétain and Marshall Carmona of Portugal, the Spanish press considered it as evidence that the neutrality so far maintained was correct. Franco remained, however, a sympathizer of the Axis powers; his government's position changed only in accordance with the war developments and was always accompanied by the Falange's pro-fascist manifestations. The Allied powers were aware of this fact; consequently the "Backbone" plan, intended for the occupation of Spain and North Africa in case of a hostile response or if Franco allowed German troops to cross through its territory, was conceived at the time of the African landing. Franco himself mistrusted both Roosevelt and the United States. In April 1943 he wrote to the pope emphasizing the Catholic features of his government and suggesting that American politics were in the hands of the Jews and Freemasons.

Throughout 1943 the Spanish position was modified according to developments in the war. The fall of Italian fascism in the summer was a major factor in speeding up the process. The State Department and above all American liberal opinion favored an uncompromising policy toward Franco's Spain, even drastically reducing supplies. Hayes was instead much more tolerant and did not think it necessary to apply too strong a pressure, especially on Jordana, whom he trusted.[27]

As early as the initial months of 1943, the United States obtained concessions from Spain in exchange for oil, but the crucial step was taken at the end of 1943 when a telegram sent from Spain to the Philippines government headed by José Laurel, which collaborated with Japan, seemed to mean a recognition by the Spanish government. In fact, it was a serious diplomatic error, but it did not carry any important political significance or mean a supporting move for Japan.[28] The State Department, however, took advantage of the incident to reveal the extent to which it disapproved of Franco's regime.

Without previous consultation with its own embassy or with Great Britain, in February 1944 the U.S. government decreed an oil embargo that lasted until May, when Franco's government yielded to most of its demands. These included surrendering all Italian ships in Spanish ports, the withdrawal of the Division Azul from the Soviet Union, the closing of the German consulate in Tangiers, and reducing Spanish wolfram exports to Germany. Urged by Churchill, the State Department insisted only that the delivery of this strategic material be gradually reduced over a limited period of time. Hayes also did his best not to make the Spanish position appear too difficult, mainly because that would only harm Jordana, who was the most neutral in the current Spanish government.

The lesson of this initial act of hardhanded policy was never forgotten by the Spanish leaders. Throughout 1944 and 1945 the attitude of the Francoist government became benevolent, almost subservient, toward the Allied powers, particularly the United States, which was even granted rights for military landings. Franco, who saw World War II as resulting from two separate conflicts—that between the Allied powers and Germany, in which he was neutral, and that between the Soviet Union and Germany, in which he sympathized with the latter—added a third element to the picture, the fight against Japan, in which he supported the Allied powers. But his change of attitude was as hurried as it was insincere. When Jordana died in June 1944, he was not replaced by another neutralist but by José Felix de Lequerica, former ambassador to Vichy and Axis sympathizer during most of the war. The Spanish government then argued that Spain had been neutral notwithstanding previous declarations to the contrary.

These were changes that American opinion did not find convincing. From January 1945 onward there were proposals for the breaking off of diplomatic ties with Franco. When Roosevelt died in April, according to the polls nearly half of the American public saw no possible cooperation of their country with Spain and a fifth wanted an immediate breaking off of relations. Hayes himself, who had resigned as ambassador, did not think Franco could last much longer, although he did not support direct intervention in Spain. Roosevelt's most eloquent text about Franco was written in this atmosphere.

Only a month before he died Roosevelt clearly outlined the U.S. position for the new ambassador, Norman Armour.[29] The document stated that the Spanish regime had been aided by Germany and Italy in its beginnings and had been shaped on their political model. For this reason a great number of Americans thought the regime suspect and would like to see an end to Spanish-American relations. While abstaining from interfering in internal affairs, Roosevelt nonetheless pointed to the official position of Spain during the war and the hostility of the Falange, and argued that the fascist character of the regime made it inadmissible to the community of nations.

This position was, after all, consistent with Roosevelt's unswerving attitude toward Franco and his political regime. The crucial and unsolved problem was not how to phrase it but how to translate it into realistic action. From the Spanish Civil War onward Roosevelt was, among the leaders of major democratic nations, the one most opposed to Franco, a fact of which he was perfectly aware. American neutrality, however, in its actual terms, indirectly benefited the Spanish dictator. During World War II the fact that Franco never took up arms in support of the Axis powers did not allow a military intervention against him, which was not advisable from the strategic point of view even if it could have been justified from a moral standing. The policy thus outlined by Roosevelt in the above-mentioned letter would be carried out by his successors, but it did not succeed either. Indeed, it was widely realized that a dictatorial government resulting from a civil war and determined to survive can be ousted only by another civil war. Democratic regimes do not usually have the capacity or the wish to intervene in order to provoke such a war.

14

EMPEROR HIROHITO AND FRANKLIN D. ROOSEVELT

Akira Iriye

What did Emperor Hirohito think of Franklin D. Roosevelt? As U.S.-Japanese relations steadily deteriorated throughout the 1930s, did the Japanese emperor do anything to affect the course of events? What role did he play in the several weeks leading up to the coming of the war? What was his perception of the United States as an enemy, of President Roosevelt as its leader?

These are intriguing questions, but unfortunately virtually impossible to answer with any degree of certainty. If the emperor expressed himself in writing, no researcher has seen such documents. Although he undoubtedly communicated his thoughts to those around him orally, few of these men kept a detailed record of such conversations, or if they have, its existence has not been revealed. It is true that several of them have published their diaries and memoirs, but they contain much hearsay, repeating what others say the emperor has said. Official transcripts of meetings by Japan's leaders in the presence of the emperor do exist, but their few statements by the emperor have a rather bland quality, as if they shield Hirohito's innermost thoughts from public scrutiny.

An added difficulty is the fact that most accounts of the emperor's role in prewar and wartime Japan tend to be polemical, even emotional, because the whole issue is bound up with the question of his war guilt. On one hand are those writers who attribute to the emperor the responsibility for important decisions. After all, according to the constitution, he was commander-in-chief, and so all questions of strategic nature had to be approved by him. As Japan's head of state, moreover, he was in a position to sanction cabinet appointments, including the choice of a prime minister. He had veto power over personnel and other matters. Under the circumstances, he was clearly in charge in prewar Japan, and must be held responsible for the government's and the military's decisions made in his name.

Another school of thought holds that under the Meiji constitution, while the emperor was sovereign, he did not rule; day-to-day affairs of state were carried out by civilian ministers, while military decisions were made by the supreme command. He might express his personal preferences one way or another on given matters, but these were not official pronouncements and therefore not to be construed as part of the decision-making process.

This second view was officially adopted at the postwar war crimes tribunal held in Tokyo, which decided not to bring the emperor to trial. The underlying assumption was that Hirohito had stood above politics and was therefore not to be held responsible for specific policy decisions. But if so, it becomes futile, even useless, to ascertain what he thought about mundane affairs, and perhaps for this reason most studies of prewar Japanese foreign policy have paid little attention to the emperor's role. At the same time, however, many of those who would exempt Hirohito from the war guilt question go on to say he was a man of peace, that he did all he could to preserve an amicable relationship with foreign, in particular Western, countries. But it would be illogical to hold this view and still argue that the emperor stood above mundane decision making, for how could one praise his efforts for peace and at the same time say he should not be held responsible for any decision of state?

Because of these difficulties, few have attempted a systematic study of the emperor's attitude toward the United States in general and toward President Roosevelt in particular. There thus exists an asymmetry in our knowledge of U.S.-Japanese relations before and during the war; we know far more about Roosevelt's than about Hirohito's thinking at a given moment. Perhaps detailed and authoritative studies similar to Robert Dallek's *Franklin D. Roosevelt and American Foreign Policy* or Waldo Heinrichs's *Threshold of War* will never be written on the Japanese side unless the papers of the Imperial Household should miraculously become available for research.

What follows, then, is a very tentative description of the emperor's ideas and action concerning the United States from 1933 to 1945 on the basis of published documents. Most of these come from the writings by the "court circle," those around the emperor who had access to him on a regular basis.

In those days there were four positions of particular closeness to the emperor: the lord keeper of the privy seal, the Imperial Household minister, the imperial aide-de-camp, and the grand chamberlain. Several of them, as well as some of their subordinates, kept diaries and other records, and it is from these sources that we obtain some idea of Hirohito's life. Perhaps the most important of them was Count Makino Shinken, lord keeper of the privy seal from 1925 to 1936. His diary is to be published in the near future and may contain valuable information not available elsewhere. But he was murdered by army radicals who planned a coup d'etat in February 1936, and so for the crucial years between 1936 and 1941 much remains obscure. Nevertheless, on the basis of the records thus far published, it is possible to obtain a rough image of at least some of the ideas the emperor may have entertained toward the United States or toward President Roosevelt.

If Hirohito expressed an opinion of Franklin D. Roosevelt when he became president in 1933, no record exists. There was much speculation in the Japanese press about Roosevelt's attitude and policy toward Japan, and the emperor is known to have been an avid reader of Japanese newspapers, so he may have wondered how Roosevelt's coming to power would affect Japanese relations with the United States. But we simply do not know. Nor is there any record of what the emperor might have thought about the New Deal, or how he might have compared Roosevelt with such European leaders as Benito Mussolini and Adolf Hitler. The diary of General Honjô Shigeru, the aide-de-camp, does reveal, however, that in November 1933 the emperor thought Japan should establish a cultural propaganda organ abroad so as to acquaint Americans and Europeans with the essences of Japan's "spiritual civilization."[1] This may be taken as an indication of the emperor's belief, which he shared with most of the elites, in Japan's unique qualities. Despite Hirohito's much-acclaimed tour of England and Western Europe when he was crown prince, it would seem that he had never embraced liberal or democratic values to the extent that a few of the senior statesmen, notably Prince Saionji Kimmochi, did. Saionji, the so-called last *genrô*, appears to have become increasingly critical of the nativist influences exerted on the emperor by those around him.[2] The recently published diary of Irie Sukemasa, who was one of the youngest chamberlains in the 1930s and who went on to serve as grand chamberlain till 1985, contains references to right-wing ideologues who had access to the court circle.[3]

Whether or not the emperor himself developed a nativist, antiliberal conception of the state is difficult to ascertain, but it is interesting to note that at that time he frequently referred to "the constitution." As historian Inoue Kiyoshi notes, it was customary for Hirohito when appointing a new prime minister to command the latter to observe the constitution.[4] By "the constitution" Hirohito seems to have meant two things: one, the specific document known as the Meiji constitution, promulgated in 1889, and the other, more broadly the structure of the Japanese polity with the emperor at the top. The written constitution defined the emperor as sovereign and as commander-in-chief, but it was widely believed that his authority preceded and transcended any such document. Emperor Hirohito seems to have thought so also, for he frequently expressed the view that in Japan emperor and nation were interchangeable.[5] That is to say, there had been an emperor as long as there had been the nation known as Japan, and it was unthinkable to separate the two. At the same time, however, this did not make Hirohito an absolute monarch or a dictator, as he himself apparently said on a number of occasions. Although no specific record of what he thought about Hitler or other dictators of the 1930s exists, it seems reasonably clear that he never quite identified with them. His identification was with Japanese national tradition, or *kokutai* (the national polity). He believed that he could not exist apart from this tradition, nor could the nation. The emperor's authority was thus derived from tradition and legitimized by the Meiji constitution. Such a perspective gave rise to exceptionalism, the idea that Japan's political system was unique, and made it difficult for the emperor, and doubtless for others, to understand or empathize with the momentous political upheavals taking place in Germany, the Soviet Union, or the United States in the 1930s. It was perhaps for this reason that there is little written evidence that the emperor ever showed much interest in those upheavals.

At the same time, however, he was quite sensitive to the relationship between the country's polity and foreign affairs. It may be more correct to say that he became concerned with foreign policy questions when they appeared to have serious implications for the constitution, in the two senses just noted. One can see this in Hirohito's evolving attitude toward the United States. During President Roosevelt's first term (1933-1937), the emperor seems to have assumed that on the whole Japanese-American relations were going well. The aggression in Manchuria had not, he apparently concluded, significantly altered the nature of Japanese foreign affairs, and he saw no reason why Japan should reconsider or redefine its relations with the United States. Thus in 1934, when Japan, America, and Britain conferred on the future of the naval disarmament agreements, the emperor told the lord keeper that he saw nothing wrong with maintaining the existing 10:7 ratio in naval arms between the United States and Britain on one hand and Japan on the other. When, nevertheless, the Japanese navy was seen to be adamant about "parity," he chose not to resist the momentum for letting the naval agreements lapse. He told the prime minister, however, that it was imperative not to provoke the powers unnecessarily.[6] He seems to have sensed that too belligerent a stand toward the Anglo-American powers would undermine the basically stable framework of Japanese relations with those countries, which in turn could destabilize the domestic polity. This was because those taking such a stand were intent on domestic "renovation" as well, a renovation that would purge the nation of individuals tinged with Western influences and create a more unified system of governance. From Hirohito's point of view, much as he believed in Japan's "spiritual civilization," such a movement could grow out of hand and even compromise the emperor system itself. It was not surprising, then, that in 1936, in the wake of the February 26 army uprising, he played an unequivocal role in suppressing the revolt, insisting that the new cabinet to be formed in the aftermath should take care not to cause undue irritation in international affairs. He was clearly aware that external complications could bring about a constitutional crisis.[7]

Unfortunately for him, the 1936 affair did not put an end to the renovationist movement, particularly with regard to Japanese foreign affairs. Even as he commanded the government not to disturb unduly the country's relations with the United States and Britain, the cabinet went ahead and signed an anti-Comintern pact with Germany and Italy, the first visible step tying Japan to the fascist states. An increasing number of military leaders as well as politicians and even imperial relatives continued to be infatuated with the German or the Italian new order, and were more than ever determined to eliminate liberal, democratic, and capitalist influences from Japan. The emperor was very much aware of this challenge to "the constitution" and constantly exhorted those around him to preserve the system, including, one infers, some framework of stable relations with the Anglo-American powers. But it became much more difficult to do so after July 1937, when war with China began.

Recent scholarship suggests that it was not so much Japan's military as civilian leaders who pushed for the escalation of the Chinese war. As Michael Barnhart, among others, points out, the army supreme command was wary of diverting national resources to China when the nation had to be prepared for a probable war with the Soviet Union.[8] Strategic logic dictated retrenchment. But the civilian leadership followed its own agendas and supported a total war on the continent, not so much for purely military as for domestic political, even cultural reasons. It apparently hoped to take advantage of the China war to establish a new order at home. How the emperor viewed such an attempt is difficult to determine, although the Irie diary conveys the atmosphere of jubilation in the imperial household in 1937 at Japan's quick military successes. The diary also provides evidence that some unpleasant news—such as Japanese attacks on innocent civilians and foreign residents in China—was kept from the emperor. Newsreels, for instance, were previewed by court officials before being edited for the emperor's viewing.[9] Thus it is difficult to ascertain how much he was aware of what was going on in China and whether he supported the long drawn-out war.

In any event, Hirohito had to recognize that, given the Chinese war, it was becoming more and more difficult to maintain stable relations with the United States and Britain. This is not the place to chronicle in detail Japan's road to war with the Anglo-American nations. Suffice it to say that, although the Japanese military was initially not very enthusiastic about fighting a total war in China, soon it came to share the view being promoted by the civilian government that the war was but part of Japan's quest for establishing a new Asian order. Such a definition, because it was inherently anti-Western, inevitably led to a crisis in Japanese relations with America, Britain, and the other European democracies. The advocates of an Asian new order looked longingly in the direction of a new order in Europe being constructed by the Axis powers, an added factor in exacerbating the situation. In the domestic context of Japan, the war in China and the new order strategy had the effect of further strengthening anti-Anglo-American forces. All these developments worried the emperor. A crisis and possible conflict with the United States and Britain would damage the political structure of the country—the constitution—by giving more power to the domestic revisionists, but it was becoming increasingly more difficult to suppress them, as he had done successfully in 1936. Any serious attempt to preserve the constitution as it had been understood, so as to check a deterioration in Japanese relations with America and Britain, would now have to entail something like a coup against the renovationists. Hirohito was unwilling to go that far, for fear that such a step could backfire and severely damage the constitution, especially the emperor system itself. In other words, to preserve the constitution, it would be necessary to conciliate the anti-Western forces at home. That was the dilemma; domestic stability became separated from stability in Japan's foreign affairs defined in terms of amity with the United States and Britain. The emperor could promote one of these objectives only at the expense of the other. The dilemma would never go away.

The emperor had to walk an extremely tight rope, trying to maintain some degree of stability in Japanese relations with America and Britain, while at the same time not alienating too much forces within the country oriented toward Germany, Italy, and fascist Spain.

It was an untenable position, made even more so by the increasingly hardening policy of the United States toward Japan during Roosevelt's second term. This was evidenced in such landmarks as the "quarantine speech" of October 1937, the embargo of aircraft to Japan in 1938, and most dramatic, the notification in July 1939 that the United States would abrogate the 1911 treaty of commerce with Japan. Regrettably, none of the published material records the emperor's exact reaction to these events. However, in August 1939, in the wake of the Nazi-Soviet nonaggression pact and the resignation by the Japanese cabinet that had negotiated with Berlin for an alliance, he did strongly express himself in opposition to any such alliance, and said the next prime minister must adopt a diplomacy of "cooperation with Britain and America."[10] Unfortunately for him, the German spring offensive of 1940 set in motion a chain of events that made the Japanese government and military once again solicitous of an Axis alliance. He openly told his aides that he was worried about American economic sanctions; at one point, he even expressed concern that a hardened American policy might adversely affect Japan's silk industry.[11] Such concerns were ignored as the government went ahead and concluded an alliance with Germany and Italy. It is clear that the emperor was aware of the consequences of such diplomacy, but he did not go beyond expressing his misgivings. He never sought decisively to reorient Japanese foreign policy, for that would have entailed domestic restructuring, to rein in the revisionists. In time he came to accept the Axis alliance, hoping that this would help stabilize the domestic polity.

Records for 1941 are somewhat more full as Marquis Kido Kôichi became lord privy seal in January of that year, and he was an avid diarist. His daily entries came increasingly to mention the United States. But the picture of the emperor one gets from the Kido diary is not very different from the preceding ones. In January the emperor expressed his concern over the financial implications of the prolonged war in China and cautioned the military against provoking Britain and the United States over Thailand, where the military was trying to establish its influence through assisting Thailand's territorial ambitions at the expense of the neighboring Indochina. In April in an enigmatic entry the emperor is quoted as expressing his satisfaction that President Roosevelt is willing to engage in detailed conversations with Ambassador Nomura Kichisaburô on the China question. The emperor, of course, was misinformed; Roosevelt had no intention of carrying on serious negotiation unless the Japanese relented on their aggressive war in China. But somehow Hirohito believed this degree of interest on the part of the United States vindicated Japan's alliance with Germany and Italy. The implication, of course, was that by associating itself with the Axis powers,

Japan succeeded in moderating American policy. This was a wrong conclusion to draw from wrong premises, and shows how removed the emperor had become from the realities of the situation.[12]

The emperor's optimism was short-lived, however. After the German invasion of the Soviet Union on 22 June, as U.S.-Japanese relations became extremely precarious because of Japan's decision to occupy the whole of Indochina and of the American freezing of Japanese assets, Hirohito had to recognize that war with America was now a real possibility. He told the navy minister at the end of July that a war with the United States would not be as easily winnable as the naval engagement against Russia in 1905. In early August, as Prime Minister Konoe Fumimaro sought to meet with President Roosevelt to dilute the crisis, the emperor cautioned that should such a meeting yield no result, then Japan would be faced with a most difficult decision. At the crucial 6 September meeting of Japan's top military and civilian leaders in the emperor's presence, Hirohito expressed hope that even as the nation prepared for war it also continue its diplomatic efforts to prevent the catastrophe. At the end of the month, he wanted to know what America's rubber stock was, as well as the amounts of rubber and tin produced in Central and South America that could be made available to the United States. On 13 October, a few days before Konoe was replaced by General Tôjô Hideki, the emperor told Kido that Japan should be thinking of ending the war with America, should it come, through the good offices of the Vatican. On 4 November, he wanted to know how Japan could deal with the enemy's expected counterattacks by air and submarine from bases in Australia. On 27 November, Hirohito held a meeting with the elder statesmen (former prime ministers) for one last time before approving the war decision. The Kido diary for 8 December, the day the Pearl Harbor attack was executed, records nothing about the emperor, but says the foreign minister informed him that the American ambassador had brought a cable from Roosevelt to the emperor. In this cable the president appealed to the emperor to prevent the coming of war. It arrived too late, and if the emperor ever read it, neither Kido nor anyone else recorded his reaction.[13]

As this summary indicates, the emperor's precise thinking toward Roosevelt is difficult to ascertain from available records, but his image of the United States emerges, at least in rough outline. He was keenly aware of Japan's inferiority in resources and was wary of going to war against a country that was far more richly endowed. This did not make the emperor pro-American for political or ideological reasons. Nowhere is there a clear indication of what he thought about the political institutions and ideologies of the United States. Rather, he seems to have viewed the latter in economic terms. This was also how the military and its civilian supporters perceived the United States, but whereas they wanted to rectify the disparity in resources and reduce Japan's dependence on richer countries by establishing control over China and ultimately over the whole of Southeast Asia, the emperor was concerned that such a scheme might backfire and bring about a severe crisis for Japan, especially for "the constitution." He sought to avoid war that would undermine the constitution, but at the same time he did not act decisively to stop war with the United States for fear that such action might also destabilize the political system of the country.

The dilemma stayed with him throughout the war. To be sure, he was initially thrilled by Japan's quick victories. He candidly told Kido in March 1942 that Japan appeared to be doing all too well. Such a state of elation did not last long, however. After the crucial battle of Midway in June 1942, as the tide steadily turned, the emperor became increasingly anxious about the course of the war, worried, as before the war, over the resources Japan had recently obtained in Southeast Asia. If they could not be held, the war was all but over.[14] He had to recognize that during the next three years the situation continued to deteriorate, so that by June 1945 he had clearly concluded that the war must be terminated as expeditiously as possible. The reason it took him three years to come to this conclusion may have in part been due to the fact that the military never told him the truth about the course of the war. Equally plausibly, he may have been worried about the implications of a defeat for the future of the "constitution" and wanted some sort of a negotiated end to the war.[15] In any event, these two—resources and political structure—remained the basic perspectives in which Hirohito viewed the war. But whereas resources could be quantified and compared, and Japan's inferiority frankly recognized, the political system was something in which the emperor had an abiding faith. It was not something that could be given up, even in military adversity and defeat. It was not because he and his aides recognized America's political or cultural superiority that they decided on ending the war. Rather, it was in order to preserve *kokutai* that they did so. As is well known, the Japanese were adamant till the very end that they would surrender only if the Allied powers promised to let Japan retain the imperial system. The Allies issued an ambiguous statement, enabling the Japanese to accept the ending of the war. But that story belongs to the post-Roosevelt era.

The day the news of Roosevelt's death reached Tokyo, Irie Sukemasa, the chamberlain, wrote in his diary that the information cheered him up considerably, since the president's passing would surely create confusion among the Allies.[16] Was this the atmosphere of the imperial palace at that time? It seems incredible that the Japanese leaders, at a time when they had all but recognized the inevitability of defeat, should have found anything to celebrate about in the death of the enemy's leader. Apart from their lack of sophistication about international affairs, the Irie diary reveals the absence of compassion, of any but the most superficial acquaintance with American politics and culture. It would be no exaggeration to say that the emperor shared this superficiality.

To conclude, it is clear that Emperor Hirohito's views of America and its leader were not very different from those held by his military and civilian advisors. They too were keenly aware of the serious gap in the two countries' economic positions. And they were quite correct on this score. In 1940, for instance, America's gross national product (GNP) was close to $100 billion, with a per capita income of over $750. The nation accounted for more than 35 percent of the world's manufacturing output, and its merchant marine for about 17 percent of the world's output. Its export trade amounted to $4.0 billion and import trade to $2.6 billion. Japan, in contrast, could boast a GNP of only about $7 billion, or less than $100 per capita. Its manufacturing output was less than one-seventh of that of the United States, and its total trade was only 22 percent of America's. The Japanese leaders, from the emperor down, were justified in viewing Japan as a much poorer country. But whereas the emperor and several civilian leaders concluded from this that Japan should not wage a war against an enormously rich country like the United States, the military was determined to reduce Japan's sense of inferiority through bold action in Asia.

Likewise, both the emperor and the top leaders shared the mystique of Japan's uniqueness, expressed in terms of the imperial institution. The institution had to be preserved at all cost, otherwise the nation would lose its soul. Sometimes this belief in the imperial system made the emperor cautious about antagonizing the Anglo-American powers, for a serious deterioration in Japanese relations with them might bring about war to the detriment of the institution. Ironically, the institution survived, even after the military suffered a crushing defeat. It was left to Roosevelt's successors and to the Japanese people after the war to determine whether or not the very existence of the institution, which Emperor Hirohito had worked so hard to preserve as an expression of Japan's "spiritual civilization," had made war with the United States all but inevitable.

Part IV

THE POSTWAR PERIOD

15

THE LEGACY OF FRANKLIN D. ROOSEVELT'S INTERNATIONALISM

Leon Gordenker

Franklin Roosevelt's ideas and decisions about world politics influenced and shaped the world that lived on after him far more than most statesmen could hope to do. But no one person, whatever his skill, insight, intelligence, and position, has ever come close to determining all that comes after him. Even the creation of institutions to give practical effect to ideas and policies by itself cannot guarantee future behavior.

Beyond these general limits, estimating the precise value of Roosevelt's legacy is complicated by his political style. It was fluid, shifting, never altogether free of obscurity, often short term, manipulative, and dependent on alliances with supporters of different stripe. Perhaps that was the only way that he could make headway toward his liberal internationalist harbor in a sea that was blocked by isolationists and narrow nationalists. A consummate politician and magnetic leader, Roosevelt—who said that a radical had both feet firmly planted in the air—could hardly be accused of impracticality and utopianism. Nor was he a philosopher king who lucidly plumbed great depths of knowledge on all important subjects. Neither was he a fussy manager of policy who left orderly, logical bureaucratic structures wherever he could. Yet his presidency, his speeches, his official activities, his proposals, his conversations, and his press conferences imply or state principles that figure in his legacy. His main ideas and the programs that grew out of some of them still shine as beacons in world politics. This chapter calls attention to the principles, decisions, and limitations that give form to FDR's legacy of internationalism.

WHAT A PRESIDENT CAN DO IN WORLD POLITICS

Whatever Franklin Roosevelt's gifts as a statesman, he operated within constraints created by the structure of the American state, the context of public attitudes of his time, and the structure of international politics then. These same factors, changing with the times and the personalities, gave contours to his legacy.

A commonplace in thinking about an American president as a leader of foreign policy stresses his relative freedom of action. On domestic policy, he is much more constrained by law and opinion. But such statements merely set out relative relationships. No matter how strong the American economy and how imposing its military establishment, the president as the senior political leader in foreign relations and commander-in-chief of the armed forces still cannot succeed in issuing binding orders to the rest of the world. He cannot even treat minor states as his country's vassals without a serious investment of might and treasure, as the last century of relationships with Central America has demonstrated. He cannot expect that even the friendliest of allies will effortlessly adjust to his tendencies, as friction between Roosevelt and Churchill more than once demonstrated. Nor can he at will work changes in policy in other governments, as Roosevelt clearly understood with regard, for instance, to the Soviet Union. He cannot even be sure that his secretary of state, formally his principal advisor and executive for foreign relations, will entirely support his policy, or that the military will accurately understand and give effect to his orders.

In fact, American politics dictates that the president *must* remain preoccupied with domestic issues and leadership of his constituencies. The country is huge, complex, and troublesome to manage. It has a constitutional structure that leads to an emphasis on alliances, consensus, and flexibility, rather than on unitary policy, hierarchical procedures, and centralization. Americans vote for or against the president, not for a specific political program. His appeal to the voters ultimately circumscribes his policies. As for foreign popularity, nationals of other states and their governments represent no votes. They are seldom of much direct help in the president's constant task of shaping a supporting constituency. And anyhow a considerable part of the American electorate regards foreigners as a rather suspect lot.

The political skills, experience, credit, and principles that a president brings to his office all help in coping with the constraints. But they do not guarantee that he can do more than put some, perhaps very little, of what is likely to be an unstated program into effect. Nor do they ensure that his attempts at leadership will succeed or endure. The foreign relations he envisions for the country, if he has ideas about them, may be low on the agenda of popular politics. His allies include congressional factions, interest and ethnic groups, opinion leaders and their followers, parts of the communication media and a hundred other fragments. Assembling a consensus, temporary or long term, out of this assortment is a challenge to any president; certainly it was to Roosevelt as he sought to overcome isolationism and later to prepare for war. Politics driven by domestic alliances inevitably means that a president will sometimes seem bold, sometimes timid, frequently tentative, not necessarily consistent or clear. His own bureaucracy will reflect this haziness, and some elements may be expected, or even encouraged, to take off on their own, to "freewheel." In coping with the difficulties inherent in the American political structure, a president with outstanding political skills and some fixed stars by which to steer his policy can transform some of these hindrances into opportunities to accomplish much. Roosevelt was such a president.

A MAP OF FDR'S INTERNATIONAL WORLD

Roosevelt's map of the future, his sketch of desirable policies, included important fixed points. Some of them developed out of his experience during the First World War in the Wilson administration, his campaign for the vice presidency, his exposure to social policy as governor of New York and as the depression president who promised a New Deal, and from his reactions to the Second World War. Some critics, including foreign affairs professionals for most of whom he had little time, accused him of shallowness.[1] Later a well-known historian in a widely read book published in 1973, when the hoped-for postwar order seemed perhaps less pertinent than Henry Kissinger's overbearing approach, declares that " . . . superficial reasoning . . . produced the Roosevelt administration's policies." Echoing a popular slogan, he says that the wartime president and his men faced the future thinking only about the last war.[2] Another more recent analysis claims that ". . . his background, experience, and expertise on diplomatic questions were seldom commensurate with his impact on external developments."[3] In short, he did not know what he was doing.

Where one analyst sees ignorance and another stabbing in the dark, it is also possible to see patterns. That is what this chapter seeks to do. Both the discoverers of historical black holes and of bright galaxies should take care, however, that they recall the pressure of political life. Little time remains at the end of a day for reflection, even among the rare civil servants who are charged with long-term planning. Roosevelt in fact had few of them indeed in his government and even less of the contemporary apparatus of think tanks and university-based policy analysts. Yet political events tumble over one another in a chaotic fashion. Scholars later perhaps can disentangle main lines, but it is also conceivable that they impose their own preferences. Despite the need for caution, some tall beacons to the future as they shone during FDR's tenure in the White House can be discerned.

In his first inaugural address, Roosevelt set the behavior of the good neighbor as a standard. Justice would be a guide to reaching that standard. (The good-neighbor idea only later became associated primarily with Latin American relations.) A good neighbor keeps his word, which is precisely what international lawyers say is an obligation on all states.[4] As most treaties are kept most of the time, it is not a farfetched notion.[5] It points to more use of an expression of justice through rules to regulate relations among states.

An unmistakable notion of justice can be found in the Four Freedoms speech and the Atlantic Charter.[6] It is also linked with opposition to colonialism and the general protection of human rights, about which more later. Furthermore, a good neighbor does not seek to swallow anyone else's land. This opposition to territorial aggrandizement figures in the Atlantic Charter.

The Four Freedoms also point to the goal of a higher standard of well-being for everyone. Perhaps this derives from the misery of the depression, but Roosevelt had come to understand the meaning of poverty earlier during his governorship. Alleviating it was a basic demand in world politics that began to be explicitly formulated during the life of the League of Nations.[7] It remains a fundamental goal.

Roosevelt understood the world as interdependent.[8] In such a world, a great deal of communication among governments is necessary. While that could promise much to foreign offices, FDR did a great deal of the informing and discussion in the surroundings of his personal office and his close advisors. He developed summit meetings to a new art in his early meetings with Churchill and those later with Churchill, Stalin, and other heads of governments. He carried on a huge, direct correspondence with some of his ambassadors and with personal acquaintances with relevant knowledge. He sought far and wide for advice on foreign policy. He avidly absorbed information. Then he insisted that important policy issues should be reserved for decision in the White House—not in the State Department or Congress. For good or ill, foreign offices everywhere probably have never quite recovered from the effects of FDR's personal diplomacy.

A Great Power in an interdependent world, Roosevelt held, had to take a committed part in international life. This view obviously directly contradicted the extreme isolationists and those who narrowly defined the use of American power. As the United States was certainly an important country before the Second World War and after it the most formidable polity in the world, it had special obligations, according to Roosevelt's approach.

It has to preserve itself, of course. No statesman on record has voluntarily taken a position in favor of the disappearance of his polity. Therefore it has to have a formidable military arm at a time when others were arming. Nevertheless, in the long term, there was little point in arms races. Therefore, great powers have to take the lead in arms control to keep weaponry at a modest, reasonable but serviceable level.

A dash of nationalism helps the government of a great power define its position. Nationalism is also related to self-determination. In any case, the national interest has to be used as a guide to good policy.

The price of greatness entails an inverse obligation to protect the weaker from other strong powers and from each other: No one dominates, as in the time-honored pattern of the balance of power. Territorial conquest is ruled out. This also was recognized in the Atlantic Charter.

As good neighbors do not push each other around, Great Powers have a special obligation to help with resolution of international friction and to suppress violence. Thus FDR's "quarantine the aggressor" speech and the idea of the Four Policemen that he repeatedly invoked.

INTERNATIONAL ORGANIZATION

Interdependence and Great Power status do not manage themselves automatically. Roosevelt favored formal, international organization, protected by international law and armed might, as an institutionalized way of managing world politics. He did not set off conventional bilateral relations as one means and international organization as its opposite. One did not obviate the other, but a Great Power could discharge its special responsibilities in international organizations.

The armed might of the Great Powers would be pooled here to keep the peace and limited to the necessary level. Others would need military establishments of a minor magnitude.

Justice would be promoted by international cooperation on economic and social issues and on human rights. A chain of appropriate international organizations would be created, or old ones revived, to deal on a specialized basis with economic and social issues.

The eventual dismantling of the colonial system would be promoted through trusteeship and the elimination of preferential trading. Beyond that, self-determination was a basic principle of this organized world.

At last the United States, a promoter of law, would be able to adhere to a world court.

YALTA: FOLLOWING THE MAP

Roosevelt followed his map at Yalta with some successes and some failures.[9] What was done there had a strong effect on the postwar world. What failed of application at that time nevertheless in many respects became the pattern. In any case, it was anything but a "sellout" as some right-wing American politicians insisted, especially during the hysterical anticommunism of the late 1940s and early 1950s when the late Senator Joseph R. McCarthy nearly dominated politics.

Perhaps the most tense issue of the Yalta Conference involved the nature of government in Eastern Europe. Firmly under the control of Soviet armed forces, Eastern Europe, and especially Poland, offered little leeway for negotiators. The Soviet Union, as Roosevelt perfectly understood, would do its best to dominate Eastern Europe and to block the participation in the Polish government of those it did not support. But he did not accept the notion of fixed spheres of influence, which Churchill and Stalin had agreed upon in 1944.[10] Consequently, he and Churchill pressed Stalin to agree to free elections in Poland. Furthermore, they successfully proposed provisions for liberated Europe to support the people in forming governments and solving their problems by democratic means and freely elected governments. This accorded with Roosevelt's notion that justice had to be part of world politics. The Soviet Union formally agreed, whatever the differences in interpretation. They were substantial, judging by the sharpness of letters soon exchanged between Roosevelt and Stalin.[11]

The Yalta Conference ironed out the remaining obstacles to placing an agreed-upon document before the San Francisco Conference, scheduled to begin in April 1945, to approve the United Nations Charter. Those obstacles included, in essence, the degree to which the permanent members would be protected by the veto in the Security Council but not the veto itself; multiple membership for the Soviet Union and its republics; and the principles of trusteeship. Whatever the precise legal details worked out at the conference, the significant point was that the "Big Three" had signed on. Soviet enthusiasm proved limited in the subsequent weeks when Moscow at first declined to send Foreign Minister Vyacheslav Molotov to the conference, but Roosevelt's pressure and after his death a plea by Averell Harriman, the American ambassador in Moscow, secured a change of mind.[12]

Despite Churchill's horrified reaction to the treatment of colonial issues in the projected UN Charter, the conferees eventually agreed that that was a proper, but limited, subject matter for international discourse. That Stalin would accept this was practically a foregone conclusion. Churchill took some persuading and needed some concessions before agreeing. But the conference ended with enough accord so that the issue of colonialism was firmly on the international agenda.

For Roosevelt a principal aim at Yalta was to secure the entry of the Soviet Union in the war against Japan. That it should become a belligerent accorded with FDR's notion of the obligations of a Great Power to defeat the destroyers of peace. This was achieved, although at some cost to China, which was not represented at Yalta or even precisely informed until later.[13] Nevertheless, Roosevelt's strong belief that China should be part of the Great Power club was ratified. Moreover, despite several varieties of doubts, France also was included. In addition, the four European victors took on special obligations for governing defeated Germany until a peace treaty should be worked out. Four Policemen still had their hands on their batons in Europe. For the rest of the world, the Chinese policeman would be added. That still is the list.

The Yalta Conference can thus be understood as generally following the road markers that Roosevelt had set out for the future. It was not a perfect performance; nor could that have been expected by anyone but an obtuse utopian. It was a rather convincing operation of statesmanlike quality and a firm consolidation of a military victor's influence.[14]

TROUBLE IN THE PASSAGE TO PERMANENT PEACE

If Roosevelt's ideas about world politics are viewed as a chart for immediately entering a peaceful, prosperous world, they obviously were faulty. By the time he died, only weeks after the Yalta Conference, he understood that the Soviet Union would balk against any chains needed to moor Great Powers to each other.[15] Why this was so was less important in the postwar setting than the fact that it was so. As for China and the United Kingdom, the war had left them with vast damage and weakness. France too had little ability to take the share that General Charles de Gaulle claimed. Then the United States and the Soviet Union soon developed a relationship of serious antagonism, only sharpened by the effects of nuclear weapons, ideological differences, the need to readjust economies, and the demands of rapidly changing societies.

On Roosevelt's death, President Harry Truman faced the tangled and dangerous issues of the postwar world with little preparation. For reasons never made entirely clear, FDR had kept him in the dark about the development of the nuclear weapon and a host of other important factors in foreign policy. Truman had not even met Edward Stettinius, who had taken over from Cordell Hull as secretary of state.[16] Truman was not part of the delegation at Yalta, received no reports on it while it was in progress, and had had no part in developing the agenda. Nor was he a close collaborator on the planning for the United Nations. In those circumstances, the very structure of policy and the officials needed to apply it offered little choice but to continue Roosevelt's course in the short term or to plunge into waters of which he was even more ignorant. Truman kept on Roosevelt's cabinet and pledged to follow his policies. He accepted that he would never be free of Roosevelt's influence.[17]

Truman immediately decided to push ahead with the San Francisco Conference. Its successful conclusion and the start-up of the new organization meant that one of the features of FDR's postwar world had been given continuing status.

Truman lost no time in exerting the prerogatives of a Great Power. He demonstrated at the Potsdam Conference with Clement Attlee and Stalin that the prestige of the United States as the strongest and richest country in the world at that time was to be respected. His decision to go ahead with the use of nuclear weapons against Japan dramatized the enormous military advantage in American hands. At the same time, he applied in his own fashion FDR's practice of personal diplomacy. He sought a friendly relationship with the Soviet Union and openly complimented Stalin, with whom he judged he could work. But when friction developed, he used American capacities as a Great Power. While he presided over victory in Japan and subsequent demobilization, Truman maintained significant American forces in Europe and Japan. He insisted in the Truman doctrine on the American interest in promoting democratic governments and self-determination. The Marshall Plan too was aimed at sustaining democratic government and ensuring self-determination. Truman justified ordering American troops into battle in Korea as a way of fulfilling obligations under the UN Charter and of protecting the prestige of the world organization.[18] In short, after taking over the presidency, he at once used much of Roosevelt's map.

When Dwight Eisenhower occupied the White House, the long dominance of the Democratic party in American politics came to an end. The visible shadow of FDR grew fainter as the years went on.[19] Ike and his successors had little ideological reason to identify with Roosevelt, the New Deal, and Rooseveltian internationalism. Later, as Democrats, John Kennedy, Lyndon Johnson and Jimmy Carter all paid tribute to Roosevelt's ideas without having completely to rebuild the main beacons. As a Republican and with Kissinger as a close associate, Richard Nixon hardly sought openly to follow FDR's lead. Even so, he discovered the importance of the International Monetary Fund early on and Kissinger later began to profit from the United Nations, especially in Africa and the Middle East. The ideological presidency that Ronald Reagan installed made much of human rights and eventually turned disdain for the UN system into at least toleration and in some cases positive support. Thus the successive generations did not flippantly reject constructions of the 1930s and 1940s, whatever their partisan or personal preferences.

AN ACCURATE CHART

Forty-five years after Roosevelt's death, this enthusiastic sailor's chart of world politics still is useful. That map did not entirely rearrange the heavens but rather suggested the navigational points for world politics. FDR's conception of international relations foresaw a liberal internationalist, orderly world in which the United States would be a leading participant. In one sense, he was following a politician's classical course. As the main elements of political firmament are given and can be changed only slowly, adaptation and accommodation are the nucleus of wisdom. Still, Roosevelt sensed the needs of the future with surprising accuracy.

More than ever before, the interdependence of all societies is obvious. Striking examples abound. The United States imports the greater part of its petroleum needs. It sells huge agricultural surpluses, aircraft, and high-technology products abroad. Japan is a leading creditor for the United States and the Third World. Banks in the rich countries have lent vast sums to the poorer countries that have difficulty in repaying their loans and face frustrating problems in overcoming poverty. Confidence in the whole world's banking system is affected. A reduced arms budget in the United States depends partly on what stance the Soviet Union assumes in Europe and East Asia and how the NATO allies react. Roosevelt had it right in assuming interdependence as a principle of world politics.

The concept of explicit Great Power leadership has been a familiar part of modern world politics since the Congress of Vienna in 1815 when the Napoleonic imperial drive was politically liquidated. Roosevelt's emphasis on the special role of the Great Powers, both as limited by law and by commitment, fits well with both fact and contemporary need. The Great Powers, especially the United States, the Soviet Union, and China, all with plentiful nuclear arms, could end civilization as we know it. Moreover, what they do short of war affects the rest of the world as if a normal child were standing in a room in a doll's house. Consequently, international relations requires constant diplomatic contact, conferring, and vigilance in order to reduce the possibility that conflict would end in war.

The means of international contact developed since the end of the Second World War were well-nigh unimaginable then. That does not mean that the connections are always or even often used well, but they exist. George Bush telephones Mikhail Gorbachev. A permanent telex link is held open between the two governments. Satellite observation provides raw intelligence and verification of other information. That too is a means of contact. Diplomatic missions have proliferated and with the independence of colonial territories there are more participants than ever—160 in the United Nations, which was started with fewer than 60 members. The number of international conferences on both specialized and general subjects runs well into five digits annually. The idea of international organization has flowered into a busy actuality. In 1951 some 120 intergovernmental organizations of various stripes were doing business. By 1989 there were 300.[20] The United Nations plans on more than 7,000 meetings in New York during the 1990-91 biennium and another 13,000 in Geneva.[21] Even when governments try to shelter their doings from outside knowledge, as the Soviet Union and its allies did in most of the postwar period and as Burma and Albania still attempt to do, they are forced into some, and usually progressively more, transnational connections. *Glasnost* in the Soviet Union represents one recent acceptance of Roosevelt's understanding of interdependence.

Roosevelt's participation in Great Power summit meetings, learned in part from Churchill, began a practice that has continued unabated. FDR understood this as an extraordinary means of diplomacy and also as a stage for his spectacular personal magnetism. It is a practice, however, which even in this time drew criticism. For better or worse, however, the critics failed to prevail. It now seems a standing feature of world political discourse. It is used routinely in the European communities, in Africa and elsewhere. It is also arguably a highly significant symbolic device even if some foreign affairs professionals distrust it as a negotiating technique.

In emphasizing the importance of an armed force as part of the equipment needed by the United States to ward off expansive behavior by the governments that became enemies, Roosevelt sought what would now be called deterrence. This was no new notion, but FDR systematically and delicately built it into American policy. With nuclear weapons, it now is an unavoidable aspect of contemporary world politics—for good or ill.

Roosevelt's hope that the Soviet Union could be brought to cooperate reasonably easily with other important governments never materialized in the crucial months after his death. Stalin and most of his successors chose policies that treated the United States and its associates as threats. Returning the compliment, the United States and its friends developed a structure of military alliances directed toward the Soviet Union. The dream of harmony disintegrated rapidly. The outbreak of war in Korea suggested that conflict could be confined but also was followed by overwhelming rearmament by the United States. Four decades later both the United States and the Soviet Union, the latter in the lead, have begun once more to turn toward cooperation and to joint treatment of fights among the smaller fry. Both are showing strong tendencies to pull back from their competitive expansiveness. For the moment, it looks again as if Roosevelt's map may apply.

Roosevelt's instincts on colonialism accurately foretold later developments. He foresaw the eventual dissolution of the system and wanted to take positive steps to manage the change. After his death, the anticolonial movement, once only a breeze, became a hurricane. His successors in the United States and in most of the rest of the world helped to speed the process, partly through the United Nations.

The end of colonialism is but one face of self-determination, an important Rooseveltian marker buoy for the future. Another face is democratic government. Not original with him and echoing Wilson's concepts, self-determination locked the Soviet Union and the United States in conflict over the treatment of Eastern Europe. Soviet domination of Eastern Europe immediately after the Second World War, the brutal suppression with Soviet troops of more relaxed governments in Hungary and Czechoslovakia, the iron hand of communist governors in East Germany, Poland, Rumania, and Bulgaria—these all proclaimed a denial of self-determination as well as democracy. During the last three or so years, that denial of self-determination has turned into an affirmation of the principle. It implies a popular movement. In Eastern Europe, the principle, it seemed in 1989 and 1990, was being applied in a purer form than ever. Even the Soviet Union appears to bend to the democratic wind. And much farther south, at the tip of Africa, after decades of agitation from inside and out, Namibia is independent and South Africa may have moved far in the direction of democracy. Roosevelt's map usually proved accurate during a long voyage.

Roosevelt did not put as much effort into personal leadership on international economic and trade issues as he did on fighting the war and seeking peace and security. But he approved the construction of a set of agreements and organizations that pointed the way toward international cooperation on trade and economic policy. By now the reciprocal trade agreements that Hull so much favored have been broadened into the General Agreement on Tariffs and Trade and have reduced tariffs throughout the world by some 90 percent. International trade has come through an unparalleled cycle of growth. The Uruguay round of negotiations represent the latest worldwide effort, with the United States as a leader, to shake off even more of the shackles on international trade. The World Bank and the International Monetary Fund have increasingly served as centers for the management and promotion of international economic relations and development, which are aims that ran parallel to the domestic approach of the New Deal.

However important the two global financial organizations and several regional bodies have become, Roosevelt's central concern in giving international relations greater order was a new agency to maintain peace. The fortunes of the United Nations system waxed and waned during the following forty-five years. At times, American involvement as well as that of other countries, including the Soviet Union and other permanent members of the Security Council, more closely approached the scornful than the positive. Yet the organization survived and at the moment is widely regarded by government leaders as highly useful in regional conflicts and promising in some other areas. It has performed a vast amount of work and, as usual in political affairs, has not satisfied all parties. But what could when dealing with, say, conflicts around Israel and the eastern Mediterranean or reducing poverty in Africa? All the same, a bold line indicating international organization on Roosevelt's map to the future was followed.

Especially in the Security Council, the translation of the early image of the Four Policemen again appears workable. When there is cooperation among the permanent members of the council, it operates with convincing effect. It has done so recently in Afghanistan, the Persian Gulf, Namibia, and Nicaragua. More ventures are on the way to add to these and some notable earlier enterprises.

The Four Freedoms find their echo in the development of an international system for the protection of human rights. FDR's widow, Eleanor, was a principal force in drafting and securing approval in the UN General Assembly in 1948 for the Universal Declaration of Human Rights. It has since become the basis of a system of treaties in which ninety countries have taken on formal obligations to protect human rights. It underlies a strong human rights regime in Europe. And in the streets of Eastern Europe and all too briefly in China, human rights have been a central demand of popular democratic movements. Linked to this was substantial progress in setting out new norms for the protection of the rights of women and children. This impressive development also harmonizes with FDR's views on colonialism and interdependence. Ironically, the United States has not acceded to the treaties for the protection of human rights although now even the last two Republican presidents favor it, even if the Senate does not.

At last the United States, along with the other 159 members of the United Nations, is a member of the World Court. Adherence to the statute of the International Court of Justice is obligatory for UN members, even if its use depends on more than mere membership. It has indeed been used, sometimes in a controversial way by the United States as in the case brought against it by Nicaragua about the mining of one of its harbors. Yet its very existence and considerable prestige in much of the world forty-five years after FDR's death is yet one more buoy on his map of the future of world politics.

CONCLUSION

Is a peaceful, secure, orderly world part of the legacy of FDR's internationalism? Much as he may have wished that it would be, of course it is not. Human society is much too complex to be managed by one leader or even by one great state or, for that matter, by one armed camp seeking to dominate another. Not even the opportunities of a great victory could ensure a fixed future. World politics merely reflects that complexity. But Roosevelt's rather unsystematic, fragmented thinking about the world after the defeat of the fascist states did have an impressive result. It set out the key issues of future American foreign policy at a time when the United States possessed a vast capacity for leadership. The way most of those issues were handled accorded rather well with FDR's mental map of world politics—at least as I have reconstructed it. Some of that map merely marked out behavior that would no doubt have occurred, whatever the other landmarks. It would, moreover, be fatuous to portray world politics after Roosevelt as a smooth, progressive, efficient development toward goals he set out and that were usually acceptable most of the time. Nor can we even be sure that coincidences between his map and contemporary politics will not soon be pulled apart. But much of the map implied a special foresightedness, not always in tune with expert opinion, about what to expect in world politics and how to shape the outcomes. By concentrating American leadership and that of other important governments on interdependence and its consequences, on the responsibility of Great Powers, on the prudent use of arms to help in that responsibility and on the creation of global institutions, FDR's approach has never ceased to guide.

ABOUT THE AUTHORS

DAVID K. ADAMS, professor of twentieth-century history, is head of the Department of American Studies and director of the David Bruce Centre at the University of Keele in England.

VALENTIN BEREZHKOV was the personal interpreter to Stalin and Molotov, a capacity in which he met, among others, Hitler, von Ribbentrop, Franklin D. Roosevelt, and Churchill. At present he is senior researcher at the Institute of U.S. and Canada Studies in Moscow.

HSI-SHENG CH'I is professor of political science and chairman of East Asian Studies Curriculum at the University of North Carolina at Chapel Hill.

IVAN CIZMIC, a specialist in the Yugoslav emigrant movement in the United States, is affiliated with the Institute for Migration and Nationalities at the University of Zagreb, Yugoslavia.

CLAUDE FOHLEN is professor emeritus of American history at the Sorbonne in Paris, France.

LEON GORDENKER is professor emeritus of politics at Princeton University, research fellow in Princeton's Center of International Studies, and visiting professor at the City University of New York.

AKIRA IRIYE is professor of history at Harvard University.

DETLEF JUNKER is professor of modern history at the University of Heidelberg, Federal Republic of Germany.

ALBERT E. KERSTEN is professor of diplomatic history at the University of Leiden and affiliated with the Institute of Netherlands History in The Hague, the Netherlands.

HENRY RAYMONT, a former journalist with the United Press in Washington and *New York Times* bureau chief in Buenos Aires, is at present senior research fellow at the Joan Shorenstein Barone Center on the Press, Politics and Public Policy at the John F. Kennedy School of Government of Harvard University.

GER VAN ROON is professor of political history at the Free University in Amsterdam, the Netherlands.

ARTHUR M. SCHLESINGER, JR., is Albert Schweitzer Professor in the Humanities at the City University of New York.

JAVIER TUSELL is professor of contemporary history of Spain at the University of Madrid, Spain.

MAURIZIO VAUDAGNA is professor of northern American history at the University of Torino, Italy.

LUBOMIR W. ZYBLIKIEWICZ is professor of history in the Department of International Relations at the University of Cracow, Poland, and at the Institute of Political Sciences of the Polish Academy of Sciences.

ABOUT THE EDITORS

CORNELIS A. VAN MINNEN is executive director of the Roosevelt Study Center in Middelburg, the Netherlands.

JOHN F. SEARS is executive director of the Franklin and Eleanor Roosevelt Institute at Hyde Park, New York.

NOTES

Franklin D. Roosevelt's Internationalism

1. Pieter Geyl, *Napoleon: For and Against* (New Haven, 1949), p. 18.
2. Edmund Ironside, *Time Unguarded: The Ironside Diaries, 1937-1940* (New York, 1962), p. 40.
3. Winston S. Churchill, *Their Finest Hour* (Boston, 1949), pp. 45-47, 54-55.
4. Samuel I. Rosenman, ed., *The Public Papers and Addresses of Franklin D. Roosevelt, 1940* (New York, 1941), pp. 198-205.
5. Robert E. Sherwood, *Roosevelt and Hopkins* (revised ed., New York, 1950), p. 882.
6. Frances Perkins, *The Roosevelt I Knew* (New York, 1946), p. 330.
7. Rosenman, *Public Papers and Addresses . . . 1928-1932* (New York, 1938), p. xiii.
8. Jefferson to Thomas Leiper, 1 January 1814, Jefferson, *Writings*, P.L. Ford, ed., (New York, 1897), vol. 9, pp. 445-446.
9. Howard K. Beale, *Theodore Roosevelt and the Rise of America to World Power* (Baltimore, 1956), p. 382.
10. FDR to Eleanor Roosevelt, n.d., 1915, Elliott Roosevelt, ed., *FDR: His Personal Letters, 1905-1928* (New York, 1948), vol. 2, p. 267.
11. Rosenman, *Public Papers and Addresses . . . 1936* (New York, 1938), p. 289.
12. Speech at the Worcester Polytechnic Institute, 23 June 1919, Roosevelt Papers.
13. Speech at Cumberland, West Virginia, 27 October 1920, Roosevelt Papers.
14. Franklin D. Roosevelt, "Our Foreign Policy: A Democratic View," *Foreign Affairs*, July 1928.
15. Rosenman, *Public Papers and Addresses . . . 1928-1932*, p. 724.
16. Anne O'Hare McCormick, "The Two Men at the Big Moment," *New York Times Magazine*, 6 November 1932.
17. Roosevelt to Ramsay MacDonald, 30 August 1933, U.S. Department of State, *Foreign Relations of the United States, 1933* (Washington, 1950), vol. 1, pp. 210-211.
18. Roosevelt to William C. Bullitt, 21 April 1935, Elliott Roosevelt and Joseph P. Lash, eds., *FDR: His Personal Letters, 1928-1945* (New York, 1950), vol. 1, p. 476.
19. Rosenman, *Public Papers and Addresses . . . 1936*, p. 12.
20. Ibid., p. 289.
21. Franklin D. Roosevelt to Elihu Root, 9 February 1935, in Roosevelt and Lash, eds., *Personal Letters*, 1928-1945, vol. 1, p. 451.
22. Rosenman, *Public Papers and Addresses . . . 1936*, p. 290.

23. Franklin D. Roosevelt to William Phillips, 17 May 1937, in Roosevelt and Lash, eds., *Personal Letters, 1928-1945*, vol. 1, p. 680.
24. Rosenman, *Public Papers and Addresses . . . 1939* (New York, 1941), p. 463.
25. Franklin D. Roosevelt to T. J. O'Brien, 25 May 1938, Roosevelt Papers.
26. Lindsay to Robert L. Craigie, 3 February 1937, Public Records Office, quoted by Richard A. Harrison, "The Runciman Visit to Washington in January 1937," *Canadian Journal of History*, August 1984.
27. La Grange to Joseph Caillaux, 21 January 1938, La Grange, "Final Report on American Trip, February 15, 1938," La Grange Papers, quoted by John McVickar Haight, Jr., *American Aid to France, 1938-1940* (New York, 1970), p. 7.
28. Anne Morrow Lindbergh, *The Wave of the Future* (New York, 1940) pp. 15, 19, 21, 34.
29. Rosenman, *Public Papers and Addresses . . . 1940*, pp. 204-205.
30. Ibid., p. 672.
31. Rosenman, *Public Papers and Addresses . . . 1941* (New York, 1950), pp. 314-315.
32. Rosenman, *Public Papers and Addresses . . . 1944-1945* (New York, 1950), p. 127.
33. Walter Lippmann Memoir, Oral History Office, Columbia University, quoted by Robert A. Divine, *Second Chance: The Triumph of Internationalism in America during World War II* (New York, 1967), p. 157.
34. Sumner Welles, *Where Are We Heading?* (New York, 1946), p. 37.
35. U.S. Department of State, *Foreign Relations of the United States: The Conferences at Cairo and Teheran, 1943* (Washington, 1961), p. 532.
36. U.S. Department of State, *Foreign Relations of the United States: The Conferences at Malta and Yalta, 1945* (Washington, 1955), p. 544.
37. Edward R. Stettinius, Jr., *Roosevelt and the Russians* (New York, 1949), p. 71; T. M. Campbell and G. C. Herring, eds., *The Diaries of Edward R. Stettinius*, Jr., *1943-1946* (New York, 1975), p. 53.

Churchill and Franklin D. Roosevelt: A Marriage of Convenience

1. For example, Robert Dallek, *Franklin D. Roosevelt and American Foreign Policy, 1932-1945* (New York, 1979); Wm. Roger Louis, *Imperialism at Bay, 1941-1945: The United States and the Decolonisation of the British Empire* (Oxford, 1977); Christopher Thorne, *Allies of a Kind: The United States, Britain and the War Against Japan, 1941-1945* (London, 1977). See also Virginia Cowles, *Winston Churchill: The Era and the Man* (London, 1953), pp. 328-350.
2. David Reynolds, *The Creation of the Anglo-American Alliance, 1937-41* (London, 1981), p. 2; D. K. Adams, "Perceptions and Prejudices: British Diplomats Confront the New Deal," in Cornelis A. van Minnen, ed., *The*

Roosevelts: Nationalism, Democracy and Internationalism (Middelburg, 1987), p. 63.

Some members of the British establishment, of course, had a greater appreciation of the United States. For example, Oliver Harvey, private secretary to Anthony Eden from January 1936 to February 1938, records in February 1937 Eden's sense of "the inestimable value to us of the goodwill of Roosevelt." John Harvey, ed., *The Diplomatic Diaries of Oliver Harvey 1937-1940* (London, 1970), p. 19. Compare the frequent references to FDR in the Earl of Avon, *The Eden Memoirs, Facing the Dictators* (London, 1962).

3. Introduction to WSC's lecture in New York, 12 December 1900, in Robert H. Pilpel, *Churchill in America 1895-1961* (New York, 1976), p. 39.
4. Churchill himself wrote: "The greatest tie of all is language," "The Union of the English-Speaking Peoples," *News of the World*, 15 May 1938. See also Allen Nevins, ed., *America Through British Eyes* (New York, 1948); Walter Allen, *TransAtlantic Crossing* (London, 1971); Christopher Mulvey, *Anglo-American Landscapes* (Cambridge, 1983).
5. Howard K. Beale, *Theodore Roosevelt and the Rise of America to World Power* (Baltimore, 1956); Bradford Perkins, *The Great Rapprochement: England and the United States 1895-1914* (New York, 1968); *Kissing Cousins* is the title of a book on British and American culture by Daniel Snowman (London, 1977).
6. Theodore Roosevelt to F. P. Dunne, 3 December 1904, cited in Henry F. Pringle, *Theodore Roosevelt* (London, 1934), p. 281.
7. Paul Kennedy, *The Rise and Fall of the Great Powers* (London, 1988).
8. Cited in Richard Heatcote Heindel, *The American Impact on Great Britain 1898-1914* (Philadelphia, 1940), p. 138; Philip S. Bagwell and G. E. Mingay, *Britain and America 1850-1930* (London, 1970); David Starr Jordan, *America's Conquest of Europe* (Boston, 1913).

   The official catalogue of the Exhibition was more restrained than *The Economist*, compare: *Official Descriptive and Illustrated Catalogue* (3 vols., London, 1851), vol.3, pp. 1431-1432.
9. David Frost and Michael Shea, *The Rich Tide* (London, 1968), pp. 197-231.
10. David Sinclair, *Dynasty: The Astors and Their Times* (London, 1983), cited in Frost and Shea, *Rich Tide* p. 332. See also Virginia Cowles, *The Astors, the Story of a TransAtlantic Family* (New York, 1979).
11. Richard Kenin, *Return to Albion: Americans in England 1760-1940* (New York, 1979), p. 140.
12. Ibid., pp. 152-163, 210-215, 139; see also Maureen E. Montgomery, *'Gilded Prostitution': Status, Money and Transatlantic Marriages, 1870-1914* (London, 1989); Ruth Brandon, *The Dollar Princesses* (London, 1980), and WSC's draft essay on Leonard Jerome in Martin Gilbert, ed., *Winston S. Churchill*, vol. 5, Companion Part 2 Documents, *The Wilderness Years 1929-1935* (London, 1981), pp. 422-423.

13. Lucius Beebe, *The Big Spenders* (Garden City, N.Y., 1966); G. W. Steevens, *The Land of the Dollar* (New York, 1897); Philip Burne-Jones, *Dollars and Diplomacy* (New York, 1904).
14. Isaiah Berlin, *Mr. Churchill in 1940* (London, 1950), pp. 31-32. Robert Rhodes James, *Churchill, A Study in Failure 1900-1939* (London, 1970), p. 348. Berlin's judgment seems more a propos than that of the admiring journalist George W. Steevens in 1898 that WSC "has the twentieth century in his marrow," "The Youngest Man in Europe" in Charles Eade, ed., *Churchill by His Contemporaries* (London, 1953), pp. 61-66.
15. Lord Moran, *Churchill: Taken from the Diaries of Lord Moran* (Boston, 1966), p. 322.
16. Pilpel, *Churchill in America*, pp. 14, 17.
17. Ibid., pp. 34-38.
18. Ibid., p. 61.
19. Ibid., pp. 48-50, 55.
20. Ted Morgan, *FDR: A Biography* (New York, 1985), p. 165; Frank Freidel, *Franklin D. Roosevelt: The Apprenticeship* (Boston, 1952), p. 354; Kay Halle suggests they "met fleetingly," *Winston Churchill on America and Britain* (New York, 1970), p. 48. In his Commons Valedictory Churchill claimed they met "only for a few minutes," *Hansard*, 17 April 1945. See also Francis L. Loewenheim, Harold D. Langley, and Manfred Jonas, eds., *Roosevelt and Churchill: Their Secret Wartime Correspondence* (New York, 1975), pp. 5-6.

    Churchill had, however, paid fulsome tribute to the United States in an article "Will America Fail Us?" *Illustrated Sunday Herald*, 30 November 1919. For this and other occasional pieces see Michael Wolff, ed., *The Collected Essays of Sir Winston Churchill*, 4 vols.(London, 1976).
21. Martin Gilbert, *Winston S. Churchill*, vol. 5, *1922-1939* (London, 1976), pp. 71, 134-135, 76, 79-81, 93, 119, 123, 304.
22. Ibid., pp. 301, 307-308, 310, 315; B.J.C. McKercher has noted Churchill's anti-Americanism during this period in *The Second Baldwin Government and the U.S. 1924-1929* (Cambridge, 1984), pp. 11, 175-176.
23. Gilbert, *Churchill*, vol. 5, pp. 338-351; Pilpel, *Churchill in America*, pp. 78-95; Phyllis Moir, *I Was Winston Churchill's Private Secretary* (New York, 1941), pp. 124-125; Moir calls Baruch Churchill's "best friend in this country," ibid., p. 109; Henry Morgenthau to WSC, 23 October 1929, in Gilbert, *Churchill*, vol. 5, Companion Part 2, p. 106; Warren F. Kimball, *Churchill and Roosevelt: The Complete Correspondence*, 3 vols. (Princeton, 1984), vol. 1, p. 23; Gilbert, *Churchill*, vol. 5, p. 334.

    Churchill had wanted to go back to the United States to observe the 1904 presidential campaign with Burke Cockran but his political duties prohibited this; Randolph S. Churchill, ed., *Winston S. Churchill*, vol. 2 Companion Part 1 (London, 1969), p. 350. Baruch discusses his friendship with WSC in Baruch, *The Public Years* (New York, 1960). See also Margaret L. Coit, *Mr. Baruch* (Boston, 1957).

24. William Manchester, *The Last Lion: Winston Spencer Churchill, vol. 1, Visions of Glory, 1874-1932* (London, 1983), p. 672; Halle, *Churchill on America*, pp. 210-215.
25. Halle, *Churchill on America*, pp. 225-237. Churchill apparently maintained some contacts with the United States. Kay Halle reports that on her first meeting with him in 1931 he told her how much he admired the American ambassador, Charles D. Dawes, and dined with him once a week. Halle, *The Irrepressible Churchill* (London ed., 1985), p. 5.
26. Manchester, *Last Lion*, pp. 715-720; Gilbert, *Churchill*, vol. 5, pp. 420-427; *Washington Post*, 14 February 1932, cited in Pilpel, *Churchill in America*, p. 111; Robert Rhodes James, *Winston S. Churchill: His Complete Speeches* (New York, 1974), vol. 5 *1928-1935*, pp. 5126-5134; Gilbert, *Churchill*, vol. 5, Companion Part 2, pp. 397-399.
27. Churchill speech of 21 April 1932, Gilbert, *Churchill*, vol. 5, p. 428; broadcast on 8 May, Gilbert, *Churchill*, vol. 5, p. 431; speech of 23 November 1932; Halle, *Churchill on America*, p. 48.
28. Gilbert, *Churchill*, vol. 5, pp. 555, 666, 700, 847.
29. Churchill to Louise J. Alber, 11 August 1933, Gilbert, *Churchill*, vol. 5, Companion Part 2, pp. 642-643; Churchill to William Chenery, 15 September 1933, ibid., pp. 653-654; notes for a broadcast, 16 January 1934, ibid., pp. 702-713.
30. Halle, *Churchill on America*, pp. 48-49; Gilbert, *Churchill*, vol. 5, Companion Part 3, p. 733, footnote 1. See also Halle, *Irrepressible Churchill*, pp. 6-7.
31. Kimball, *Churchill and Roosevelt*, vol. 1, p. 23; Gilbert, *Churchill*, vol. 5, Companion Part 2, pp. 692-693.
32. Churchill to Aylmer Vallance, 20 May 1933, Gilbert, Vol. V, Companion Part 2, pp. 605-606. The article was published in *Collier's*, 4 November 1933.
33. Churchill to William Chenery, 13 September 1954, Gilbert, *Churchill*, vol. 5, Companion Part 2, p. 870; Halle, *Churchill on America*, pp. 267-277; Winston S. Churchill, *Great Contemporaries* (London, 1937). The essay on Roosevelt was apparently added with two others to the second printing. A volume of the same title appeared in London in 1935 by an anonymous editor containing a profile of FDR by Ernest K. Lindley.
34. Sir Ronald Lindsay to WSC, 4 December 1933, Gilbert, *Churchill*, vol. 5, Companion Part 2, p. 688; Charles Scribner to WSC, 8 August 1935, ibid., p. 1229.
35. Gilbert, *Churchill*, vol. 5, Companion Part 3, *The Coming of War, 1936-1939* (London, 1982), pp. 732-733; Churchill is also reported to have referred to the "dollar sterling" in 1944; Halle, *Irrepressible Churchill*, p. 6, fn. 2.
36. Gilbert, *Churchill*, vol. 5, p. 679; *Churchill*, vol. 5, Companion Part 3, pp. 34, 311, 351-352, 516, 520-522, 592, 734, 1109, 1116, 1488-1489; "Amer-

ica Looks at Europe," *Evening Standard,* 31 May 1937, reprinted in Winston S. Churchill, *Step by Step 1936-1939* (London, 1939), pp. 134-137.

37. Gilbert, *Churchill,* vol. 5, Companion Part 3, p. 782; James, *Collected Speeches,* vol. 6, pp. 5894-5896; Sir Archibald Sinclair may also have been referring to the quarantine speech when he wrote on 10 October 1937 that "Our maternal cousins are waking up," *Step by Step,* pp. 193-196; Gilbert, *Churchill,* vol. 5, Companion Part 3, pp. 786-787, 865-866; "What Japan Thinks of US," Churchill, *Step by Step,* pp. 205-208. See also "Can America Keep Out of War?," *Collier's,* 2 October 1937.
38. Winston S. Churchill, *The Second World War,* Vol. 1: *The Gathering Storm* (London, 1948), p. 199; James, *Collected Speeches,* vol. 6, p. 5915.
39. "The Union of the English-speaking Peoples," *News of the World,* 15 May 1938; Halle, *Churchill in America,* pp. 288-300; R. W. B. Clarke to Brendan Bracken, 24 April 1938, Gilbert, *Churchill,* vol. 5, Companion Part 3, p. 1005; WSC to Clementine Churchill, 8 July 1938, ibid., p. 1094.
40. WSC to Ludwig Noe, 26 July 1938; WSC conversation with Major von Kleist, 19 August 1938, Gilbert, *Churchill,* vol. 5, pp. 957, 963-964; "The United States and Europe," *Daily Telegraph,* 4 August 1938, Gilbert, *Churchill,* vol. 5, p. 957, n. 1; *Churchill, Step by Step,* pp. 267-271.
41. Harold R. Peat to WSC, 23 August 1938, Gilbert, *Churchill,* vol. 5, Companion Part 3, pp. 1124-1125; Samuel I. Rosenman, ed., *The Public Papers and Addresses of Franklin D. Roosevelt, 1938* (New York, 1941), pp. 495-499.
42. Gilbert, *Churchill,* vol. 6, p. 967; WSC to Lord Halifax, 31 August 1938, Gilbert, *Churchill,* vol. 5, Companion Part 3, pp. 1130-1131; Churchill, *Gathering Storm,* pp. 228-229. For FDR's overtures to Britain in the late summer of 1938, see, for example, Joseph P. Lash, *Roosevelt and Churchill 1939-1941* (New York, 1976), pp. 25-28.
43. Gilbert, *Churchill,* vol. 5, p. 982; Gilbert, *Churchill,* vol. 5, Companion Part 3, p. 1183. Baruch repeated his offer in April 1939, ibid., p. 1431; Gilbert, *Churchill,* vol. 5, p. 1034; WSC to Clementine Churchill, 8 January 1939, Gilbert, *Churchill,* vol. 5, Companion Part 3, pp. 1342-1344; see also WSC to Clementine Churchill, 18 January 1939, Gilbert, *Churchill,* vol. 5, Companion part 3, pp. 1346-1349. Clementine was holidaying in the West Indies. Chamberlain had endorsed FDR's Annual Message to Congress, 4 January 1939; for text see Rosenman, *Public Papers and Addresses...* 1939, pp. 1-12.

    Sometime about March 1939 Baruch reported to Hopkins and Roosevelt on the European situation, and gave Churchill's comment that "War is coming very soon. We will be in it and you [the United States] will be in it." Robert E. Sherwood, *The White House Papers of Harry L. Hopkins* (London ed., 1948), p. 111.
44. Broadcast to the United States, 28 April 1939, Gilbert, *Churchill,* vol. 5, Companion Part 3, pp. 1478-1480; Rosenman, *Public Papers and Addresses . . . 1939,* pp. 201-205. In an article of 20 April 1939 Churchill called Roosevelt's appeal "a weighty contribution to the cause of collective

security;" *Churchill, Step by Step*, pp. 352-356; James, *Collected Speeches*, vol. 6, pp. 6068, 6144.

45. Keith V. Gordon, *North America Sees Our King and Queen* (London, 1939); Lash, *Roosevelt and Churchill*, pp. 63-64.
46. Kimball, vol. 1, pp. 24-25; Gilbert, *Churchill*, vol. 6, p. 52; Manchester, *The Caged Lion: Winston Spencer Churchill 1932-1940* (London ed., 1988), pp. 551-552; Kimball, Churchill and Roosevelt, vol. 1, p. 5; Gilbert, *Churchill*, vol. 6, pp. 53-55; Manchester, *Caged Lion*, p. 549.
47. Manchester, *Caged Lion*, p. 550.
48. For developments of the relationship see Lash, *Roosevelt and Churchill*; Herbert Feis, *Churchill-Roosevelt-Stalin* (Princeton, 1957); Kimball, *Churchill and Roosevelt.*
49. Churchill, "The United States and Europe," 4 August 1938, *Step by Step*, p. 267.
50. Michael R. Beschloss, *Kennedy and Roosevelt* (New York, 1980) p. 200; see also p. 230. Churchill's "lording it" was a general characteristic. A friend of the family has written: "The Age of the Common Man had very little appeal for Mr. Churchill," Cowles, *Winston Churchill*, p. 276.

De Gaulle and Franklin D. Roosevelt

1. William Leahy, *I was there. The Personal Story of the Chief of Staff to Presidents Roosevelt and Truman, based on his notes and diaries made at the time* (New York, 1950).
2. Quoted from Frank Freidel, *Franklin D. Roosevelt. A Rendezvous with Destiny* (Boston, 1990), p. 462. Churchill made this joke, answering a query: "Oh, let's don't speak of him. We call him Jeanne d'Arc and we're looking for some bishops to burn him."
3. Quoted in Freidel, *Franklin D. Roosevelt. A Rendezvous with Destiny.*, p. 460.
4. Quoted in Robert Dallek, *Franklin D. Roosevelt and American Foreign Policy, 1932-1945* (New York, 1979), pp. 377-378.
5. Freidel, *Franklin D. Roosevelt. A Rendezvous with Destiny.*, p. 460.
6. Jean Monnet, *Memoires*, (Paris, 1976) passim, and André Kaspi, *La mission de Jean Monnet à Alger, mars-octobre 1943* (Paris, 1971), p. 70.
7. Papiers Jean Monnet, quoted by Kaspi *La mission*, p. 71.
8. Kaspi, *La mission*, p. 71, n. 1.
9. Dallek, *Roosevelt and American Foreign Policy.*, p. 406.
10. Charles de Gaulle, *Memoires de guerre, II, l'Unité, 1942-1944* (Paris, 1956), p. 116. "Do you remember that, during the last war, France played a similar role, as a supplier of armaments, to that played now by the United States? . . . Yes, during World War I, you Americans used only French guns, drove only French armored cars and flew only French airplanes. Did we require, in return, from Belgium, Serbia, Russia, Rumania, did we require

from the United States the appointment of this or that leader or institute this or that political system?"

11. Quoted by Dallek, *Roosevelt and American Foreign Policy*, p. 459.
12. Freidel, *Franklin D. Roosevelt. A Rendezvous with Destiny*, p. 527.
13. De Gaulle, *Mémoires*, pp. 238-240. "Such an organization, according to him, implies the location of American forces on bases scattered all over the world, some of them on French territory .... The discourse of the American president convinces me once more that, in the relations between states, logic and feelings weigh rather little when compared to the realities of power, . . . that France, to regain her place, must rely on herself. I told him this. He smiled and concluded: 'We shall do what we can, but it is true that to help France, nobody can replace the French people."
14. André Kaspi, *Franklin D. Roosevelt* (Paris, 1988), p. 536.
15. Charles de Gaulle, *Mémoires de guerre, III, Le salut, 1944-1946* (Paris, 1959) p. 82. "One knew that our people was eager to take part in the victory. One measured how good was our reborn army. One saw me back in Paris and surrounded by the fervor of the nation. But was the United States convinced that France was able to become again a great power? Were they truly ready to help her?"
16. Department of State Bulletin, 4 March 1945.
17. De Gaulle, *Vol. III*, pp. 87-88. "[FDR] decided on the place of our meeting. It would be Algiers. Had I accepted to go, he would have decided on the date. The invitation of FDR seemed to me unacceptable . . . Why did the American President invite the French President to visit him in France? . . . It is true that, for Franklin D. Roosevelt, Algiers perhaps was not France. One more reason to remind him .... The sovereignty, the dignity of a great nation must be intangible, I was in charge of those of France."
18. "When, on April 12, death came to remove him from his huge task, whereas victory was in sight, I carried wholeheartedly to his memory my regrets and my admiration."
19. Ted Morgan, *FDR. A Biography* (New York, 1985), p. 718.
20. For Leahy, see note 1. Robert D. Murphy, *Diplomat among Warriors* (New York, 1964).
21. Morgan, *FDR. A Biography*, p. 720.
22. Robert A. Divine, *Roosevelt and World War II* (Baltimore, 1969), p. 4.
23. Freidel, Franklin D. Roosevelt. *A Rendezvous with Destiny*, p. 596.

Stalin and Franklin D. Roosevelt

1. U.S. Department of State, *Foreign Relations of the United States*, 1941 vol. 1, pp. 766-767 (hereafter FRUS).
2. *Sovetsko-angliyskiye otnosheniya vo vrema Velikoy Otechestvennoy voyny 1941-1945* [Soviet-English Relations During the Great Patriotic War 1941-1945] (Moscow, 1983), vol. 1, pp. 151-157.

3. *Sovetsko-amerikanskiye otnosheniya vo vremya Velikoy Otechestvennoy voyny 1941-1945* [Soviet-American Relations During the Great Patriotic War 1941-1945] (Moscow, 1984), vol. 1, pp. 147-148.
4. Ibid., p. 149.
5. James MacGregor Burns, *Roosevelt, the Soldier of Freedom* (New York, 1970), p. 230.
6. *Perepiska Predsedatelya Soveta Ministrov SSSR s prezidentami SShA i prem'yer-ministrami Velikobritanii vo vremya Velikoy Otechestvennoy voyny 1941-1945 gg.* [Correspondence of the Chairman, USSR Council of Ministers, with the Presidents of the U.S. and Prime Ministers of Great Britain During the Great Patriotic War 1941-1945], 2nd ed., vol. 2, pp. 17-18.
7. *Sovetsko-amerikanskiye otnosheniya*, vol. 1, p. 179.
8. *FRUS*, 1942, Roosevelt-Molotov Discussions, vol. 3 (Washington, 1961), pp. 566-583.
9. *Sovetsko-amerikanskiye otnosheniya*, vol. 1, p. 203.
10. Elliott Roosevelt, *As He Saw It* (Westport, Conn., 1946), pp. 54-55.
11. *FRUS*, The Conferences at Cairo and Teheran, 1943 (Washington, 1961), pp. 254-255.
12. *Sovetski Soyuz na mezhdunarodnykh konferentsiyakh perioda Velikoy Otechestvennoy voyny 1941-1945 gg., Tegeranskaya konferentsiya rukovoditeley trekh soyuznykh derzhav—SSSR, SShA i Velikobritanii. 28 noyabrya-1 dekabrya 1943 g.* [The Soviet Union in International Conferences in the Period of the Great Patriotic War 1941-1945, the Tehran Conference of the Leaders of the Three Allied Powers—USSR, U.S. and Great Britain. 28 November-1 December 1943] (Moscow, 1984), p. 150.
13. Edward Rozek, *Allied Wartime Diplomacy: A Pattern in Poland* (New York, 1958), pp. 222-223.
14. E. Stettinius, *Roosevelt and the Russians. The Yalta Conference* (Garden City, N.Y., 1949), p. 303.
15. Testimony of Leslie Groves in the Matter of J. Robert Oppenheimer—Transcript of Hearings Before Personnel Security Board, Washington 12 April to 6 May 1954 (Washington, 1954), p. 173.
16. *FRUS*, The Conferences at Washington and Québec 1943, (Washington, 1970), p. 638; J. W. Pickersgill and D. F. Foster, The MacKenzie King Record, 1944-1948 (Toronto, 1968), p. 532.
17. President's Map Room Papers. Naval Aide's File Box 172. General Folder, Manuscript Department, FDR Library, Hyde Park, New York.
18. Churchill to Eden, 25 March 1945, Premier 3, Records number 139/6. Public Records Office, Library of Congress.
19. Perepiska, vol. 2, pp. 211-212.
20. Ibid., p. 214.
21. Anthony Cave Brown, *The Last Hero. Wild Bill Donovan* (New York, 1984), pp. 371-372.
22. Perepiska, vol. 2, pp. 228-229.

Sikorski, Mikolajczyk, and Franklin D. Roosevelt, 1939-1945

1. I do not consider the third Polish prime minister, Tomasz Archiszewski, who took office in December 1944 because by then the relations between the two governments were almost nonexistent.
2. See Anita Prazmowska, *Britain, Poland and the Eastern Front 1939* (Cambridge, 1987).
3. See *Polonia amerykanska: przesziosc i wspolczesnosc*, ed. Hieronim Kubiak (Wroclaw, 1988), a collection of work by Polish and American scholars.
4. U.S. Department of State, *Foreign Relations of the United States, 1941*, (Washington) vol. 1, pp. 232-234 (hereafter FRUS).
5. Jan Ciechanowski, *Defeat in Victory* (London, 1948), pp. 30-31. During Sikorski's speaking tour he addressed Americans of Polish descent in Chicago, Detroit, Buffalo, and New York.
6. Sikorski's numerous works include *Modern Warfare*, a thoughtful book on the character of the future war, issued in Poland in 1934, and then, in translation, in France in 1935, twice in the Soviet Union up to 1936, in Britain in 1942, and in the United States in 1943 with a note by George C. Marshall.
7. Jan Ciechanowski, the Polish ambassador during the war years, left a rather vivid political portrait of himself in his memoirs, the image of a man too often taken aback. He presented his credentials in March 1941, but he had already served as a minister to the United States from 1922 to 1929. See a more lenient assessment of his role in *A Question of Trust. The Origins of the U.S.-Soviet Diplomatic Relations: The Memoirs of Loy W. Henderson* (Palo Alto, Calif., 1986), pp. 517-519.
8. Edward W. Raczynski, *W sojuszniczym Londynie. Dziennik Ambasadora . . . 1939-1945* (London, 1960). The author was also acting as the Polish foreign minister at the time.
9. Sarah Meiklejohn Terry's *Poland's Place in Europe. General Sikorski and the Origin of the Oder-Neisse Line, 1939-1943* (Princeton, N.J., 1983) contains a rich picture of the debate on the future of Poland's western frontier, although the conclusions she draws are not quite convincing.
10. *FRUS, 1942*, vol. 3, pp. 108-110. See also Stanislaw Stronski, *General Sikorski's Achievement* (Glasgow, 1944), p. 21.
11. Elliott Roosevelt and Joseph P. Lash, eds., *FDR: His Personal Letters, 1928-1945* (New York, 1950), vol. 2, p. 1290.
12. *FRUS, 1942*, vol. 3, pp. 123-133.
13. Ibid., pp. 136-137. Terry is right in saying that "the irony of Sikorski's program was that its greatest strength was also its greatest weakness. While every element reinforced the others so that progress in any area tended to promote all, they were so closely interwoven that if any one of those elements was removed the whole structure began to come unstuck" (*Poland's Place in Europe*, p. 144). This flaw was so fundamental that after

the March 1942 meeting with Roosevelt we can observe the unraveling of Sikorski's political program.

14. But even Ciechanowski noticed during two conversations on 24 and 26 March that Roosevelt was "entirely engrossed in matters of war strategy . . . anxious to obtain the opinion of General Sikorski on various aspects of military problems" and, in the ambassador's words, "had relegated international problems to a later date." Ciechanowski, *Defeat in Victory*, pp. 110-111.
15. Especially worthy of note is the report of the U.S. ambassador to the Polish government, sent to the president, the secretary, and under secretary of state on 9 November. *FRUS, 1942*, vol. 3, pp. 197-198. Nevertheless, I would argue with Terry's characterization of Sikorski's last visit as "a last desperate effort" Terry, *Poland's Place in Europe*, p. 298.
16. Terry, *Poland's Place in Europe*, p. 109; Ciechanowski, *Defeat in Victory*, pp. 134-147. It seems that the date of departure was changed at the last moment, and instead of leaving on 7 January, Sikorski left three days later. See Welles's memo of 4 January 1943 in *FRUS, 1943*, vol. 3, p. 318.
17. He is reported to have said: "I do not ask for a definite answer in these matters. I know that they are touchy for you at this moment, Mr. President. I ask only for serious consideration of our arguments and [that you] undertake discussion of these subjects with us at the appropriate time." But this reticence included more than the question of Poland's western boundary cited by Terry, *Poland's Place in Europe*, p. 112.
18. *FRUS, 1942*, vol. 3, pp. 199-202.
19. Ibid., pp. 204-208.
20. Robert E. Sherwood, *The White House Papers of Harry L. Hopkins. An Intimate History*, vol. 2, January 1942-July 1945 (London, 1949), p. 707.
21. *FRUS, 1943*, vol. 3, pp. 320-321.
22. A. Polonsky, ed., *The Great Powers and the Polish Question 1941-1945. A Documentary Study in Cold War Origins* (London, 1976), pp. 113-114.
23. His behavior, at least in regard to the letter addressed to him by Roosevelt, does not justify Terry's characterization of him as "naively optimistic." *Poland's Place in Europe*, p. 118.
24. Ciechanowski, *Defeat in Victory*, p. 147.
25. T. Romer, *Moja misja jako Ambasadora R.P. w Zwiazku Sowieckim, Zeszyty Historyczne* (Paryz, z. 30), p. 164. M. Sokolnicki, *Dziennik ankarski 1939-1943* (London, 1965), p. 543.
26. *FRUS, 1944*, vol. 3, pp. 1402-1403, 1409-1411; Ciechanowski, *Defeat in Victory*, pp. 311-312.
27. *FRUS, 1944*, vol. 3, pp. 1272-1274; L. E. Davis, *The Cold War Begins. Soviet-American Conflict over Eastern Europe* (Princeton, N.J., 1974), pp. 104-107.

Review of American-Yugoslav Relations in World War II

1. The following works provide a partial review of American-Yugoslav relations: Dusan Plenca, *Medunarodni odnosi Jugoslavije u toko drugog svjetskog rata* [Yugoslav International Relations during the Second World War] (Belgrade, 1963); Slobodan Nesovic, *Inostranstvo i nova Jugoslavija 1941-1945* [Foreign Nations and the New Yugoslavia 1941-1945] (Belgrade, 1964), and *Diplomatska igra oko Jugoslavije 1944-1945* [The Diplomatic game and Yugoslavia, 1944-1945] (Zagreb, 1977); Mihajlo Maric, *Kralj i vlada u emigraciji* [King and Government in Exile] (Zagreb, 1966); Sava Kosanovic, *Sta se moglo videti iz emigracije* [What Could Be Seen from Exile] (Belgrade, 1954); Vojimir Kljakovic, "Jugoslovenska vlada u emigraciji i Saveznici prema pitanju Hrvatske 1941-1944" [The Yugoslav Government in Exile, the Allies, and the Croatian Question, 1941-1944], *Casopis za suvremenu povijest* nos. 2-3, (Zagreb, 1971), and no. 1, (1973).
2. *Zajednicar* [The Fraternalist], Pittsburgh, 9 April 1941.
3. Immediately after the war began, the American government established the President's War Relief Control Board to collect aid for states in the anti-Hitlerian coalition. The War Relief Board was supposed to form a special committee for each such country, which would receive a fixed amount of aid from the general fund. Using his connections in Washington, K. Fotic, the Yugoslav envoy, succeeded in establishing the United Yugoslav War Relief Fund. Many famous Americans joined this committee. The committee reported on its activity in *The News Bulletin of the United Yugoslav Relief Fund,* which was published in New York. Much later, on 16 December 1944, a much more successful fund for the collection of aid was established under the name The War Relief Fund of Americans of South Slavic Descent. Before its dissolution in 1949, this fund had collected goods and money totaling $3,264,649.
4. See Plenca, *Medunarodni odnosi Jugoslavije*, p. 36.
5. Ibid., p. 13.
6. Bogdan Radica, "O radu Hrvata u USA za vrijeme proslog rata" [The Work of Croats in the USA during the Last War], *Hrvatska revija*, vol.1, year VII, p. 55 (Buenos Aires, March 1957). On the visit of the king to the United States, see Plenca, *Medunarodni odnosi Jugoslavije*, p. 136, and Maric, *Kralj i vlada,* p. 217.
7. *Zajednicar*, 30 September 1942. According to FDR's statement, he always instructed Elmer Davis to portray the guerilla activity in Yugoslavia as Yugoslav, which was meant to refer to everyone in the country who offered resistance to the Axis forces. According to Roosevelt, every individual would be rewarded at the end of the war in accordance with his services. See Kljakovic, *Jugoslovenska vlada*, p. 121.
8. *Zajednicar*, 30 September 1942.
9. Adamic Collection, Immigration History Research Center, St. Paul, Minnesota. In April 1917 President Wilson founded the Committee on Public

Information whose goal was not only to make public everything that the government considered necessary during the war but also to give the government itself a source of information. George Creel was put in charge of the office. The office had subcommittees, among which was the Yugoslav Bureau Committee on Public Information, which was run by Peter Mladineo. In 1922 the Committee on Public Information was transformed into the Foreign Language Information Service (FLIS), which had the following purposes: to supply foreign-language speakers in the United States with accurate information in their own languages and to establish connections between the American government and these immigrants. The head of the Yugoslav department was Ivan Mladineo. FLIS was reformed in 1939. The agency had its own official publication, *Common Ground*, which Adamic edited until his resignation.

10. Sava Kosanovic, the minister of the Yugoslav government, lived in exile in the United States.
11. Kosanovic, *Sta se moglo videti*, p. 16.
12. It is necessary to emphasize that President Roosevelt condemned the behavior of both the Germans and the Pavelic regime in his message to Yugoslavs in January 1942. He stressed that "the majority of Croats are peaceful followers of the legitimate leaders, Dr. Vlatko Macek" and that "all famous people who have abstained from supporting Pavelic have been sent to concentration camps." See Kljakovic, *"Jugoslovenska vlada,"* p. 116.
13. Kosanovic, "Jugoslovenska vlada," p. 16.
14. B. Radica, "O radu Hrvata u USA," p. 57. In January 1942 President Roosevelt stated to Sumner Welles, the American Under Secretary of State, that a plebiscite would be carried out in Yugoslavia after the war so that the question of "friction between [Yugoslavia's] peoples, especially between the Serbs and the Croats" would be resolved once and for all. See Sumner Welles, *Seven Decisions* (New York, 1951), p. 136, and Plenca, *Medunarodni odnosi Jugoslavije*, p. 138.
15. See Nesovic, *Diplomatska igra*, and Plenca, *Medunarodni odnosi Jugoslavije*.
16. Vladimir Dedijer, *Beleske iz Amerike* [Notes from America] (Belgrade, 1945), p. 145. The Yugoslav government in London exerted great effort to attain American protection for the chetniks. In April 1943 S. Jovanovic called Ambassador Fotic to London for consultation. On May 5, after his return to Washington, Fotic visited Roosevelt, who expressed the hope that an agreement could be reached whereby the partisans and the chetniks would be active in separate zones in order to avoid further fratricidal warfare. See Plenca, *Medunarodni odnosi Jugoslavije*, p. 179.
17. Dedijer, *Beleske*, p. 45.
18. Ibid, p. 50.
19. Kosanovic, *Jugoslovenska vlada*, p. 68.

20. Nesovic provides an excellent summary of the writing in the American press about events in Yugoslavia during the war. In addition, he translated and published a large number of these articles in Serbo-Croation.
21. The United Committee of South Slavic Americans published the pamphlet in May 1944 in New York.
22. Dedijer, *Beleske*, p. 173.
23. Ibid., p. 165.
24. Winifred N. Hadsel, "The Struggle for Yugoslavia," *Foreign Policy Reports,* Foreign Policy Association, 19, no. 24 (1944), pp. 314-27.

Wilhelmina and Franklin D. Roosevelt: A Wartime Relationship

1. The private papers of Queen Wilhelmina could not be researched for this chapter. The director of the Royal Archives made available some copies of correspondence between Queen Wilhelmina and President Roosevelt to the author.
2. A general survey of the Dutch international position until the loss of the Indies appears in March 1942 in A. F. Manning, "The Position of the Dutch Government in London up to 1942," *Journal of Contemporary History* 13 (1978), pp. 117-135.
3. A. E. Kersten, "Van Kleffens' plan voor regionale veiligheidsorganisaties," *Jaarboek van het Departement van Buitenlandse Zaken 1980-1981* ('s-Gravenhage, 1981), pp. 157-164.
4. E. N. van Kleffens, *Belevenissen, vol. 2, 1940-1958* (Alphen aan den Rijn, 1983), p. 105.
5. Wilhelmina, *Eenzaam maar niet alleen* (Baarn, 1959), p. 333. Published in English as *Lonely But Not Alone* (New York, 1960).
6. Elliott Roosevelt and Joseph P. Lash, eds., *FDR: His Personal Letters, 1928-1945* (New York, 1950), vol. 2, p. 953.
7. A. F. Manning, "Koningin Wilhelmina," in C. A. Tamse, ed., *Nassau en Oranje in de Nederlandse Geschiedenis* (Alphen aan den Rijn, 1979), pp. 382-383.
8. Royal Archives (The Hague): file A50-VIIb-V2a, report Gordon to Roosevelt, 14 November 1939.
9. Ibid., Wilhelmina to Roosevelt, 12 February 1940.
10. Queen Wilhelmina put great pressure on Prince Bernhard to leave Holland together with Princess Juliana and their daughters, and she threatened to commit suicide in case he refused to do so. *NRC-Handelsblad*, 9 May 1990.
11. L. de Jong, *Het Koninkrijk der Nederlanden in de Tweede Wereldoorlog. vol. 9: Londen* ('s-Gravenhage, 1979), pp. 12-15; Roosevelt and Lash, eds., *FDR*, vol. 2, p. 1027.
12. FDR's correspondence with Queen Wilhelmina and other members of the royal family has been preserved in the F. D. Roosevelt Library at Hyde Park (N.Y.), President's Secretary File, box 62, folder: Netherlands.

13. Documenten betreffende de Buitenlandse Politiek van Nederland 1919-1945. Periode C: 1940-1945 (hereafter referred to: *DBPN, C)*, vol. 5 ('s-Gravenhage, 1987), pp. 58-60.
14. Roosevelt and Lash, eds., *FDR*, vol. 2, pp. 1377-1378.
15. J. Roosevelt and S. Shalett, *Affectionately FDR* (New York, 1959), p. 318.
16. W. D. Hassett, *Off the Record with F.D.R. 1942-1945* (New Brunswick, 1958), p. 76.
17. Roosevelt and Lash, eds., FDR, vol. 2, p. 953.
18. De Jong, *Het Koninkrijk,* vol. 9, pp. 1099-1100.
19. *DBPN, C,* vol. 3, pp. 234-235; De Jong, *Het Koninkrijk,* vol. 9, pp. 110-111.
20. Van Kleffens, *Belevenissen, vol. 2*, p. 105.
21. Ibid., p. 106.
22. Ibid., pp. 106-107; *DBPN, C,* vol. 5, p. 60.
23. Archives of the Netherlands Ministry for Foreign Affairs Washington Embassy archives, file: A7/42.3, cypher telegram no. 1189-1190, 23 June 1943 from Washington Embassy to Ministry for Foreign Affairs London.
24. G. van der Ham, *Wilhelmina in Londen 1940-1945* (Haarlem, 1980), p. 26.
25. Manning, "Koningin Wilhelmina," p. 387.
26. *DBPN, C,* vol. 4, pp. 607-608 and p. 610.
27. *DBPN, C,* vol. 5, pp. 650-656; De Jong, *Het Koninkrijk,* vol. 9, p. 1099.
28. De Jong, *Het Koninkrijk,* vol. 9, p. 1102.
29. *DBPN, C,* vol. 5, p. 220.
30. Ibid., pp. 729-932. On the origins of the queen's address see C. Fasseur, "Een wissel op de toekomst: de rede van Koningin Wilhelmina van 6/7 December 1942," in F. van Anrooij et al., eds., *Between People and Statistics. Essays in Modern Indonesian History. Presented to P. Creutzberg* (The Hague, 1979), pp. 267-281. On the Dutch reactions to American anti-colonialism during World War II, see A. E. Kersten, "The Dutch and the American Anti-Colonialist Tide 1942-1945," in R. Jeffreys-Jones, ed., *Eagle against Empire: American opposition to European Imperialism 1914-1982* (Aix-en-Provence, 1983), pp. 91-116.
31. C. G. Thorne, *Allies of a Kind. The United States, Great Britain and the War against Japan 1941-1945* (London, 1978), pp. 218-219.
32. Franklin D. Roosevelt Library, Hyde Park (N.Y.); President's Secretary File, folder: Netherlands: letter Queen Wilhelmina, 7 November 1942.
33. Ibid., 6 March 1943.
34. Ibid.
35. Archives of the Netherlands Ministry for Foreign Affairs, Washington Embassy Archives: file A7/42.3, cypher telegram no.1189-1190, 23 June 1943.
36. Roosevelt and Lash, eds., *FDR*, vol. 2, pp. 1534-1535.
37. Franklin D. Roosevelt Library, President's Personal File, box 693, folder Wehle, 4 December 1944; Hoover Institution on War, Revolution and Peace

at Stanford (Calif.), Stanley K. Hornbeck Papers, box 470, folder November 1944, memorandum 20 November 1944.

38. Wilhelmina, *Eenzaam*, pp. 325-326.
39. Hornbeck Papers, memorandum 20 November 1944.

The Oslo States and Franklin D. Roosevelt

1. Quotation from Robert Dallek, *Franklin D. Roosevelt and American Foreign Policy, 1932-1945* (New York, 1979), p. 207.
2. Ibid., p. 211.
3. Author of *The Rise and Fall of the Great Powers* (New York, 1987).
4. See Ger van Roon, *Small States in Years of Depression. The Oslo Alliance 1930-1940* (Assen, Netherlands, 1989).
5. Trip to Ruys de Beerenbrouck, 24 April 1933, Dutch State Archives (hereafter ARA), files Ruys de Beerenbrouck.
6. Samuel I. Rosenman, ed., *The Public Papers and Addresses of Franklin D. Roosevelt, 1933* (New York, 1938), p. 192.
7. Haakon to Roosevelt, 17 May 1933, National Archives (hereafter NA), State Department (hereafter SD) 500.Al5a5/1970.
8. Christian to Roosevelt, 17 May 1933, NA, SD 500.Al5A4/1969.
9. Gustav to Roosevelt, 17 May 1933, NA, SD 500.Al5a4/1971.
10. Albert to Roosevelt, 18 May 1933, NA, SD 500.Al5a4/1976.
11. Wilhelmina to Roosevelt, 17 May 1933, NA, SD 500.Al5a4/1968.
12. Crocker to Hull, 24 May 1933, NA, SD 500.Al5a4/2087.
13. Gibson to Hull, 20 May 1933, NA, SD 500.Al5a4/1924.
14. See Walter Lippman, ed., *The United States in World Affairs, 1933: An Account of American Foreign Relations* (New York, 1934), pp. 96-97.
15. Michael Anthony Butler, "*The Neutrals, 1933-1940: The United States, the Oslo Nations and the response to Hitler*" (thesis, M.A. University of Virginia, 1980), pp. 123ff.
16. Van Roon, *Small States*, p. 168.
17. Report of Norwegian envoy, 21 June, 1937, Archives of the Department of Foreign Affairs, Oslo (UDO,H 12 A 2/30).
18. Report of A.Th. Lamping, director of trade agreements, on talks held in Washington, 1 July 1937, ARA, Department of Foreign Affairs (hereafter BuZa), Economic Affairs Section (hereafter DEZ), no. 110.
19. "Fundamental Principles of International Policy," Washington 1937.
20. Ibid., p. 53-54.
21. Walter to Hull, 7 August 1937, NA, SD 711.00, Statement 16 July 1937/120.
22. "Need for a new Constructive Effort in the Field of International Economic Relations," Public Record Office, London (PRO,T 188,148).
23. Henry to Delbos, 7 July 1937, French Department of Foreign Affairs, Paris (AEP), Commercial Relations (Rel. Comm.), vol. 92.
24. Note pour le Ministre, 19 July 1937, ibid.

25. ". . . il semble intéressant d'examiner les perspectives d'une coopération plus large entre l'Amérique et l'Europe . . ." ibid., 9 July 1937.
26. Van Haersma de With to Patijn, 2 February 1938, copy, Dutch Archives of the former Colonial Department (Kol.), V, 7.3.1938-32.
27. Van Limburg Stirum to Patijn, 31 December 1937, copy ARA, BuZa, Legation London.
28. See Dallek, *Franklin D. Roosevelt*, pp. 152-153.
29. Ibid., P. 155.
30. Hull to Johnson, 28 January 1938, NA, SD 865 D.01/366.
31. Butler, "The Neutrals," p. 306.
32. Ibid., p. 307.
33. Général van Overstraeten, *Albert I-Léopold III, Vingt ans de politique militaire belge* (Paris-Bruxelles, n.d.).
34. M.A. Butler, "The Neutrals," p. 320.
35. Gordon to Hull, 27 and 28 September 1938, NA, SD 760 F.62/1205 and 1215.
36. Gordon to Hull, 29 September 1938, NA, SD 760F. 62/1292.
37. Ibid.
38. Diary of J. E. Meyer Ranneft, senior Netherlands naval attaché in Washington, 4 January 1939, Dutch Ministry of Defence, Naval Archives (Mar.,Hist., Ec.-l).
39. Text of the telegram in ibid. (Mar., Hist., JC-3/9; see diary of Meyer Ranneft, 25 January 1939).
40. Van Overstraeten, Albert I-Léopold III, p. 262.
41. Ibid., p. 306.
42. Ibid., p. 330.
43. Waller to Hull, 4 November 1938, NA, SD 500 C/952.
44. Butler, *"The Neutrals,"* p. 336.
45. Herry to Brussels, 18 April 1939, Belgian Foreign Affairs Archives, Brussels (AEB), Série 11.179-7.
46. Van Roon, *Small States*, p. 284.
47. Text in archives of the Foreign Ministry Helsinki, Fb 7:10 7B.
48. Dallek, *Franklin D. Roosevelt*, p. 197.
49. See John A. Garraty, "The New Deal, National Socialism and the Great Depression," *American Historical Review* 784 (1973): 917; Richard W. Steele, "The Pulse of the People. Franklin D. Roosevelt and the Gauging of American Public Opinion," *Journal of Contemporary History*, 9 (1974): 195.
50. "The President intends to discuss with the Belgian Ambassador and myself the possibility of a safe zone to allow shipping flying a neutral flag to reach the ports of Antwerp and Rotterdam. Please wire me your views" (Loudon to Van Kleffens, 28 August 1939, copy ARA, BuZa, legation Washington.
51. Dated 31 August 1939, ibid.

52. Van Kleffens to Harinxma, 30 September 1939, copy ARA, BuZa, legation London.
53. Memorandum, 28 September 1939 (annex to copy referred to in ibid.)
54. Reports on this in NA, SD 740.00112 Navicert, 3/10 and 5/10; see also Loudon to Van Kleffens, 29 September 1939, copy ARA, BuZa, legation Washington.
55. See Van Roon, *Small States*, p. 322.
56. "The President warned . . ." Dutch Ministry of Defence, Naval Archives, Diary Meijer Ranneft, 18 October 1939.
57. Loudon to Van Kleffens, 23 October 1939, copy ARA, BuZa, legation Washington.
58. Note by Moffat, 29 October 1939, NA, SD 760D.61/356.
59. See Van Roon, *Small States*, pp. 333 ff.
60. Sterling to Hull, 13 February 1940, NA, SD 500.A21/22.
61. Spaak to Cudahy, 6 March 1940, copy Luxembourg State Archives (hereafter AE Lux.), Archives of the Department of Foreign Affairs (hereafter AE) 3785.
62. Loudon to Van Kleffens, 2 April 1940, copy ARA, BuZa, legation Washington.
63. Loudon to Van Kleffens, 29 March 1940, copy in ibid.
64. Bech to Waller, 7 May 1940, copy AE Lux., AE 3785.
65. Butler, *"The Neutrals,"* p. 248.

Latin America and Franklin D. Roosevelt

1. Arthur M. Schlesinger, Jr., "Franklin D. Roosevelt: The Education of a Statesman," in Cornelis A. van Minnen, ed., *The Roosevelts: Nationalism, Democracy and Internationalism*, Roosevelt Study Center Publications no. 4 (Middelburg, 1987), p. 43.
2. Cordell Hull, *The Memoirs of Cordell Hull*, 2 vols. (New York, 1948).
3. República de Colombia, *Política Internacional* (1936) p. 130.
4. La Nación, Buenos Aires, 30 November 1936.
5. Alfonso Aguilar, *Pan Americanism: A View From the Other Side* (Monthly Review Press, 1965), p. 69.
6. V. Andrade, *My Mission for Revolutionary Bolivia* (University of Pittsburgh, 1976) p. 54.
7. Frank Freidel, *Franklin D. Roosevelt: The Apprenticeship* (Boston, 1952).
8. Arthur M. Schlesinger, Jr., *The Cycles of American History* (Boston, 1986).
9. A. Gomez Robledo, *Reflexiones*: Idea y Experiencia de America (Fondo de Cultura Económica, Mexico, 1958).
10. Interview with author, Saenz's home, Tepoztlan, Morelos, 13 August 1989.
11. Interview with author, Carlos Fuentes' home, Mexico City, 17 August 1989.
12. Octavio Paz, *Tiempo Nublado* (Mexico, 1987) p.82.

Chiang Kai-shek and Franklin D. Roosevelt

* The author wishes to thank the Faculty Council of the University of North Carolina at Chapel Hill for its financial support of this research.

1. Chiang Kai-shek [hereafter CKS] talk with Currie, 22 July 1942, in *Chung-hua min-kuo chung-yao shih-liao ts'u-pien, tui Jih k'ang-chan shih-ch'i*, part 3, *Chan-shih wai-chiao* [hereafter *Wartime Diplomacy*], vol. 1, pp. 635-636; CKS talk with Currie, 4 August 1942, *ibid.*, vol. 1, pp. 698-703.
2. CKS talk with Currie, 4 August 1942, *Wartime Diplomacy*, vol. 1, pp. 698-703.
3. CKS cable to Mme. Chiang, 26 March 1943, *Wartime Diplomacy*, vol. 1, pp. 817-818.
4. Foreign Minister Wang Ch'ung-hui cable to CKS, 21 November 1938, *Wartime Diplomacy*, vol. 1, p. 81; Ambassador Wang Cheng-t'ing cable to Chinese foreign ministry, 18 September 1937, *ibid.*, vol. 1, p. 409.
5. Yen Hui-ch'ing cable to CKS, 3 November 1939, *Wartime Diplomacy*, vol. 1, pp. 89-90.
6. *Wartime Diplomacy*, vol. 1, pp. 78-79; Willys Peck to Hull, 19 July 1937, U.S. Department of State, *Foreign Relations of the United States* [hereafter *FRUS*], *1937*, vol. 3, p. 206; memorandum by Hornbeck, 12 July 1937, *ibid.*, p. 144.
7. FDR cable to CKS, 10 November 1938, *Tsung-t'ung Chiang kung ta-shih ch'ang-pien ts'u-kao* [hereafter *CKS Chronicle]*, vol. 4, p. 265.
8. Hu Shih to CKS, 1 December 1940, *Wartime Diplomacy*, vol. 1, p. 125; pp. 121-125.
9. Report by Currie to Roosevelt, 15 March 1941, President's Secretary's File, Box 427, Roosevelt Papers.
10. Ch'en Li-wen, *Sung Tze-wen yu chan-shih wai-chiao*, pp. 136, 140-141.
11. *CKS Chronicle*, vol. 5, pp. 420-424; CKS cable to FDR, 13 November 1943, *ibid.*, p. 430.
12. Entry of 13 April 1945, *Wang Shih-chieh Diary*.
13. Chiang's diary entry on 31 May 1939, *CKS Chronicle*, vol. 4, pp. 358-359.
14. *CKS Chronicle*, vol. 4, p. 112.
15. Hu Sung-ping, ed., *Hu Shih-chih hsien-sheng nien-p'u ch'ang-pien ts'u-kao*, vol. 5, pp. 1646-1647.
16. Ibid., p. 1650.
17. Hu Shih's cable to Chiang on 20 October 1938, in Hu Sung-ping, Hu Shih-chin, vol. 5, pp. 1648-1649; Hu Shih cable to Chinese foreign ministry, 12 October 1940, in ibid., p. 1710.
18. CKS talk with U.S. ambassador on 29 August 1939, in *CKS Chronicle*, vol. 4, pp. 255-256, 264, 404.
19. *Hu Shih jen chu Mei ta-shih ch'i-chien wanglai tienkao*, p. 50.
20. CKS talk with British ambassador on 14 October 1940, *CKS Chronicle*, vol. 4, p. 586; CKS talk with U.S. ambassador Johnson on 18 October 1940, ibid., pp. 587-588.
21. CKS proposal dated 9 November 1940, *CKS Chronicle*, vol. 4, p. 595.

22. *CKS Chronicle,* vol. 4, p. 611.
23. CKS cable to T. V. Soong in D.C., 21 June 1942, *Wartime Diplomacy,* vol. 1, pp. 156-157.
24. CKS talk with Currie, 15 February 1941. *Wartime Diplomacy,* vol. 1, pp. 558-559.
25. Chiang cable to T. V. Soong in D.C., 21 June 1942. *Wartime Diplomacy,* vol. 1, pp. 156-157.
26. CKS cable to Mme. Chiang, 12 February 1943, *Wartime Diplomacy,* vol. 1, pp. 790-791.
27. CKS cable to FDR, 16 November 1942, *Wartime Diplomacy,* vol. 1, p. 781.
28. For a sample of Mme. CKS's assessment, see her cable from New York to CKS, 28 November 1942, *Wartime Diplomacy,* vol. 1, pp. 782-783.
29. Mme. Chiang from New York to CKS, 28 November 1942, *Wartime Diplomacy,* vol. 1, pp. 782-783; Mme. CKS cable to CKS, 1 March 1943, *CKS Chronicle,* vol. 5, pp. 286-287.
30. CKS talk with Currie, 26 February 1941, *Wartime Diplomacy,* vol. 1, pp. 591-595.
31. T. V. Soong cable to CKS, 3 June 1941, *Wartime Diplomacy,* vol. 1, pp. 725-726.
32. *Wartime Diplomacy,* vol. 1, pp. 827-829.
33. CKS talk with Lattimore, 31 July 1941, *Wartime Diplomacy,* vol. 1, pp. 730-732.
34. CKS talk with Lattimore, 31 July 1941, *Wartime Diplomacy,* vol. 1, pp. 730-732; Lattimore letter to Mme. Chiang, 1 August 1941, ibid., vol. 1, pp. 732-734.
35. CKS talk with Wallace, 8 July 1944, *Wartime Diplomacy,* vol. 1, pp. 875-876.
36. Ross Koen, *The China Lobby in American Politics;* Stanley Bachrack, *The Committee of One Million: "China Lobby" Politics,* 1953-1971.
37. FDR message to CKS, January (date not given) 1944, in FDR President's Personal File #7308.
38. CKS cable to FDR, 17 June 1944, *Wartime Diplomacy,* vol. 1, pp. 172-173.
39. CKS cable to FDR, 17 June 1944, *Wartime Diplomacy* , vol. 1, pp. 172-173; CKS talk with Wallace, 8 July 1944, ibid., pp. 875-876.
40. CKS cable to FDR, 12 January 1942, *Wartime Diplomacy,* vol. 1, pp. 738-739.
41. Lattimore from D.C. to CKS, 28 December 1942, *Wartime Diplomacy,* vol. 1, pp. 747-748.
42. Michael Schaller, *The U.S. Crusade in China, 1938-1945,* pp. 148-149; Elliot Roosevelt, *As He Saw It,* pp. 152-164; Hurley to FDR, 20 November 1943, *FRUS, 1943, China,* pp. 163-166.
43. FDR cable to CKS, 4 July 1942, *Wartime Diplomacy,* vol. 1, pp. 627-628.
44. H. H. K'ung cable to CKS from New York, 17 August 1944, *Wartime Diplomacy,* vol. 1, pp. 176-177; Schaller, pp. 148-149; Roosevelt, *As He Saw It,* pp. 152-164; Hurley to FDR, 20 November 1943, *FRUS, 1943, China,* pp. 163-166.

45. *Wartime Diplomacy,* vol. 1, pp. 467-478.
46. Currie conversation with CKS, 22 July 1942, *Wartime Diplomacy,* vol. 1, p. 13.
47. CKS talk with Currie, 22 July 1942, *Wartime Diplomacy,* vol. 1, p. 13.
48. CKS cable to T. V. Soong, 10 July 1940, *Wartime Diplomacy,* vol. 1, pp. 415, 421, 113.
49. Schaller, *U.S. Crusade,* pp. 36-37.
50. Currie cable to Lattimore, 26 November 1941, *Wartime Diplomacy,* vol. 1, p. 736. Also see: Memorandum of Hull, 27 May 1942, *FRUS, 1942, China,* p. 571; *Wartime Diplomacy,* vol. 1, pp. 504, 669-670; Cordell Hull, *The Memoirs of Cordell Hull,* p. 318; Memorandum of T. V. Soong, 2 June 1941, T. V. Soong Files, Box 24.
51. FDR letter to CKS, 19 December 1943, *CKS Chronicle,* vol. 5, p. 459.
52. FDR cable to CKS, 4 July 1942, *Wartime Diplomacy,* vol. 1, pp. 627-628.
53. As an example see H. H. K'ung cable from D.C. to CKS, 7 November 1944, *Wartime Diplomacy,* vol. 1, p. 199.
54. FDR to Marshall, 8 March 1943, in Romanus and Sunderland, *Stilwell's Mission to China,* pp. 279-282.
55. Ambassador Wei Tao-ming cable to CKS, 11 May 1944, *Wartime Diplomacy,* vol. 1, pp. 171-172.
56. Chiang was told by K'ung that while the U.S. government and press had made many harsh attacks against China, FDR understood the real situation and calmly handled the problem, which alleviated the situation significantly. See: H. H. K'ung cable from D.C. to CKS, 7 November 1944, *Wartime Diplomacy,* vol. 1, p. 199.
57. *CKS Chronicle,* vol. 5, p. 696.
58. CKS talk with Hurley, 24 April 1945, *Wartime Diplomacy,* vol. 1, pp. 210-217.

Hitler's Perception of Franklin D. Roosevelt and the United States of America

1. For a recent bibliography on German-American relations from 1933 to 1945, see Detlef Junker, *Kampf um die Weltmacht. Die USA und das Dritte Reich 1933-1945* (Düsseldorf, 1988), pp. 173-179. On Hitler's perception of the United States and Franklin D. Roosevelt, see James V. Compton, *Hitler und die USA. Die Amerikapolitik des Dritten Reiches und die Ursprünge des Zweiten Weltkrieges* (Oldenburg/Hamburg, 1968); Saul Friedländer, *Auftakt zum Untergang. Hitler und die Vereinigten Staaten 1939-1941* (Stuttgart, 1965); Joachim Remak, "Hitlers Amerikapolitik," *Aussenpolitik* 6 (1955): 706-714; Gerhard L. Weinberg, "Hitler's Image of the United States," in Gerhard L. Weinberg, *World in the Balance. Behind the Scenes of World War II* (Hannover, 1981), pp. 53-74; Harald Frisch, *Das Deutsche Rooseveltbild 1933-1941* (Berlin, 1967); Andreas Hillgruber, "Der Faktor Amerika in Hitlers Strategie 1938-1941," in Andreas Hillgru-

ber, *Deutsche Grossmacht- und Weltpolitik im 19. und 20. Jahrhundert* (Düsseldorf, 1977), pp. 197-222; Andreas Hillgruber, "Hitler und die USA 1933-1945," in Detlef Junker, guest ed., *Deutschland und die USA 1890-1985*. Heidelberg American Studies Background Paper No. 2 (Heidelberg, 1986), pp. 27-41. Gordon A. Craig, "Roosevelt and Hitler: The Problem of Perception," in Klaus Hildebrand and Reiner Pommerin, eds., *Deutsche Frage und Europäisches Gleichgewicht. Festschrift für A. Hillgruber* (Köln, 1985), pp. 169-194. Robert Edwin Herzstein, *Roosevelt & Hitler. Prelude to War* (New York, 1989).

2. Quoted in Holger H. Herwig, *Politics of Frustration: The United States in German Naval Planning, 1889-1941* (Boston, 1976), p. 188.
3. Adolf Hitler, *Mein Kampf*, XVI. Aufl. (München, 1932), vol. 1, pp. 313-314, vol. 2, pp. 490, 721-723.
4. *Hitlers Zweites Buch. Ein Dokument aus dem Jahre 1928*. Eingeleitet und kommentiert von Gerhard L. Weinberg (Stuttgart, 1961), pp. 120-132.
5. Rainer Zitelmann, *Hitler. Selbstverständnis eines Revolutionärs* (Hamburg, 1987), pp. 320-324; see Peter Krüger, "Zu Hitlers 'nationalsozialistischen Wirtschaftserkenntnissen,'" *Geschichte und Gesellschaft* 6 (1980): 263-282.
6. *Hitlers Zweites Buch*, pp. 122, 130.
7. See Hitler's statements in 1941: Adolf Hitler, *Monologe im Führerhauptquartier 1941-1944. Die Aufzeichnungen Heinrich Heims*, edited by Werner Jochmann (Hamburg, 1980), pp. 47, 56, 78; *Akten zur Deutschen Auswärtigen Politik* (hereafter *ADAP*), Serie D, 1937-1941, vol. 13, no. 2, pp. 566-568, 695-696, 703-705.
8. U.S. Department of State, *Foreign Relations of the United States* (hereafter *FRUS*), *1937*, vol. 1, p. 173.
9. See Andreas Hillgruber, "Hitler und die USA 1933-1945," p. 27; Craig, "Roosevelt and Hitler," p. 185; Weinberg, "Hitler's Image," pp. 61-63; Enrico Syring, "Hitlers Kriegserklärung an Amerika vom 11. Dezember 1941," in Wolfgang Michalka, ed., *Der Zweite Weltkrieg* (München, 1989), p. 683, emphasizes the fact that there is no contemporary evidence for this assumption.
10. See Hans Jürgen Schröder, *Deutschland und die Vereinigten Staaten 1933-1939* (Wiesbaden, 1970), pp. 95-119; Frisch, *Das Deutsche Rooseveltbild*, pp. 31-44.
11. Hermann Rauschning, *Gespräche mit Hitler* (Zürich, 1940); Ernst Hanfstaengel, *Zwichen Weissem und Braunem Haus. Erinnerungen eines politischen Aussenseiters* (München, 1970).
12. Schröder, *Deutschland und die Vereinigten Staaten*, p. 98.
13. *FRUS, 1933*, vol. 1, pp. 143-145; *ADAP*, Serie C: 1933-1937, vol. 1, no. 2, pp. 445-450; an English translation of Hitler's speech in John W. Wheeler-Bennett, ed., *Documents on International Affairs, 1933* (London, 1933), pp. 196-208.
14. Hitler's message and Roosevelt's noncommittal reply in *FRUS, 1934*, vol. 2, p. 419.

15. *Völkischer Beobachter*, 7 June 1933. Quoted in Schröder, *Deutschland und die Vereinigten Staaten*, p. 102.
16. Nikolaus von Below, *Als Hitlers Adjutant* (Mainz, 1980), p. 47; Hitler's speech 11 December 1941, in Max Domarus, ed., *Hitler, Reden und Proklamationen 1932-1945*, vol. 2, no. 2 (München, 1965), pp. 1794-1811.
17. Below, *Als Hitlers Adjutant*, p. 47f.; *Die Tagebücher von Josef Goebbels. Sämtliche Fragmente*. Herausgegeben von Elke Fröhlich im Auftrag des Instituts für Zeitgeschichte und in Verbindung mit dem Bundesarchiv, vol. 3, 1937-1939 (München, 1987), p. 391 (entry 1 January 1938).
18. Detlef Junker, ed., *Deutsche Parlamentsdebatten*, vol. 2, 1919-1933, p. 282, (in Eberhard Jäckel, Detlef Junker, and Axel Kuhn, eds., *Deutsche Parlamentsdebatten*, 3 vols. (Frankfurt, 1970/71).
19. *Staatmänner und Diplomaten bei Hitler. Vertrauliche Aufzeichnungen über Unterredungen mit Vertretern des Auslandes 1939-1941*, herausgegeben und erläutert von Andreas Hillgruber, vol. 1, (Frankfurt, 1967), p. 566; see Hitler, *Monologe*, p. 70f. (9 September 1941) and p. 78 (10 October 1941).
20. Domarus, *Hitler, Reden und Proklamationen*, p. 1803f.
21. See Junker, *Kampf um die Weltmacht*, pp. 39-42.
22. Domarus, *Hitler, Reden und Proklamationen*, pp. 1804, 1807, 1808; see Hitler's speech of 30 January 1939, in Junker, *Deutsche Parlamentsdebatten*, vol. 2, pp. 288-295. Very similar was Hitler's reaction on the Lend-Lease Act. See *Heeresadjutant bei Hitler 1938-1943. Aufzeichnungen des Major Engel*. Herausgegeben von Hildegard von Kotze (Stuttgart, 1974), p. 99.
23. Entries of June 22 and August 23, 1940. See entries 18, 20, and 24 November 1938; 17 December 1938; 24 January 1939; 12 November 1939; 17 June 1940; 5 September 1940; 8 October 1940; 1 February 1941; 17 March 1941; 27 April 1941; 8 June 1941. *Die Tagebücher von Josef Goebbels*, vols. 3 and 4.
24. Domarus, *Hitler. Reden und Proklamationen*, p. 1807.
25. *ADAP*, Serie D., 1937-1945, vol. 6, p. 215.
26. Domarus, *Hitler, Reden und Proklamationen*, p. 1807.
27. Junker, *Deutsche Parlamentsdebatten*, vol. 2, p. 284.
28. *ADAP*, Serie D, 1937-1941, vol. 13, no. 2, p. 712.
29. Domarus, *Hitler, Reden und Proklamationen*, p. 1801f.
30. Hitler, *Monologe*, p. 184. Documentation of Hitler's most important statements about Roosevelt and the United States from 1942 to 1945 in Junker, *Kampf um die Weltmacht*, pp. 157-164.
31. *Hitlers politisches Testament. Die Bormann Diktate vom Februar und April 1945. Mit einem Essay von Hugh R. Trevor-Roper und einem Nachwort von André François-Poncet* (Hamburg, 1981), p. 103f.
32. Generaloberst (Franz) Halder, *Kriegstagebuch*, vol. 2, bearbeitet von Hans-Adolf Jakobsen (Stuttgart, 1963), p. 49; *Staatsmänner und Diplomaten bei Hitler*, vol. 2, p. 550.

33. *Staatmänner und Diplomaten bei Hitler*, vol. 2, p. 41. For the debate about Hitler's declaration of war see Junker, *Kampf um die Weltmacht*; Syring, "Hitlers Kriegserklärung"; Hillgruber, "Der Faktor Amerika"; Hillgruber, "Hitler und die USA"; Eberhard Jäckel, "Die deutsche Kriegserklärung an die Vereinigten Staaten von 1941," in Friedrich H. Kroneck and Thomas Opperman, eds., *Im Dienste Deutschlands und des Rechts. Festschrift für Wilhelm Grewe zum 70. Geburtstag*, pp. 117-137; Peter Herde, *Italien, Deutschland und der Weg in den Krieg im Pazifik 1941* (Wiesbaden, 1983); Gerhard L. Weinberg, "Germany's Declaration of War on the United States. A New Look," in Hans L. Trefousse, ed., *Germany and America. Essays on Problems of International Relations and Immigration* (New York, 1980), pp. 54-70.

Mussolini and Franklin D. Roosevelt

1. Louis A. DeSanti, "U.S. Relations with Italy under Mussolini" (Ph.D. diss., Columbia University, 1952), p. 292. See also Renzo De Felice, *Mussolini il Duce. Lo Stato Totalitario* (Torino, 1981), pp. 446-447.
2. John P. Diggins, *Mussolini and Fascism. The View from America* (Princeton, N.J., 1972), p. 281. On their political culture, see Maurizio Vaudagna, "The New Order and the Historical Myth. Notions of Fall and Revival in the Public Addresses of Franklin D. Roosevelt and Benito Mussolini," Paper presented at the Toronto International Conference, American Studies Association, 2-5 November 1989, pp. 5-6.
3. Loretta Valtz Mannucci, "Giornalisti e diplomatici italiani di fronte alla campagna presidenziale di Franklin D. Roosevelt (1932)," in Giorgio Spini, Gian Giacome Migone, and Massimo Teodori, eds., *Italia e America dalla Grande Guerra a oggi*," (Roma, 1976), p. 70. On "Americanization in Europe, see Frank Costigliola, *Awkward Dominion. American Political, Economic and Cultural Relations with Europe, 1919-1933* (Ithaca, N.Y., 1984); E. S. Roosenberg, *Spreading the American Dream. American Economic and Cultural Expansion, 1890-1945* (New York, 1982); Victoria De Grazia, "Mass Culture and Sovereignity: The American Challenge to European Cinemas, 1920-1960," *Journal of Modern History* 61 (March 1989): 53-87.
4. Anna Maria Martellone, "'Blood against Gold': Anti-American Propaganda in Fascist Italy," *Storia Nordamericana* 3, no. 2 (1986): 55-56.
5. Arthur M. Schlesinger, Jr., *The Age of Roosevelt. The Politics of Upheaval* (Boston, 1960), vol. 3, p. 648.
6. Diggins, *Mussolini*, p. 279.
7. Giovanni Pastore, "Interpretazioni fasciste e confindustriali del New Deal," *Italia e Stati Uniti dall'Indipendenza americana a oggi (1776-1976)* (Genova, 1978), p. 373. See also *Scritti e Discorsi di Benito Mussolini* (Milano, 1936), 17 August 1934.
8. DeSanti, "U.S. Relations," p. 326.

9. Gian Giacomo Migone, *Gli Stati Uniti e il fascimo. Alle origini dell' egemonia americana in Italia* (Milano, 1980); C. Damiani, *Mussolini e gli Stati Uniti* (Bologna, 1980); Gian Giacomo Migone, *Problemi di Storia nei rapporti tra Italia e Stati Uniti* (Torino, 1971); Maurizio Vaudagna, *Corporativismo e New Deal* (Torino, 1981); Daria Frezza, "Il rapporto Italia-USA nel periodo fascista," *Studi Storici* 1 (1974): 184-194.
10. Michela Nacci, *L'antiamericanismo in Italia negli anni trenta* (Torino, 1989); Michela Nacci, "I rivoluzionari dell'Apocalisse. Società e politica nella cultura della crisi francese fra le due guerre," *Intersezioni* 4, no. 1 (1984): 85-123; Jeffrey Herf, *Reactionary Modernism. Technology, Culture and Politics in Weimar and the Third Reich* (New York, 1984); Martin J. Wiener, *English Culture and the Decline of the Industrial Spirit* (Cambridge, 1981).
11. Antonello Gerbi, *La disputa del Nuovo Mondo. Storia di una polemica, 1750-1890* (Milano, 1983, orig.ed. 1955); Tiziano Bonazzi, ed., *Europa-America: la circolazione delle idee* (Bologna, 1976); R. A. Billington, *Land of Savagery, Land of Promise. The European Image of the American Frontier* (New York, 1981); J. Evans, *America. The View from Europe* (New York, 1976); C. L. Sanford, *The Quest for Paradise. Europe and the American Moral Imagination* (Urbana, Ill., 1961); Sigmund Skard, *The American Myth and the European Mind* (New York, 1961); Denis Lacorne, Jacques Rupnik, and Marie-France Toinet, *L'Amérique dans les têtes. Un siècle de fascinations et d'aversions* (Paris, 1986); H. Honour, *The New Golden Land. European Images of America from the Discoveries to the Present Time* (London, 1976); Ugo Rubeo, *Mal d'America* (Roma, 1987); David Ellwood and Adrian Lyttelton, eds., *L'America arriva in Italia, Quaderni Storici*, 58 (special issue) (1985).
12. Nacci, *L'antiamericanismo*; Martellone, "'Blood against Gold'"; Bruno Wanrooj, "Progress without Change: The Ambiguities of Modernization in Fascist Italy," *Storia Nordamericana*, 3, no. 2 (1986), pp. 33-49.
13. Maurizio Vaudagna, ed., *L'estetica della Politica. Europa ed America negli anni trenta* (Bari, 1989); George L. Mosse, *The Nationalization of the Masses* (New York, 1975); Luisa Passerini, "L'immagine di Mussolini: specchio dell'immaginario e promessa di identità," *Rivista di Storia Contemporanea* 3 (1986): 323ff.; Remo Bodei, "Dal parlamento alla piazza. Rappresentanza emotiva e miti politici nei teorici della psicologia delle folle," *Rivista di Storia Contemporanea* 3 (1986): 313ff.; Alberto Aquarone e Maurizio Vernassa, *Il Regime fascista* (Bologna, 1974); Renzo De Felice, *Mussolini il Duce. Gli anni del consenso, 1929-1936* (Torino, 1974); P. V. Cannistraro, *La Fabbrica del consenso. Fascismo e mass media* (Bari, 1975); Victoria De Grazia, *Consenso e cultura di massa nell' Italia fascista* (Bari, 1981).
14. Maurizio Vaudagna, "New Deal e corporativismo nelle riviste politiche e economiche italiane," in Spini, Migone, and Teodori, eds., *Italia e America*, pp. 101-140; Maurizio Vaudagna, "Il corporativismo nel giudizio dei diplomatici americani a Roma," *Studi Storici* 16, no. 3 (1975): 764-796;

Franco Catalano, "New Deal e corporativismo fascista di fronte alle conseguenze della grande crisi. Discussioni storiografiche," *Il Movimento di Liberazione in Italia* 2 (1967): 3-34.

15. DeSanti, *U.S. Relations*, pp. 206-207. See also Diggins, *Mussolini*, pp. 278-279.
16. Valtz Mannucci, "Giornalisti," p. 72; Adolfo Martini, "Il New Deal nell'immagine della stampa italiana, 1932-1936" (Ph.D. diss., University of Torino, 1985-86), p. 244.
17. *Scritti e discorsi*, 8, 7 July 1933, p. 234; Pastore, "Interpretazioni," p. 370; Valtz Mannucci, "Giornalisti," pp. 169-170; Maurizio Vaudagna, "The New Deal and Corporativism in Italy," *Radical History Review* 4, nos. 2-3 (1977): 4-5.
18. Pastore, "Interpretazioni," p. 371.
19. Charles E. Sherrill, *Kamal, Roosevelt, Mussolini* (Bologna, 1936), pp. 53-54; Maurizio Vaudagna, "'Drammatizzare l'America.' I simboli politici del New Deal," in Vaudagna, *L'estetica*, pp. 77-102.
20. Vaudagna, "The New Deal and Corporativism," p. 4.
21. Vaudagna, *Corporativismo*, pp. 198-201.
22. Pastore, "Interpretazioni," p. 373. Vaudagna, "The New Deal and Corporativism," pp. 4-7; Martini, "Il New Deal," pp. 113-127.
23. Pastore, "Interpretazioni," p. 370; Martini, "Il New Deal," pp. 54, 102.
24. Migone, *Gli Stati Uniti*, p. 306; Vaudagna, "The New Deal and Corporativism," p. 7; Diggins, *Mussolini*, pp. 258-261.
25. DeSanti, "U.S. Relations," p. 259. See also Brice Harris, Jr., *The United States and the Italo-Ethiopian Crisis* (Stanford, Calif., 1964); John Norman, "Italo-American Opinion in the Ethiopian Crisis: A Study in Fascist Propaganda" (Ph.D. diss., Clark University, 1942).
26. Pier Giorgio Zunino, *L'ideologia del Fascismo. Miti, credenze e valori nella stabilizzazione del regime* (Bologna, 1985), pp. 322-332; Wanrooj, "Progress," p. 48.
27. Pastore, "Interpretazioni," p. 372.
28. Martini, "Il New Deal," p. 219.
29. Ibid., p. 232.
30. Martellone, "'Blood against Gold'," p. 60; Martini, "Il New Deal," p. 233.
31. Martini, "Il New Deal," p. 246.
32. Martellone, "'Blood against Gold'," p. 65.
33. Ibid., p. 66.
34. Robert Dallek, *Franklin D. Roosevelt and American Foreign Policy* (New York, 1979), p. 186.
35. Martellone, "'Blood against Gold,'" p. 66.
36. Nacci, *L'antiamericanismo*, p. 23.
37. Martini, "Il New Deal," p. 149.
38. Dallek, *Franklin D. Roosevelt*, p. 312.

39. Ennio Di Nolfo, *Vaticano e Stati Uniti, 1939-1952. Dalle Carte di Myron C. Taylor* (Milano, 1979), p. 124.

Franco and Franklin D. Roosevelt

1. Douglas Little, *Malevolent Neutrality. The United States, Great Britain, and the Origins of the Spanish Civil War* (Ithaca, N.Y., 1985).
2. See Claude G. Bowers, *My Mission to Spain. Watching the Rehearsal for World War II* (New York, 1945). The correspondence between Bowers and Roosevelt is in *FDR Papers,* Hyde Park, PSF, Box 69. A discussion of his work as ambassador appears in Douglas Little, "Claude Bowers and His Mission to Spain: The Diplomacy of a Jeffersonian Democrat," in Kenneth P. Jones, *US Diplomats in Europe, 1919-1941* (Santa Barbara, Calif., 1983), pp. 129-146.
3. Robert Dallek, *Franklin D. Roosevelt and American Foreign Policy, 1932-1945* (New York, 1979), p. 530.
4. On the United States and the Spanish Civil War, see, for the Spanish point of view, Antonio Marquina, "Estados Unidos y la guerra de España" in *La guerra civil, Historia 16,* vol. 18, pp. 80-89. For the American point of view, see Allen Guttmann, *American Neutrality and the Spanish Civil War* (Lexington, KY, 1968); Taylor F. Jay, *The United States and the Spanish Civil War* (New York, 1956); and Richard P. Traina, *American Diplomacy and the Spanish Civil War* (Bloomington, Ind., 1968).
5. *U.S. Department of State, Foreign Relations of the United States, 1939,* Washington, vol. 2, p. 716. (hereafter cited as FRUS)
6. Cordell Hull, *The Memoirs of Cordell Hull,* 2 vols., esp. pp. 479, 485, 513, and 517 (New York, 1948).
7. *FRUS, 1936,* vol. 2, pp. 437ff.
8. *FDR: His Personal Letters, 1928-1945*, ed. Elliott Roosevelt (New York, 1950), vol. 1, pp. 614-615.
9. Dallek, *Franklin D. Roosevelt*, pp. 136, 140.
10. Wayne S. Cole, *Roosevelt and the Isolationists* (Lincoln, Neb., 1983), esp. p. 224.
11. Hull, *Memoirs, vol.* 1, pp. 511-514.
12. *FDR Papers,* PSF, Box 69, Roosevelt to Bowers, 31 August 1938.
13. Hull, *Memoirs,* vol. 1, pp. 516-517; Dallek, *Franklin D. Roosevelt,* pp. 178-180.
14. Allen Guttmann, *The Wound in the Heart of America and the Spanish Civil War* (New York, 1962).
15. Ted Morgan, *F.D.R. A Biography* (New York, 1985), p. 438.
16. John David Yalaik, "In the Days Before Ecumenism: American Catholics, Antisemitism and the Spanish Civil War," *Journal of Church and State,* 13, no. 3, (1971): 465-477, and "American Catholic Dissenters and the Spanish Civil War" in *Church History Review,* 53, no.4, (January 1968): 537-555.
17. *FDR. His Personal Letters,* vol. 2, p. 875.

18. Willard L. Beaulac, *Franco, Silent Ally in World War II* (Carbondale, Ill., 1986), p. 46. Among the memoirs of American diplomats in Spain during the first stages, see also Herbert Feis, *The Spanish Story: Franco and the Nations at War* (New York, 1948).
19. On the Spanish position toward the conflict, see especially Antonio Marquina, *España en la politica de seguridad occidental* (Madrid, 1986), Xavier Tusell and Genoveva Garcia Queipo de Llano, *Franco y Mussolini. La politica española durante la segunda guerra mundial* (Barcelona, 1985).
20. On this matter as a whole, see James W. Cortada, *Relaciones España-USA, 1941-1945* (Barcelona, 1973); Juan Dura, *US Policy Toward Dictatorship and Democracy in Spain* (Ph.D. diss. University of California, Berkeley, 1979); C. R. Halstead, *Spain, the Powers and the Second World War* (Ph.D. diss. University of Virginia, 1962); Allan W. Bert, *American Diplomacy and Spain During World War II* (Ph.D. diss. George Washington University, 1975).
21. Hull, *Memoirs*, vol. 1, p. 881, and vol. 2, p. 1334.
22. On this period see Charles R. Halstead, "Diligent Diplomat: Alexander W. Weddell as American Ambassador to Spain, 1939-1942," *Virginia Magazine of History and Biography*, January 1974. The correspondence between Weddell and Roosevelt in *FDR Papers*, PSF, Box 69, and that of Weddell's successor as well.
23. *FRUS, 1940*, vol. 2, p. 810.
24. *FRUS, 1940, vol.* 2, pp. 820-826.
25. Hull, *Memoirs, vol.* 2, p. 1187.
26. On his period see Charles R. Halstead, "Historians in Politics: Carlton J.H. Hayes as American Ambassador to Spain, 1942-1945," *Journal of Contemporary History*, *7*, no.3, (1975): 383ff., and mainly his memoirs, *Wartime Mission in Spain* (Toronto, 1945).
27. *FRUS, 1942, vol. 2*, pp. 729-731.
28. James W. Cortada, "Spain and the Second World War: The Laurel Incident," *Journal of Contemporary History*, 15, no. 4, (1980): 65ff.; Hull, *Memoirs*, vol. 2, pp. 1326-1332.
29. It was later published in the *New York Times*, 15 September 1945.

Emperor Hirohito and Franklin D. Roosevelt

1. *Honjô nikki* (Honjô diary) (Tokyo, 1967), p. 176.
2. Harada Kumao, *Saionji kô to seikyoku* (Prince Saionji and politics) (Tokyo, 1950-56), vol. 4, pp. 28-29.
3. *Irie Sukemasa nikki* (Irie Sukemasa diary; Tokyo, 1990), vol. 1, p. 116.
4. Inoue Kiyoshi, *Shôwa tennô no sensô sekinin* (The war responsibility of the Showa emperor) (Tokyo, 1989), pp. 35-40.
5. Ibid., pp. 44-46.
6. *Kido Kôichi nikki* (Kido Kôichi diary) (Tokyo, 1966), vol. 1, pp. 354, 370.

7. Ibid., p. 474.
8. Michael Barnhart, *Japan Prepares for Total War* (Ithaca, N.Y., 1986).
9. *Irie nikki*, vol. 1, p. 138.
10. *Kido nikki,* vol. 2, p. 743.
11. Ibid., vol. 2, pp. 802, 814, 822.
12. Ibid., vol. 2, pp. 849, 850, 870.
13. Ibid., vol. 2, pp. 895-96, 900-901, 905, 910, 914, 921, 926-27, 932.
14. Fujiwara Akira et al, *Tennô no Shôwa-shi* (The emperor's history of the Showa era) (Tokyo, 1984), pp. 86-87.
15. Ibid., pp. 91-93.
16. *Irie nikki*, vol. 1, p. 422.

The Legacy of Franklin D. Roosevelt's Internationalism

1. As usual, George Kennan expressed this view with eloquence: ". . . I firmly believe that we could make much more effective use of the principle of professionalism in the conduct of foreign policy . . . this runs counter to strong prejudices and preconceptions in sections of our public mind . . . and for this reason we are probably condemned to continue relying almost exclusively on what we might call 'diplomacy by dilettantism.'" George F. Kennan, *American Diplomacy 1900-1950* (New York, 1951), p. 81. See the rejoinder to these thoughts by his ambassadorial colleague, Charles E. Bohlen, also an expert on the Soviet Union: ". . . foreign policy in a democracy must take into account the emotions, beliefs, and goals of the people. The most carefully thought-out plans of the experts, even though 100 percent correct in theory, will fail without broad public support. The good leader in foreign affairs formulates his policy on expert advice and creates a climate of public opinion to support it." Charles E. Bohlen, *Witness to History 1929-1969* (New York, W.W. Norton, 1973), p. 177.
2. Ernest R. May, *"Lessons" of the Past: the Use and Misuse of History in American Foreign Policy* (New York, 1975), p. 18.
3. Cecil V. Crabb, Jr., and Kevin V. Mulcahy, *Presidents and Foreign Policy Making: From FDR to Reagan* (Baton Rouge, 1986), p. 93.
4. The rule is *pacta sunt servanda,* ". . . a general principle of international law: a treaty in force is binding upon the parties . . ." Ian Brownlie, *Principles of Public International Law,* 3rd ed. (Oxford, 1979), p. 613.
5. Kennan strongly opposes reliance on law to regulate the behavior of governments. See Kennan, *American Diplomacy*, pp. 83-89.
6. The Four Freedoms were set out in Roosevelt's annual message to Congress, 6 January 1941. See account of FDR's personal draft of the language in Samuel I. Rosenman, *Working with Roosevelt* (New York, 1952), p. 263. The Atlantic Charter is contained in a Joint Statement by Roosevelt and Prime Minister Churchill on 14 August 1941. For details of its drafting, see U.S. Department of State, *Foreign Relations of the United States, 1941*, vol. 1 (Washington, 1958), pp. 354-369 (hereafter *FRUS*).

7. F. S. Northedge, *The League of Nations: Its Life and Times 1920-1946* (New York, 1986), pp. 177-181. The United States moreover was a member of the International Labor Organization, which dealt with parts of this subject, but the fear of the isolationist groups loomed so high that Secretary of State Cordell Hull turned down an ILO request for shelter after the fall of France isolated Geneva. It eventually found asylum in Canada. Anthony Alcock, *History of the International Labour Organisation* (London, 1971), pp. 158-160. On the League's economic and social functions, see F. P. Walters, *A History of the League of Nations* (London, 1952), pp. 748-762. The offices of the League Secretariat dealing with economic, financial, and transportation programs was invited by Princeton University, the Institute for Advanced Study, and the Rockefeller Foundation to come to Princeton. The narcotic drugs staff went to Washington. Ibid., p. 809. There are no indications that these refugee secretariats had a strong influence on the postwar planning, although President Roosevelt, who made a personal appeal to Stalin to send delegates to the International Labour Conference in 1944 in Philadelphia, certainly was aware of vigorous activities of the ILO. Alcock, *History of the International Labour Organisation*, p. 182.
8. By interdependent, I mean that what one government does affects the lives and futures of other societies in unequal proportions. Clearly the policies of a government with the capacities of those of the United States can inadvertently affect its smaller partners, even when no such result is intended. But the United States does not exist alone and in varying proportions depends on its relations with other polities for essentials of modern existence. For an extended conceptual treatment of interdependence, see Robert O. Keohane and Joseph S. Nye, *Power and Interdependence* (Boston, 1977), pp. 8-11 and *passim.*
9. James MacGregor Burns, *Roosevelt, the Soldier of Freedom* (New York, 1970), p. 580. See Robert James Maddox, *The End of an Alliance: James F. Byrnes, Roosevelt, Truman and the Origins of the Cold War* (Chapel Hill, 1982), pp. 49-70. The main documents relating to Yalta are to be found in U.S. Department of State, *FRUS: The Conferences at Malta and Yalta* (Washington, 1955).
10. Bohlen, *Witness to History*, p. 163.
11. Burns, *Roosevelt*, pp. 582-587. See also Maddox, *End of an Alliance.*
12. Robert E. Sherwood, *Roosevelt and Hopkins* (New York, 1948), pp. 883-884.
13. Bohlen, *Witness to History*, pp. 198-199. *FRUS: Conferences at Malta and Yalta*, pp. 874-875.
14. Bohlen, *Witness to History*, pp. 200-201. Robert Dallek, *Franklin D. Roosevelt and American Foreign Policy, 1932-1945* (New York, 1979), pp. 520-521.
15. Dallek, *Franklin D. Roosevelt*, pp. 533-534. Maddox, *End of an Alliance*, pp. 41-45.
16. William E. Leuchtenburg, *In the Shadow of FDR: From Harry Truman to Ronald Reagan*, rev. ed. (Ithaca, N.Y., 1989), p. 6.

17. Ibid., p. 4.
18. Dean Acheson, *Present at the Creation* (New York, 1969), p. 409. Robert J. Donovan, *Tumultuous Years* (New York, 1982), pp. 197, 199.
19. Leuchtenburg, *In the Shadow of FDR, passim.*
20. Union of International Associations, *Yearbook of International Organizations,* (München, 1989), vol. 2, p. 1597.
21. United Nations, *General Assembly, Official Records: 44th Session,* Supplement no. 6, vol. 11 (New York, 1989), pp. 13, 29.

Other Works Consulted

Basil Rauch, *Roosevelt from Munich to Pearl Harbor: A Study in the Creation of a Foreign Policy* (New York, 1950). Herbert D. Rosenbaum and Elizabeth Bartelme, eds., *Franklin D. Roosevelt: The Man, the Myth, the Era, 1882-1945* (New York, 1987). Pierre de Senarclens, *Yalta* (New Brunswick, N.J., 1988). Sumner Welles, *Seven Decisions That Shaped History* (New York , 1950).

Index